Truth may seem, but cannot be:
Beauty brag, but 'tis not she;
Truth and beauty buried be.

To this urn let those repair
That are either true or fair;
For these dead birds sigh a prayer.

Bacon

TWENTIETH CENTURY TEXT-BOOKS

EDITED BY

A. F. NIGHTINGALE, Ph. D., LL.D.

SUPERINTENDENT OF SCHOOLS, COOK COUNTY, ILLINOIS
FORMERLY SUPERINTENDENT OF HIGH SCHOOLS, CHICAGO

MAXIMILIAN.

TWENTIETH CENTURY TEXT-BOOKS

A HISTORY OF MODERN EUROPE

BY

MERRICK WHITCOMB

PROFESSOR OF HISTORY, UNIVERSITY OF CINCINNATI

WITH MAPS AND ILLUSTRATIONS

PREFACE

THE text which follows differs from the many interesting and valuable school histories which have preceded it in laying greater emphasis upon the Contemporary Period. This change of values reflects, I think, the tendency of American schools of history, and these in turn are responding to the growing world-interests of the American people. An expansion of the Nineteenth Century implies a corresponding contraction in the earlier centuries, the period of historical instruction remaining constant. It is a pity, when the history of Europe is everywhere so attractive; but it is inevitable. Our forefathers were content with classical, and often with mythical personages; we have been made to comprehend our Luther and Loyola, our Mirabeau and Napoleon; and our children will have to make more room for their Cavour, their Bismarck, and their Gladstone. It is a choice of benefits, and there are many substantial reasons why, in the building up of a system of popular education, the present should not be sacrificed to the past.

I take pleasure in acknowledging my obligation to Dr. A. F. Nightingale, of Chicago, and to Professor Dana Carleton Munro, of the University of Wisconsin, for valuable suggestions; also, by way of reference to their works,

M115449

to Professors C. M. Andrews and S. M. Macvane, and to MM. Seignobos, Lavisse, Rambaud, Monod, Driault, and de Crozals, who have done so much of late toward solving the vexed problems of historical presentation.

MERRICK WHITCOMB.

CONTENTS.

LIST OF ILLUSTRATIONS
AND MAPS.

A HISTORY OF MODERN EUROPE

CHAPTER I

The Modern Nations

§ 1. FRANCE

No sharp line of division separates the Middle Ages from modern times. The beginnings of the modern era, as distinguished from the medieval, must be sought far back in the general political disorder of the fourteenth and fifteenth centuries. The modern spirit is, however, none the less real because its beginnings are so closely interwoven with the declining medieval institutions. The ideas to which it gives rise, as they gradually free themselves from the grasp of feudalism and ecclesiastical control, struggle forward to become those typical features of modern life, the development and perfection of which have been the task of western civilization up to the present time.

The modern spirit.

One of the distinctive features of the new times is the modern idea of government. In feudal times the sovereign was little more than an over-lord, the greatest noble of the realm. His contact with his subjects was not immediate, but only through the medium of his feudal barons. The task of the new movement, the transition from feudal to modern government, was the substitution of a uniform central administration for the numerous little states, independent in fact, even though subject to the king in feudal theory;

Modern government.

2   1

a gathering together into one hand of the scattered forces of the kingdom. That the establishment of this later form of government was at the expense of feudalism is evident; so that the rise of the modern state, the establishment of a central power, is coincident with the decline of the feudal system.

Modern government includes among others two great functions: *the right of administering justice; and the right of levying taxes.* In his gradual asser-

The king's justice.
tion of the right of justice the king was greatly assisted by the legists, a body of men, chiefly of the middle class, who devoted themselves to the study of law. These men were the product of the revival

THE KING AND HIS COUNCILORS.

of interest in the Roman Law, which began in the twelfth century at Bologna. This study spread into France, and furnished men trained in the principles of a legal system, who, on account of their ability to solve the difficult problems of justice in accordance with equity and with the authority of a written law, soon became the necessary agents of the king. The principles of the Roman Law were opposed to the principles of feudalism. The Roman Law contemplated a ruler whose authority should extend throughout the length and breadth of his kingdom, unhindered by the trammels of feudalism. This was the ideal of the legists, and it became the ambition of the king whom they advised. "The king's will is law;" "All justice emanates from the king:" such were the maxims of the legists, and they are also the fundamental principles of modern government.

The entering wedge was the "case reserved to the King's Bench." Gradually, through the interpretation of the legists, the number of these cases became greater, until the king's authority was everywhere established. His men, called *baillis*, were distributed throughout the provinces, to safeguard the royal interests, judicial and otherwise. This was the beginning of a royal administration, which, strengthened and extended by the kings of France, became the centralized monarchy of modern times.

The authorities of the church were less inclined than the feudal nobles to yield to the king's assumption of judicial rights, and they were better organized for resistance, with a head at Rome.

Ecclesiastical and civil courts.

To conservative men of the time it seemed questionable, no doubt, whether the rights of people in general, which had found their best protection for centuries in the courts of the church, might safely be entrusted to a temporal prince. Much less were they willing to permit the exercise of such rights over the persons of the clergy.

At the close of the thirteenth century the issue was joined between the church and the rising royal power of France. Philip the Fair, continuing the work of his predecessors in extending the royal power, came into hostile contact with Pope Boniface VIII. The pope denied the right of Philip to tax the lands of the church, or to sit in justice over a clerical person. A bitter strife ensued, in which, although Philip was forced to abandon the right of taxing the clergy, and to accept from them a free gift of money in its place, he nevertheless terminated the struggle in a manner which greatly injured the papal power for a long time. Fomenting an insurrection at Rome, he overthrew

Pope Boniface with violence, and on his speedy death caused to be elected a pope of French sympathies, and saw to it that the seat of the papacy was removed to Avignon, in the midst of French territory. Here the popes lived for nearly seventy years, 1309–1377, subject to French influence, and making no further resistance to the extension of French power.

The reign of Philip the Fair (1285–1314) gave rise to another great modern institution. Up to his time the Estates of the king had consisted of the great lords and prelates, to whom he looked for aid and counsel. In the struggle with Pope Boniface, Philip, in order to strengthen his position, called into the Estates the representatives of the cities, making of them a Third Estate. In this manner the king allied to himself the new and growing commercial and industrial element, whose prosperity was dependent on an orderly and uniform administration, and opposed to the disorders of feudalism. The Estates General of France, which in their origin resemble the Parliament of England, were destined to play no such grand part in the constitutional development of France. Now and then, at intervals when the crown was weak, they came forward to the relief of France ; but for the most part they were subordinated to the overwhelming power of the strong monarchy which governed France.

The political development of France was interrupted by a long period of warfare, arising out of the claims of English kings to the French throne. With varying fortunes, the English at one time possessed the northern and southwestern parts of France, including Paris ; and the French king was driven from his capital. At this moment of greatest peril to the crown of France, a simple peasant girl, Joan of Arc, impelled by visions which she thought divine, came to the relief of her king, Charles VII, and infused new courage

The Third Estate.

The Hundred Years' War (1346–1453).

into the spirits of her countrymen. The tide was turned against the English, and step by step they were driven back, until, except the fortress of Calais, they had no longer any

ENACTMENT OF THE ROYAL EDICT.

possessions in France. Charles VII (1422–1461), delivered from his foe, took up again the centralizing projects of his predecessors, and in his reign the absolute monarchy advanced a long way toward its perfection.

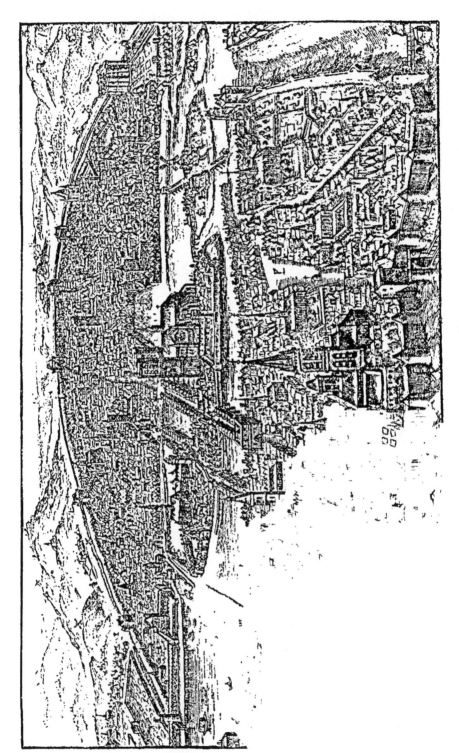

PARIS IN THE FIFTEENTH CENTURY.

SOURCE REVIEW

I. Instructions to a *bailli.*—"If you are knowing to any abuse committed by the spiritual lords, it is your duty to inform the king. If the nobles are about to betake themselves to violence, you shall not suffer it ; and if the lawyers are devouring the people, it is your duty to give information against them, and send them before the king."

STRUGGLE OF PHILIP THE FAIR WITH BONIFACE VIII.

II. Extract from Bull "*Unam Sanctam,*" [1] **defining the authority of the church over the state:** "In this church and in its power are two swords—to-wit, a spiritual and a temporal —and this we are taught by the words of the Gospel, for when the Apostle said, 'Behold, here are two swords (in the church, namely, since the apostles were speaking), the Lord did not reply that it was too many, but enough. And surely he who claims that the temporal sword is not in the power of Peter has but ill understood the word of our Lord when he said : 'Put up thy sword in its scabbard.' Both, therefore—the spiritual and the material swords—are in the power of the church, the latter indeed to be used for the church, the former by the church ; the one by the priest, the other by the hand of kings and soldiers, but by the will and sufferance of the priest. It is fitting, moreover, that one sword should be under the other and the temporal authority subject to the spiritual power."

REFERENCES

Adams : *The Growth of the French Nation*, Chapters VIII., IX. ; Lodge : *The Close of the Middle Ages*, pp. 49–65.

§ 2. GERMANY

In Germany the progress toward a modern form of government met with insuperable obstacles. Many things

---

[1] A leaden disk, called in Latin "bulla," engraved with the Papal emblem, was attached to the document with thongs or bands, and was especially prominent; hence the name. Bulls are named from the opening words of the text.

prevented the Emperor from consolidating and extending his power, as the King of France had done so successfully.

The Empire and its limitations. In France the long period of subjection to authority in Roman times established a habit of obedience to a supreme power, which the disordered conditions of feudal times had not wholly extinguished. In the countries east of the Rhine the people had never been subjected to the unifying influences of Roman administration, and here in German lands the old tribal spirit, the separatist tendency, was the stronger. Men were Swabians, Saxons, Bavarians, and Austrians in practical affairs, and Germans only by sentiment. Then, too, the Emperor, if he aspired to weld the German states into a united monarchy, was seriously hampered by the fact that his office was elective, not hereditary. The individual German states were too nearly equal in power, too jealous of authority, to permit the Empire to become anything substantial. Therefore the Empire came to be, as we approach modern times, a mere shadow of supremacy. Yet, unsubstantial as it was, its mere existence prevented, until its dissolution in the nineteenth century, any other progressive German power from rising to a position of leadership.

The connection of the Empire with the Papacy was also a bar to the development of German unity. Since the memorable event of Christmas Day, 800,[1] when the Empire took its rise, the Papacy had claimed the right to interfere in the affairs of the Empire. Of the seven great princes who elected the Emperor, in accordance with the provisions of the " Golden Bull " (1356), three were spiritual princes, who owed allegiance first of all to Rome. The papal coronation was generally thought to be necessary to the com-

The Empire and the Papacy.

---

[1] The coronation of Charles the Great; the beginning of the medieval Empire.

plete possession of the imperial dignity; and although the Emperor Lewis the Bavarian at one time (1338) formally declared the voice of the electors sufficient, yet later Emperors found it profitable to seek their coronation at the hands of the pope. Such foreign interference made it impossible for the Emperor to legislate, as Philip the Fair had done in France, against the interference of the church in the judicial and financial affairs of his territory. The formation of a modern state made necessary the transference of the affairs of government from the hands of the clergy to the king's agents, and this was impossible in the Empire, where, in addition to the three spiritual electors, quite one-third of the princes who assembled in the Imperial Diet (or Estates) were clergymen, dependent for their offices on the pope.

With the Empire in this condition of weakness, it was the individual states, such as Brandenburg, Saxony, Bavaria, Austria, and others less important, that **The German states.** were touched with the spirit of modern sovereignty.

Their dukes and princes set about the task which resulted in the conversion of their feudal territories into states in the modern sense. They sought to bring under their immediate control all the feudal elements within their boundaries: the free cities, little republics, looking to the Emperor as their lord; the free imperial knights, the remnant of medieval chivalry, who,

IMPERIAL GERMAN CITY.

while holding estates within the ducal territories, yet claimed allegiance only to the Emperor, and refused to share the common burdens of taxes and military duty laid upon them by the ducal officers. Thus, in miniature, the dukes and princes of the Empire were doing what the King of France had accomplished on a larger scale. The result in Germany was a group of small states, whose independence was limited only by the shadowy authority of the Emperor, with mutual jealousies and warring policies. Such have been the characteristics of German political life down to our times, when a partial unity has at last been achieved under the leadership of ancient Brandenburg.

With Albert II (1438) the imperial crown passed to the House of Hapsburg, there to remain, with one brief interruption,[1] so long as the Empire lasted. At this time the Hapsburgs, although rich in territory, were poor in revenue. They had lost Switzerland, but they had gained Bohemia and Hungary. Frederick III (1440–1493), cousin and successor of Albert, is said to have driven about through his possessions with an ox-team, soliciting offerings from his great vassals. In Frederick's time, however, came the first of a series of great marriages, which made the family rich and powerful. His son Maximilian married, in 1478, Mary, daughter and heiress of Charles the Bold, of Burgundy, thereby adding to the Hapsburg lands the provinces of the Netherlands, rich with commerce and industry. Maximilian's son Philip married Joanna, daughter of Ferdinand and Isabella of Spain, and, although Philip died before his father Maximilian, the child of the Spanish marriage, Charles, united the lands of Spain, Burgundy, and Austria, building up a vast empire, the fortunes of which we shall follow in the history of the Reformation.

The House of Hapsburg.

---

[1] 1742–1745 the Emperor was a Bavarian, Charles VII. On his death, in 1745, the line of Hapsburg was continued through Maria Theresa until the imperial title was laid aside in 1806.

THE YOUNG MAXIMILIAN INSTRUCTED IN THE MYSTERIES OF THE
BLACK ART.

SOURCE REVIEW

I. Constitution of the German Empire:
(*a*) Holy Roman Emperor.
(*b*) Imperial Diet, consisting of three chambers :
    1. Seven Electors : Archbishop of Mayence.
                            Archbishop of Cologne.
                            Archbishop of Treves.
                            Electoral Duke of Saxony.

>Margrave of Brandenburg.
>Elector Palatine of the Rhine.
>King of Bohemia.

2. Chamber of Princes, spiritual and lay.

3. Chamber of imperial cities.

(c) Imperial Supreme Court of Justice, for the adjustment of interstate affairs. [Note.—In the inability of this court to settle the affairs of the individual states, and thereby to give peace to the Empire, is seen most clearly the impotence of the imperial power.]

II. **Extract from the edict of Lewis the Bavarian, declaring the Empire independent of the Papacy** (1338): "We, therefore, with the counsel and approbation of the electors and other princes of the Empire, do declare that the imperial dignity and power is derived immediately from God alone, and that, according to the law and custom of the Empire, approved from of old, after anyone shall be chosen Emperor or King by the electors of the Empire, either unanimously, or by the greater part of them, he is straightway, from the simple fact of his election, to be considered and entitled true King and Emperor of the Romans, and should be obeyed by all subject to the Empire. He should, moreover, possess full power in administering the laws of the Empire, and in doing all those things which appertain to a true Emperor, nor does he require the approbation, confirmation, authority, or consent of the Pope, the Apostolic See, or of anyone whatsoever."

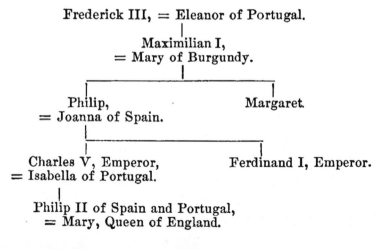

Frederick III, = Eleanor of Portugal.

Maximilian I,
= Mary of Burgundy.

Philip,
= Joanna of Spain.

Margaret.

Charles V, Emperor,
= Isabella of Portugal.

Ferdinand I, Emperor.

Philip II of Spain and Portugal,
= Mary, Queen of England.

REFERENCES

Seebohm : *Era of the Protestant Revolution*, pp. 26–33 ; Johnson : *Europe in the Sixteenth Century*, pp. 106–128 ; Lodge : *The Close of the Middle Ages*, pp. 394–418.

§ 3. SPAIN AND ENGLAND

In Spain the impulse toward national consolidation was aided by external conditions. The mountain kingdoms,

Christians
and Moors.

which had struggled side by side against the common foe, the Mohammedans of the South, were welded together by their united effort. On the decline of the Moorish power this union was made permanent in the marriage of Ferdinand and Isabella, uniting the two great Christian kingdoms of the Spanish peninsula, Aragon and Castile. In 1492, the year of the discovery of America, the last of the Moorish states of southern Spain, Granada, was overthrown. By the terms of the surrender of Granada, freedom of worship and of education, Mohammedan laws and judges were promised to the Moors. These terms were violated. Persecutions led to a series of revolts during the years 1500–1501, and on the suppression of the rebellion in 1502 a royal Spanish decree offered to the Moors the choice of baptism or exile. Meanwhile the bigotry engendered by centuries of religious strife burst forth against the Jews, who were ordered to leave the country in 1492. The exile of these industrious peoples was a severe blow to Spain. The discovery of America and the consequent influx of precious metals seemed for a time to offset the loss ; but this source of sudden wealth was fleeting, and served rather to discourage habits of thrift and industry than otherwise. At a time when other nations were laying the foundations of modern industry the Spanish mind was turned toward adventure and rapacious methods of gaining wealth.

In organizing the royal power the rulers of Spain met

with many obstacles. In no country of Europe were constitutional privileges, limiting the power of the crown, so

Internal policy of Ferdinand and Isabella. numerous and powerful as in Spain. The Cortes, or National Estates, were more vigorous than any similar body in France or Germany. In Aragon an official called the Justiciar, elected by the Cortes, claimed the right of hearing appeals,

CROWN OF QUEEN ISABELLA.

inquiring into the legality of arrests and advising the king on constitutional questions. In addition to this there were powerful military orders, with wealth and authority similar to the Templars in France. To overcome these obstacles to their power the rulers of Aragon and Castile first brought the cities to their aid. The principal cities of Castile had organized an association, called the Holy Brotherhood, for the purpose of protecting themselves against the arbitrary demands of kings and nobles. They had established courts for the trial of offenses of violence, with mounted police to carry out the orders of the courts. This association was taken under royal control, and its system of justice used in the interests of the rulers, to curb the nobles.

The fact that for two centuries the wars of Spain had been crusades against the unbelieving Moors caused the

The Crown and the Church. relations between church and state to be unusually close in Spain. The crown was given the right of nomination to the great offices and dignities of the church, and they made use of this privilege in filling the great bishoprics with men devoted to the interests of the king, instead of filling them with proud and independent nobles. This led to the elevation of able men, of whom Francisco Ximenes, Archbishop of Toledo in 1492, is perhaps the most notable. He became High Chancellor of Castile, and his ability contributed much to the work of national unity and the building up of a strong centralized government in the modern sense. At the death of Ferdinand the Spanish possessions, handed over to the Spanish-Hapsburg Charles, embraced the whole peninsula, with the exception of Portugal, with conquered territories in north Africa and south Italy, and infinite possibilities of extension in the western hemisphere. The Spanish army, drilled by able generals like Gonzalvo, was the ablest fighting force in Europe, and Spain was rapidly nearing the zenith of her brilliant but brief career.

PSALTER OF QUEEN ISABELLA.

The beginnings of modern England are to be found in the failure to secure the French crown in the struggle of the Hundred Years' War. This fortunate event threw England back upon her island possessions; her kings became English kings with English aims, and her characteristic development was begun. The bitter contest between the rival houses of York and Lancaster, known as the Wars of the Roses (1455–1485), weakened the English nobility, and paved the way for the coming of a strong monarchy. The old

England.

nobility was almost blotted out, with slaughter, exile, and impoverishment, and new families came to the front with less prestige and power, and less inclined to champion feudal rights against the rising monarchy. The common people, less affected by the wars, were advancing in trade and manufacture, and welcomed a strong hand at the helm of state. Parliament had declined in power and influence, and offered few obstacles to strong government. When Henry Tudor came to the throne as Henry VII (1485) the ground was cleared for the erection of a modern state.

SOURCE REVIEW

Revenues of the King of Spain.—Extract from the report of the Venetian ambassador to Spain: "From New Spain are obtained gold and silver, cochineal (little insects like flies), from which crimson dye is made, leather, cotton, sugar, and other things; but from Peru nothing is obtained except minerals. The fifth part of all that is produced goes to the king, but since the gold and silver is brought to Spain, and he has a tenth part of all that which goes to the mint and is refined and coined, he eventually gets one-fourth of the whole sum, which fourth does not exceed in all four or five hundred thousand ducats, although it is commonly reckoned not alone at a million, but at millions of pounds.

"From these, his realms, his majesty receives every year an income of five millions of gold in time of peace : one and one-half millions from Spain ; a half million from the Indies ; one from Naples and Sicily, and another from Flanders and the Low Countries. But his expenses are six millions, and this excess is covered by extraordinary taxes according to his pleasure."

REFERENCES

(For Spain) Seebohm: *Era of Protestant Revolution*, pp. 34–40; Johnson: *Europe in the Sixteenth Century*, pp. 91–106; Lodge: *The Close of the Middle Ages*, pp. 468–493. (For England) Seebohm, pp. 46–55; Adams, *European History*, pp. 236–244; Green: *Short History of the English People*, pp. 281–288.

CHAPTER II

The Renaissance

§ 4. Renaissance in Italy

The contribution of Italy to modern life was rather intellectual than political. Italy did not achieve a national unity after the manner of France, Spain, and England ; with her, as with Germany, the separatist tendencies were too strong to be overcome. In the Middle Ages many cities in northern Italy threw off the feudal yoke and became little republics, devoted to commerce and industry. Toward the end of the Middle Ages the democratic spirit waned. With the accumulation of wealth derived from commerce with the East, Venice and Genoa lost their spirit of liberty. Republics in name, they became in fact oligarchies, suppressing the voice of the people. Other states, like Milan, lost their freedom through violence. As republics they permitted a decline of their military spirit, and relied for defense upon bands of mercenaries, led by professional captains, *condottieri*. These men in many instances seized upon the powers they were hired to protect.

Political condition of Italy.

Florence came by another route to the same end. A manufacturing city, thronged with artisans, the political progress of Florence was toward a greater degree of democracy. A clever political trickster, a genuine "boss," Cosimo de' Medici, holding no office in the state, succeeded, by means of money and persuasion, in getting control of the government, and, what is more remarkable, in passing this control to his descendants. There was no employment of force, and

Florence.

Cosimo's rule was endured, because it brought prosperity and splendor to Florence.

CosIMO DE' MEDICI, 1389–1464.

In southern Italy the kingdom of Naples, long a subject of dispute between France and Spain, was joined at last to the Spanish crown. Midway of the peninsula lay the Papal States. The Pope, their ruler, a spiritual lord throughout the rest of Christendom, was in the Papal States a temporal ruler as well. With his vague claims upon the lands of Italy, the Pope, in his Italian policy, was opposed to unity or to the erection of a power superior to his own.

The Renaissance, as its name implies, is a re-birth ; in this instance a re-birth of the old Greek and Roman manner of looking at man and the world in which he lives. It was, then, an escape from the narrowness of view which characterized the Middle Ages. The impetus toward the new ideas came from the recovery of the writings of the Greeks and Romans. It is not to be supposed that these writings were lost during the Middle Ages ; they were merely unappreciated. With the establishment of Christianity in the Roman Empire they came to share in the general abhorrence felt toward things of pagan origin. As the Middle Ages advanced, the peculiar type of mind, developed under the discipline of the church, had nothing in common with the literary products of Greece and Rome ; consequently they were neglected and left to moulder in the dusty corners of monastic libraries. When in Italy, with the general advance of culture, a higher order of intellect was developed which turned with sympathy to the life and

The Renaissance.

thought of ancient times, the hidden treasures were soon brought to light. The man who typifies this higher development in Italy is Francesco Petrarch, 1304–1372, "the first modern scholar and man of letters." To Petrarch we owe the recovery of many priceless Latin works, and his enthusiasm was communicated to others, who carried on the work : to Poggio, who explored the cloisters of Germany ; and to Boccaccio, 1313–1375, who prepared books of mythology, classical geography and biography, for the better understanding of the works already recovered.

The revival of the Latin classics led rapidly to a desire for Greek. Students of Roman literature soon perceived that in their higher development the Romans **Greek Literature.** sought their inspiration from the Greeks. In response to the Italian demand men of Byzantine culture came westward in Venetian and Genoese galleys, bringing with them a knowledge of ancient Greek and the manuscripts of the classical writings. Before the fall of Constantinople, in 1453, so much of Greek literature as still existed in the East had been transplanted into Italy. Thus, while the Latin manuscripts were rescued piecemeal from their dusty hiding-places, the literature of Greece was recovered with less toil. Its recovery led to an advance in philosophical speculation, and in the time of Cosimo de' Medici the Florentine Academy was established for the study and discussion of the works of Plato.

The effects of the discovery of the ancient literatures were far-reaching, and may be said to mark the opening of the modern era. In the annals of Rome were portrayed a highly developed civil administration, and a complete system of laws. These afforded a stimulus to modern princes, striving to establish their authority against the trammels of the feudal system. The bold, inquiring spirit of Greek philosophy broke down the narrow limitations of medieval thought, hemmed in with the authority of the Schools. Men saw, in the exploits of the Greeks and Romans, such possibilities as were not dreamed of in the days when this world was thought to be little else than a dreary pilgrimage toward the life to come.

Effects of the Renaissance.

With the revival of classical learning came a revival of classical art. The importance assigned to art in the life of the Greeks and Romans was reflected in the efforts of their Italian admirers, who eagerly sought and preserved such master-pieces as had escaped the pillage of Italian cities. The group of the Laocoön, the Apollo of the Belvidere, and other triumphs of Greek art revealed new possibilities of pictorial representation to the artists who flourished under the patronage of wealthy popes and princes. The works of Raphael, 1483–1520, and of Michael Angelo, 1475–1564, in painting and in sculpture were the results.

Art of the Renaissance.

SOURCE REVIEW

I. The making of a library.—Extract from Vespasiano's Life of Cosimo de' Medici : "XII. When he had finished the residence and a good part of the church, he fell to thinking how he should have the place peopled with honest men of letters ; and in this way it occurred to him to found a fine library ; and one day, when I happened to be present in his chamber, he said to me, "In what way would you furnish this library?" I replied that as for buying the books it would be impossible, for they were not to be had. Then he said : "How is it possible, then, to furnish it?" I told him that it would be necessary to have the books copied. He asked in reply if I would be willing to undertake the work. I answered him that I was willing. He told me to commence my work and he would leave everything to me ; and as for the money that would be necessary, he would refer the matter to Don Archangel, then prior of the monastery, who would draw bills upon the bank, which should be paid. The library was commenced at once, for it was his pleasure that it should be done with the utmost possible celerity, and as I did not lack for money, I collected in a short time forty-five writers, and finished 200 volumes in twenty-two months ; in which work we made use of an excellent arrangement, that of the library of Pope Nicholas, which he had given to Cosimo, in the form of a catalogue made out with his own hands."

(Noble and wealthy book collectors looked with suspicion upon the new printed books. Vespasiano, speaking of the library of the Duke of Urbino, says : "All the volumes are of perfect beauty, are written by skilled scribes, on parchment, and many of them adorned with exquisite miniatures. The collection does not contain a single printed book. The Duke would be ashamed to have a printed book in his library."

Trithemius, Abbot of Sponheim, a German scholar, writes (1494): "A work written on parchment could be preserved a thousand years, while it is probable that no volume printed on paper will last for more than two centuries. Many important works have not been printed, and the copies required of these must be prepared by scribes. The scribe who ceases his labors because of the invention of the printing-press can be no true lover of books, in that, regarding only the present, he gives no due thought to the intellectual cultivation of succeeding generations. The printer has no care for beauty and the artistic form of books, while with the scribe this is a labor of love.")

REFERENCES

Paul Van Dyke: *The Age of the Renascence*, Chapters XI and XII ; Adams: *European History*, pp. 259–282; Seebohm: *Era of the Protestant Revolution*, pp. 66–74. For the political history of Italy in the Renaissance period see Lodge: *The Close of the Middle Ages*, Chapters VIII, XIV.

§ 5. The Renaissance North of the Alps

Italy was the first country of Europe to receive the new light. This was largely due to the accumulation of wealth in the Italian cities, the result of commerce and industry; because wealth gives leisure, and leisure turns toward the refinement of life. The same conditions were slower in reaching Germany, but about the middle of the fifteenth century the South German cities, enriched with the trade in Eastern goods, which crossed the Alps from Venice and found their way down the Rhine, began to take an interest in the intellectual development of the South. Young men of German patrician families sought the universities of Pavia and Bologna, and brought back to Germany the new Latin and Greek culture.

In Germany.

The New Learning, as it came to Germany, was modified by the character and ideals of the German people. A simple folk, with deep religious feeling, the Germans did not follow the subtle Italians into the intricacies of Platonic philosophy; their earnest and practical minds sought rather to apply the principles of the New Learning to the affairs of life. The fifteenth century saw a reorganization of the school system. The towns were thronged with students, many of them subsisting from public charity. Throughout the German lands, from Holland to Switzerland, and from the Rhine to Silesia, the impulse toward a higher education seemed to permeate all classes of society. Men of Italian learning set themselves to work to produce text-books, to replace the clumsy medieval manuals with books better adapted for the instruction of youth. The study of Greek and even of Hebrew was introduced into the preparatory schools.

Character of German Humanism.

In Germany the universities were the centers of the New Learning. Many of them sprang into existence in response to the new spirit; and in all of them the medieval course of study was much modified. Students deserted the lecture-rooms of the professors of theology and law, and flocked to the "Humanities," greatly to the disgust of the older instructors, who were dependent for their income upon the tuition-money paid by the students. Some of the univer-

The universities.

BILIBALDI·PIRKEYMHERI·EFFIGIES
·AETATIS·SVAE·ANNO·L·III·
VIVITVR·INGENIO·CAETERA·MORTIS·
·ERVNT·
·M·D·XX·I·V

A GERMAN PATRICIAN.

sities, in which the theological element was the stronger, held out vigorously against the new tendencies. Such was Cologne, where the influence of the Dominican order was supreme. Erfurt, on the contrary, was wholly given to the New Learning, and Heidelberg was favorably inclined.

In France conditions were unfavorable to the reception of the New Learning. The nobles were interested in

The Renaissance in France.

military exploits and the exercise of arms, and little disposed toward letters. Besides this, the University of Paris, the greatest of all universities, had been for centuries the stronghold of conservative theology, a source of authority in doctrinal matters second only to Rome itself. As such it was not likely to look with favor upon an intellectual movement, the chief spirit of which was that of questioning and criticism. The artistic side of the Renaissance appealed more strongly to the French, and its influence is to be found in the palatial buildings erected by French kings of the fifteenth and sixteenth centuries, those " *châteaux* " which have been the admiration of posterity.

In England the movement had a deeper meaning. The spirit of criticism which scholarly Englishmen imbibed

The Renaissance in England.

in foreign travel and study, particularly in Italy, increased their dissatisfaction with the institutions of the medieval church. The University of Oxford became the center of a movement looking toward a reform of the clergy and a reorganization of the schools. John Colet, who founded St. Paul's School in London (1510), and Thomas More, who became Lord Chancellor under Henry VIII, were the leaders of the Oxford group. They sought, in careful study of the New Testament and of the early Christian writers, to learn the true character of the early church, that later errors might be corrected and removed.

The finest product and best representative of the deeper spirit of the Renaissance was Desiderius Erasmus of Rot-

terdam. Although of Dutch birth, he was a citizen of
the Christian world.   His education was acquired in Ger-
Erasmus
(1467-1536).many, later at the University of Paris and
in England.   A close friend of Colet and
More during his English residence at the
close of the fifteenth century, he entered with zeal into
their projects of reform, and this became the leading motive of his life.   His years
were full of literary labors.
His translation of the New
Testament from Greek in-
to Latin opened the way
for a closer study of the
sacred texts.   The influence of his popular writ-
ings was even wider.   In
the *Praise of Folly* and
the *Familiar Colloquies* he
scourged with a bitter pen
the shortcomings of the
clergy, and by these means,
no doubt, prepared the
way for Luther.   Indeed,
his enemies said with

ERASMUS.

much truth that "Erasmus laid the egg, and Luther
hatched it."   Yet his sympathies were not with Luther.
He loved the church of Rome and sought its reformation;
and when he saw that Luther's movement tended to break
the church in two, he recoiled, with the great body of Hu-
manists, from a remedy which seemed to him more fatal
than the disease it sought to cure.

SOURCE REVIEW

I. German idea of higher learning.   From the *Adoles-
centia* of Jacob Wimpheling: "Everyone should strive for
learning and virtue, which alone confer nobility. The youth,

therefore, especially when he comes of distinguished parents, should be frequently reminded that he should value the soul's advantage and not the gifts of fortune and physical accomplishments. Each day he should exert himself, in order that he may not become an awkward, stupid, foolish, wanton fellow, as in our day most of the noble-born are ; but that he shall be intelligent and educated ; that he be well instructed from his youth and not ignorant of the humanities ; that he shall apply himself to the reading of the Holy Writ ; that he may be well-bred, just, gentle, and pious, and a friend of clever, cultured men."

II. Italian opinion of the French at the beginning of the sixteenth century. From *The Courtier* of Baldassare Castiglione (an English translation of 1588). —"But besides goodness the true and principall ornament of the minde in every man (I believe) are letters, although ye Frenchmen know only the nobleness of armes, and passe for nothing beside ; so that they not only doe not set by letters, but they rather abhorre them and all learned men they doe count very rascalles, and they think it a great villany when any one of them is called a clarke."

III. Extract from letter of Erasmus, 1518, renewing progress of learning in Germany on the eve of the Reformation: "Learning is springing up all round out of the soil ; languages, physics, mathematics, each department thriving. Even theology is showing signs of improvement. All looks brighter now. Three languages are publicly taught in the schools. I myself, insignificant I, have contributed something. I have at least stirred the bile of those who would not have the world grow wiser, and only fools now snarl at me. . . . But the clouds are passing away. My share in the work must be near finished. I do not want the popular theology to be abolished. I want it enriched and enlarged from earlier sources. When the theologians know more of Holy Scriptures, they will find their consequence undiminished, perhaps increased. All promises well, so far as I can see. My chief fear is that with the revival of Greek literature there may be a revival of paganism. There are Christians who are Christians only in name, and are Gentiles at heart ; and, again, the study of Hebrew may lead to Judaism, which would be worse still. I wish there could be an end of scholastic subtleties, or, if not an end, that they could be thrust into a second place, and Christ be taught plainly and simply. The reading of the Bible and the Early Fathers will have this effect. Doctrines are taught now which have no affinity with Christ and only darken our eyes.''

REFERENCES

Paul van Dyke : *Age of the Renascence*, Chapters XIV and XX. (For Erasmus) J. A. Froude : *Life and Letters of Erasmus* (many letters translated) ; Merrick Whitcomb : *Select Colloquies of Erasmus.*

§ 6. INVENTION AND DISCOVERY

The widening of the intellectual horizon led to invention and discovery. If this life were worth the living, as the Greeks and Romans thought, then it was worth while to make it as good and grand as possible. The chains of authority which bound the medieval man were broken, and free range given to individual effort. As a result, the end of the fifteenth century was marked by inventions and by material progress, which are the true indications of the modern spirit.

Invention.

For centuries the sailor was the slave of the land. Even after he had learned to steer his course by the stars, the dangers of cloudy nights and foggy days limited his voyages. Even in the Mediterranean navigators crept

The Compass.

SHIP. TIME OF FIRST ATLANTIC VOYAGES.

from cape to cape. The magnetic needle was known to the Chinese from high antiquity. Its use came westward, transmitted by the Arabs, perhaps, and reached the Mediterranean sometime about the period of the second Crusade (1150). At first the needle, floating freely on the surface of water, could only be used in times of calm. Step by step it was improved—mounted upon a pivot, set in gimbals, to neutralize the action of the waves—and in the fourteenth century it became a practical instrument of navigation. To this invention is due our knowledge of two-thirds of the world ; thanks to this infallible guide, the sailor could now entrust himself without fear to the trackless wastes of the high seas.

As early as the tenth century the Chinese practised the art of reproducing writing by impression ; and in the first half of the fifteenth century books were made after this manner in Europe. Whole pages were cut in wood, and from each engraved block a number of copies were printed. The next great step was the invention of movable letters. This came about the middle of the fifteenth century, and is generally ascribed to Gutenberg of Mayence. Even this advance, however, did not constitute printing in its modern form. The engraving of the separate types was still a matter of great expense. It was the casting of the movable types that brought the art to perfection. Thus, with a single engraved mould, a vast number of types could be cheaply made. About the same time was invented typemetal, a mixture of lead and antimony, strong enough to resist pressure, yet not sharp enough to cut the paper. It is also said that Gutenberg invented the printing-press. Formerly the paper was laid upon the types and pressed against them with a brush or tool called "frotton." Printing was the gift of Germany to the Renaissance.

The ancient world used *papyrus* made from an Egyptian rush-like plant, for its books; also parchment, made from the skins of animals. In the Middle Ages these materials were dear, and it is to their high cost that the destruction of classical manuscripts is due, the parchments on which they were written having been used a second time for literary purposes. Cotton paper was introduced from the East by the Venetians in the tenth century. It was heavy, spongy, and dark, and ill-adapted for permanent records. In 1221 the Emperor Frederick forbade its use for official writings, ordering them to be copied upon parchment. Finally, toward the beginning of the fourteenth century, the use of linen rags furnished a material that could be indefinitely renewed. Without a satisfactory paper, at a moderate price, the invention of printing would not have been such a boon to humanity.

Paper.

The Middle Ages made little progress in geographical knowledge. Life centered about the Mediterranean; to the West beyond was the trackless ocean, where the evening sun extinguished its fires. Timid mariners, venturing beyond the Straits of Gibraltar, feared to follow the African coast to the southward. The heat increased, it was thought, and made life impossible; the sea became thick and impassable on account of the rapid evaporation. It was only when Portugal, shut off from expansion inland by the rise of Spain, turned her energy toward the sea that the fancied obstacles were overcome. Prince Henry the Navigator, collecting all existing information regarding the west coast of Africa, pushed the exploration southward. Step by step the coast was won. In 1450 the name of Cape Verde, given to the limit of exploration, expresses the surprise of mariners at finding verdure where life was thought to be impossible. In 1452 the Gulf of Guinea was reached, and the zest for gold added to the love of adventure. In 1487 Diaz, reaching the extreme point of Africa, was blown around the Cape of Good Hope. Finally, in 1497,

Portuguese discoveries.

Vasco da Gama, doubling the Cape, reached Mozambique, and opened a new route to the Indies.

Very different from the series of ventures just chronicled was the daring project of Columbus. It is his
Columbus. faith in his ideas and his power in action that mark Columbus as a high type of the modern man. His purpose, "to seek the Orient by means of the Occident," was inspired by the words of Aristotle:

TERRORS OF THE DEEP.

"The earth is round, but at the same time it is not very large." With this in mind, he calculated the distance from Europe to India to be 90 degrees, or 1,100 Spanish leagues, about five weeks' sailing for vessels of his time. Fortunately he did not know that it was more than twice as far, or four months' journey. For such an expedition he would not have found a company, even if his own courage had been equal to the venture. Aided by

the sovereigns of Spain, he found his Indies, as he supposed, and "gave a new world to Castile and Leon." In
1519 Spanish ships, under the command of the Portuguese
Magellan, circumnavigated the earth, thereby actually
demonstrating its sphericity.

Medieval conceptions of the universe, like those of the
terrestrial globe, yielded to the questioning instinct of the
new age. At the beginning of the sixteenth
Copernicus. century Copernicus, a Polish astronomer,
in his work upon the revolutions of the celestial spheres,
affirmed that the sun was a fixed star, surrounded by
planets, of which the earth was one ; described the double
movement of the earth's motion, and fixed the position
of the moon as a satellite of the earth. As a corollary
of his conclusions, the earth was no longer the center
of the universe, nor man the prime object of creation.
Fearful of the effect of his discoveries, seeming, as they
did, to oppose the teaching and tradition of the church,
Copernicus delayed the publication of his book until his
death in 1543.

SOURCE REVIEW

I. The primitive compass ; from a description by Vincent
de Beauvais in the twelfth century.—"When the mariners are
unable to find the course that should conduct them safe into
port, they rub the point of a needle upon the magnet, fasten
it to a straw, and place it in a vessel of water, around which
they carry the magnet. The point of the needle turns ever
toward the magnet, and when by this means they have made
the needle turn completely around, then they take away the
magnet all at once. Thereupon the point of the needle turns
toward the star, and moves not thence."

II. Columbus's account of his first voyage. San Do-
mingo.—"The lands are high, and there are many very lofty
mountains. They are all most beautiful, of a thousand different shapes, accessible, and covered with trees of a thousand
kinds, of such great height that they seem to reach the skies.

I am told that the trees never lose their foliage, and I can well understand it, for I observed that they were as green and luxuriant as in Spain in the month of May. Some were in bloom, others bearing fruit, and others otherwise according to their nature. The nightingale was singing, as well as other birds of a thousand different kinds ; and that in November, the month in which I myself was roaming among them. There are palm-trees of six or eight kinds, wonderful in their beautiful variety ; but this is the case with all the other trees and fruits and grasses ; trees, plants, or fruits filled us with admiration. It contains extraordinary pine groves, and very extensive plains. There is also honey, a great variety of birds, and many different kinds of fruits. In the interior there are many mines of metal and a population innumerable. . . . It is extremely rich in gold ; and I bring with me Indians taken from these different islands, who will testify to all these things. Finally, and speaking only of what has taken place in this voyage, which has been so hasty, their Highnesses may see that I shall give them all the gold they require, if they will give me but a very little assistance ; spices also, and cotton, as much as their Highnesses shall command to be shipped ; aloes-wood, as much as their Highnesses shall command to be shipped ; slaves, as many of these idolators as their Highnesses shall command to be shipped. I think also I have found rhubarb and cinnamon, and I shall find a thousand other valuable things by means of the men I have left behind me, for I tarried at no point so long as the wind allowed me to proceed.

REFERENCES

Adams : *European History,* pp. 273-282.

ADMINISTRATION OF THE SACRAMENTS.

CHAPTER III

The Reformation

§ 7. PERIOD OF THE COUNCILS

IN the contest of Philip the Fair with Boniface VIII the papacy, which had for centuries been the supreme influence in European affairs, suffered defeat

Decline of
the papacy.

at the hands of the modern government of France. Boniface was assaulted by French agents in his palace, and died of chagrin. After his death French influence secured the election of a series of French popes, who removed the seat of papal power to Avignon on the Rhône, where it remained for seventy years under

French control. This period is called the "Babylonian Captivity." Finally, in 1377, Gregory XI, yielding to the entreaties of the Christian world, and moved as well by the decay of his power in the Papal States during the absence at Avignon, returned to Rome. But matters went from bad to worse. Upon the death of Gregory, the cardinals, vacillating between Roman and French influences, elected first Urban VI, who took his seat at Rome ; then Clement VII, who returned to Avignon. This was the beginning of the Great Schism of the West, which endured until 1417. The prestige of the papacy was greatly weakened. It was inconceivable to Christian men that there should be two heads of the church, two successors of St. Peter. Christendom was divided in its allegiance, some nations holding to Urban, others to Clement.

One result of the schism was to give free rein to independent thinkers. Wyclif (1327–1384), in England, voiced the sentiments of a party of his compatriots, who were jealous of the interference of the papal power in England, desiring to cut their island off from Roman control. The debasement of the papacy was Wyclif's opportunity, and he came forward as the champion of English independence. Although he was condemned by a council of English prelates, and although his party did not succeed in establishing the ecclesiastical independence of England, yet the movement of which he was the spiritual leader produced a series of legislative acts, which greatly limited the exercise of papal authority in England.

Results of the schism : heresy.

The ideas of Wyclif were carried to the continent, and reached a fuller development in Bohemia, under the leadership of John Huss (1369–1415) and Jerome of Prague. Bohemia was for many years a seat of armed rebellion against the church, and it was only by means of substantial concessions that the Bohemian heretics were finally brought to submit themselves to the Roman See.

Another result of the schism was the formation of a party of reform. Conservative men, who loved the church, set to work to remedy its misfortunes. The center of the reform party was in France, its leaders, John Gerson and Peter d'Ailly, both of them associated with the University of Paris. They sought, first of all, to heal the schism, to restore a single head to the divided church. In this they were successful only after many struggles. Their first effort was to bring about a simultaneous resignation of the two popes, and then to proceed with a clear field to a new election. This the rival popes were unwilling to do. A general council of the church was then called by the combined colleges of cardinals, who had abandoned their respective popes. This was the Council of Pisa, where the rival popes were deposed, and a new pope elected in their place. The new pope did not, however, meet with general obedience. Christendom doubted the authority of a council called without the voice of either emperor or pope. Thus the Council of Pisa brought it about that three popes reigned instead of two (1409).

Results of the schism: reform.

But the reformers persevered. In 1414 circumstances were more favorable. Sigismund, the Emperor, and John XXIII, pope of the Pisan line, joined in summoning a council at Constance, beyond the Alps. The first act of the council was to clear the field of papal claimants. Gregory XII voluntarily resigned; the others were deposed, and for more than two years the council remained at the head of the church, the papal See being vacant.

The Council of Constance.

The council next turned its attention to the extirpation of the Bohemian heresy. John Huss was summoned from Prague, and came to Constance, bearing letters of safe-conduct from the emperor. He was tried for heresy and condemned; and when, after long and persistent efforts had been made to convince him of his errors, he remained obstinate, he was stripped of his priestly garb and, in a penitent's gown, turned over to the temporal authorities. By them he was burned at the stake, in accordance with the general law for the punishment of heretics, and his ashes cast into the Rhine. Sigismund had some doubt about this treatment of his safe-conduct; but was assured

BURNING OF JOHN HUSS.

by the theological doctors that no contract with a heretic could be binding.

In 1417, when impending wars seemed likely to interrupt the council, that body proceeded to the election of a pope, upon whom it might confer its authority. Its choice was a member of the Roman family of Colonna, who came to the throne as Martin V. The first great object of the reform party was fulfilled: the papacy was restored; Christendom acknowledged the new pope.

The aims of the reformers, however, were wider. Fearing a return of disorders in the papacy, they sought to make the council a supreme governing body in the church, providing by decree for a succession of councils at stated intervals. This the popes, their power being restored, jealous of a limitation of their authority, resisted, and neglected the assembling of the councils. Tenacious of their ideas, the reform party again came forward and forced the pope to summon a new council at Basel in 1431. Seeking to assert its supremacy, the Council of Basel quarreled with Pope Eugene IV and deposed him, as had been done with the earlier popes at Constance. But the verdict of Christendom was with the pope against the council. With the papacy on the verge of ruin a council might intervene; but with the head of the church well established the sympathy of Christians was with the pope. Pope Eugene won ; the Council of Basel dwindled into insignificance, and the conciliar idea, the supremacy of the councils over the papacy, vanished with the necessity which called it forth.

The conciliar idea.

In addition to the restoration of the papacy and the establishment of the authority of the councils, the reform party had still another aim : the purification of the church from certain abuses which had grown up along with the widening of the church's influence and work. It is not to be supposed that these abuses were in the nature of personal immorality. It is altogether likely that the clergy, rank for rank, were better than any other class of people of the time, and that the institutions of the church were more wisely and cleanly conducted than the institutions of laymen.

Reform.

The real abuses against which the reformers protested were connected with the finances of the Roman court. During the Middle Ages, when the church had a general oversight of the affairs of Christendom, the Roman court had come to be the great clearing-house for the public business of western Europe. The thousand clerks and secretaries who performed this work must be paid, and an elaborate system of fees grew up, which drew to Rome the

HUSSITE WARS IN BOHEMIA.

money of Christendom, much to the dissatisfaction of local princes, who wished to collect this money for their own needs. More than this, the papacy, to increase its income, assumed the right of granting fat church livings throughout Europe to high officials who remained at Rome and left the livings vacant. Thus the offices of the church were neglected; churches fell into ruins because their incomes were diverted to Rome. Out of this system grew two evils : the money of Christendom was drained away to Rome ; and the offices of the church abroad were unfilled.

SOURCE REVIEW

I.—The Financial Abuse.—Extract from the *Downfall of the Church*, by Nicholas Clemanges, one of the Reform Party :
"To the same cause is to be ascribed the ruin of numerous churches and monasteries and the leveling with the ground, in so many places, of sacred edifices, while the money which used to go for their restoration is exhausted in paying these taxes. But it even happens, as some well know, that holy relics in not a few churches, crosses, chalices, feretories, and other precious articles, go to make up this tribute."

II.—Extracts from Decrees of the Council of Constance:

1. *From the Decree "Sacrosancta," establishing the supreme authority of the Council.*—"It first declares that this same council, legitimately assembled in the Holy Ghost, forming a general council, and representing the Catholic Church militant, has its power immediately from Christ, and everyone, even if it be the papal dignity itself, is bound to obey it in all those things which pertain to the faith and the healing of the said schism, and to the general reformation of the Church of God, in head and members."

2. *From the Decree "Frequens," arranging for regular future councils.*— "Therefore, by a perpetual edict, we sanction, decree, establish, and ordain that general councils shall be celebrated in the following manner, so that the next one shall follow the close of this present council at the end of five years. The second one shall follow the close of that, at the end of seven years, and councils shall thereafter be celebrated every ten years in such places as the pope shall be required to designate and assign, with the consent and approbation of the council, one month before the close of the council in question, and which, in his absence, the council itself shall designate. Thus, with a certain continuity, a council will always be either in session, or be expected at the expiration of a definite time."

III.—Popes of the Great Schism

Roman Line.		Avignon Line.
Urban VI, 1378–1389.		Clement VII, 1378–1394.
Boniface IX, 1389–1404.		
Innocent VII, 1404–1406.	Council of Pisa (1409) deposed Gregory XII and Benedict XIII and elected Alexander V, 1409–1410.	
Gregory XII, 1406–1415 (resigned).		Benedict XIII, 1394–1424.
	John XXIII, 1410–1415 (deposed).	
	The Council of Constance (1414) accepted resignation of Gregory XII, deposed John XXIII, and elected Martin V, 1417–1431.	Clement VIII, 1424–1429 · (resigned).

REFERENCES

Adams: *European History*, pp. 283–288; Paul van Dyke: *Age of the Renaissance*, Chapters VII, VIII, IX; Lodge: *The Close of the Middle Ages*, Chapters IX, X, XI.

§ 8.   The Reformation in Germany

The failure of the effort for reform occasioned widespread dissatisfaction throughout northern Europe; but nowhere so much as in Germany, where the lack of a strong central government exposed the country to the exploitation of the Roman financial system.   To the hatred of Italian control thus aroused was added the spirit of intellectual independence, the product of the Renaissance.   The Reformation is to be regarded as an application of the Renaissance spirit to religion, a rejection of authority in this particular sphere, as it had been rejected in others; a splitting up into groups, as a result of the exercise of the right of critical investigation in religious as in secular matters.   At length

Causes of the Reformation.

Martin Luther.

a champion of this right of intellectual and spiritual freedom came forth in the person of Martin Luther.

Luther (1483–1546) was the son of a humble family.   His father was a miner in Thuringia. Thanks to the ambition of his parents, no pains were spared in his education.   At the humanistic university of Erfurt he acquired such education as Germany afforded.   His nature was deeply religious, and during his Erfurt residence he abandoned his professional career and became an Augustinian

Martin Luther.

monk. But his abilities were too marked to escape notice, and he was invited to the newly founded university of Wittenberg, in Electoral Saxony, where he became professor of theology. In the development of his religious views Luther was attracted to the doctrine of "justification by faith," as set forth by St. Augustine, in whose honor the order of which Luther was a member had received its name.

The church of the Middle Ages, while by no means neglecting the element of faith, had departed from the Augustinian system, in laying a stronger emphasis upon the efficacy of "works" in securing eventual salvation. By works are to be understood the various duties, penitential and otherwise, prescribed by the clergy. No doubt, for the medieval man these tangible means of securing the soul's well-being were quite as effectual as a more spiritual method. A man of Luther's character, however, confident of his ability to achieve his soul's salvation through direct contact with the Divine Spirit, rejected these material means of justification, and laid the emphasis upon faith, by means of which this contact might be assured. Here are to be seen the workings of the individualistic tendency, the personality of man's relation with God; the rejection of that authority by which the church sought to guide Heavenward the lives of men by constant ministrations.

Justification by faith or works.

This sentiment was strengthened by Luther's visit to Rome in 1510. As he approached the Eternal City, after a weary journey, he cried aloud his greeting to the "city sanctified with the blood of the holy martyrs." But the result of his journey was bitterness. He was shocked at the luxury and cynicism of the place. It was the ever-present antagonism of the rustic toward the town, intensified with the enormous contrast between German and Italian life and culture. With Luther embroidered garments and marble palaces were evidences of

Visit to Rome.

vice ; he thought this splendor out of place in the successor of the meek and lowly Saviour. It must be remembered that, in the minds of all German thinkers of the sixteenth century, luxury of living was regarded as a departure from virtue.

An event was needed to fire the train of discontent, and this was furnished by the publication of a special indulgence for the building of St. Peter's church at Rome. The contributions of the faithful were solicited for this purpose, and in return a letter of grace and pardon was conferred, by means of which certain penalties of sin were removed, providing always that the applicant had previously with contrite heart confessed his sin and received absolution from the priest. Luther's antagonism was aroused by this indulgence for the following reasons :

The sale of indulgences.

1. With the emphasis which he placed upon faith as a means of grace he was inclined against the system of indulgences, although not yet prepared to deny wholly their efficacy.

2. He was enraged at the financial exploitation of the country, the drain of wealth toward Rome.

3. The sale of this general indulgence must have interfered with the proceeds of a local indulgence at Wittenberg, which contributed to the support of the religious institutions connected with the university.

4. He believed that Tetzel, who had charge of the sale of the indulgence in the neighborhood of Wittenberg, was claiming virtues for the indulgence beyond what the theory of the church justified.

Moved by these considerations, Luther, on October 31, 1517, following a well-established university custom, posted upon the door of the castle church at Wittenberg, Ninety-five Theses, criticizing the indulgence and the manner and motives of its sale. The Ninety-five Theses were the first blow in the great battle of the Reformation ; but Luther did not intend them as such. He had no idea of breaking away from the church, and was dismayed at the storm he had raised. The truth is, Germany was ripe for revolt, and needed only the signal.

AN INDULGENCE.

Pope Leo X was not disposed to give the matter his attention. It was merely a quarrel of monks, he said; but when he was at length persuaded of its gravity, he sum-

moned Luther to Rome. Fortunately for Luther, his
prince and patron, Frederick the Wise, Elector of Saxony,
intervened, requesting a hearing for Luther
Luther driven to
revolt.
in Germany. A hearing was accorded, and
many efforts made from the papal side to
quiet Luther, but none of them were permanently successful. A temporary truce was broken by Dr. Eck, an eminent
German scholar, who espoused the cause of the papacy, and
tempted Luther into more radical admissions at the Dis-
putation of Leipzig (1519). Meanwhile Luther had studied
much and developed his ideas; and now wrote vigorously
against the papacy, rousing the German nation to a breach
with Rome. His pamphlets called forth a bull of excommunication from Pope Leo, which Luther promptly burned'
in public, a formal dec-
laration that his ties with
Rome were broken.

The Emperor Charles
V, who succeeded his
grandfather
The Diet at
Worms.
Maximilian
in 1519, un-
dertook to silence the
controversy. Luther was
commanded to appear be-
fore him at the Diet of
1521, held at Worms, the
first Diet convened by the
Emperor since his elec-
tion. , The Emperor was
Spanish bred, without
sympathy with German
sentiment or a knowledge
of German conditions.

EMPEROR CHARLES V. AT THE TIME
OF IIIS ELECTION (1519).

Luther had no chance with Charles ; but his figure, as he
stood there, a single man before that mighty concourse,

·CHRISTO · SACRVM·

ILLe·Dei·verbo·MAGNA·PIETATE·FAVEBAT·
·PERPETVA·DIGNVS·POSTERITATE·COLI·

D·FRIDR·DVCI·SAXON·S·R·IMP·
·ARCHIM·ELECTORI·
·ALBERTVS·DVRER·NVR·FACIEBAT·
·B·M·F·V·V·
·M·D·XXIIII·

FREDERICK THE WISE, ELECTOR OF SAXONY. LUTHER'S PROTECTOR.

confronting an Emperor, lord of half the world, was heroic. When called upon to retract he replied that, until he was persuaded of the error of his way, he could not retire from the position he had taken.

According to the terms of the Emperor's safe-conduct Luther was permitted to retire from Worms ; but Charles launched against him the *Decree of Worms,* placing him under the ban of the Empire, and ordering the destruction of his books.   Meanwhile his friends, fearing to defy openly the imperial authority, hurried him to a place of safety in the castle of Wartburg, where he remained in seclusion until the following spring.

The *Decree of Worms* was never carried out.   Foreign complications and domestic difficulties kept Charles from proceeding against Luther.   More than once the Emperor was forced to ask aid of the Protestant princes, Luther's protectors, against the French and Turks.   When at length the opportunity came it was too late ; Germany was divided into two great hostile camps—the Lutherans and the Catholics.

SOURCE REVIEW

I.—The Value of Indulgences.—Extract from a sermon by Tetzel : " How many mortal sins are committed in a day, how many in a week, how many in a month, how many in a year, how many in the whole extent of life?   They are well-nigh numberless, and they that commit them must needs suffer endless punishment in the burning pains of purgatory.

"But with these confessional letters you will be able at any time in life to obtain indulgence for all penalties imposed upon you, in all cases except the four reserved to the Apostolic See.   Therefore, throughout your whole life, whenever you wish to make confession, you may receive the same remission, except in cases reserved to the Pope, and afterward, at the hour of death, a full indulgence as to all penalties and sins and your share of all spiritual blessings that exist in the church militant and all its members.

"Do you know that when it is necessary for any one to go

to Rome, or undertake any other dangerous journey, he takes his money to a broker and gives a certain per cent.—five or six or ten—in order that at Rome or elsewhere he may receive again his funds intact, by means of the letter of this same broker? Are you not willing, then, for the fourth part of a florin, to obtain these letters, by virtue of which you may bring, not your money, but your divine and immortal soul, safe and sound into the land of Paradise?"

II.—The Journey to Worms.—Relation of Luther: "The little city of Wittenberg was in the utmost consternation when the imperial summons arrived. Apprehensive for my safety, my beloved fellow citizens crowded to my residence, and would have dissuaded me from entertaining the idea for a moment of thus wilfully putting myself into the hands of my enemies. They besought me to recollect that I lived for them as well as for myself; that my life was of more importance to them than that of a thousand popes; that I would be seized by my adversaries, and sacrificed to their vengeance. They reminded me of those holy martyrs, Huss and Jerome, whose safe-conducts had been violated without scruple. I heard my beloved friends in all their remonstrances; and while I admitted the truth of all they advanced, I nevertheless resolved to obey the Emperor's mandate, and appear before that great assembly of dukes, barons, counts, knights, and other noblemen, both temporal and spiritual. 'I am called,' I said to them; 'it is decreed and ordered that I proceed to Worms, in the name of the Lord Jesus Christ; and thither I shall go, if there were as many devils in that city as there are tiles on its houses. Were I to refuse, my enemies would not only triumph, but ascribe my conduct to cowardice, and that I was not able to maintain what I had so often asserted. Fear in my case would only be a suggestion of Satan, who, apprehending the approaching ruin of his kingdom, was anxious to avoid a public defeat before such a great and illustrious assembly as that of Worms.'"

REFERENCES

Adams: *European History,* pp. 303–315; Seebohm: *Era of the Protestant Revolution,* pp. 94–130; Myers: *Medieval and Modern History,* pp. 363–370; Johnson: *Europe in the Sixteenth Century,* pp. 153–160.

§ 9. THE LATER REFORMATION

The blow struck by Luther against spiritual authority was felt throughout Europe. Among the Germanic peoples the revolt was most complete. The Swiss of Zürich under the leadership of Huldreich Zwingli, threw off the allegiance to Rome (1524) and were followed by other Swiss cities and cantons. Zwingli differed from Luther in many points of doctrine, and all efforts to unite the two Protestant factions were unavailing. The Zürich reformation led to civil war in Switzerland, with the result that each canton was permitted to select its own religion, and this division between Catholic and Protestant has survived down to the present day.

Switzerland.

The right of individual interpretation, championed by Luther, led to the rise of numerous sects in Germany. Many, particularly of the lower classes, where life was hard under the old conditions, looked forward to a reconstruction of society, along the lines of equality and universal brotherhood, such as they thought to find in the spirit and organization of the primitive church. The leaders of these sects, repelled by the conservatism of Luther, who saw in this Utopian movement the seeds of anarchy and the destruction of his own cause, scattered among the peasantry, and by their preaching brought about a social and agrarian revolution, the Peasants' War of 1525, in which the peasants were defeated and flung back into a still deeper abyss of serfdom.

The Anabaptists.

At the outbreak of the Lutheran revolt the English King, Henry VIII, espoused the papal cause, wrote a book against Luther, and in recognition of his orthodoxy received from the pope the special title of "Defender of the Faith." Reasons of state brought a change in Henry's views. Desiring to perpetu-

England.

ate his line with a male heir, he sought from the pope an annulment of his marriage with Catharine of Aragon, daughter of Ferdinand and Isabella. The pope refused to grant the king's request, and Henry procured his release at the hands of an English ecclesiastical court, with the sanction of the Archbishop of Canterbury. Resenting this defiance of his power, Pope Clement VII launched a bull of excommunication against Henry VIII, and in the controversy that ensued English independence of Rome again asserted itself, and a vote of Parliament proclaimed the king "the only Supreme Head on Earth of the Church of England (1535)."

HENRY VIII.

Although this step made England independent of the papacy, yet it did not immediately change the character of the English religion. In England the political changes came first and the change in doctrine and method of worship afterward. During Henry's reign the forms and spirit of religion suffered little change. In the brief reign of his successor, Edward VI, a child at the time of his accession to the throne, the Lutheran spirit made itself manifest. The English Prayer-Book was introduced and church services conducted in the English tongue. Edward was followed on the throne, in default of male heirs, by his sister Mary, (1553), daughter of Catharine of Aragon, and a devoted Catholic. With the assistance of the Catholic party Queen Mary sought to restore the old faith; but her effort, if indeed it could have been successful under any circumstances, was rendered doubly unpopular by her marriage with Philip II of Spain, which aroused the

5

English jealousy of foreign interference and control. After a short reign Mary was succeeded by her sister Elizabeth (1558), who easily restored Protestant institutions and her own supremacy in the church. In her reign Protestantism became the religion of the English people.

The religion thus established in England was more conservative than the reformed religions of the continent, and preserved more generally the forms of the ancient church. It satisfied, however, the desire for church reform, long since demanded by Wyclif and others. It preserved an ecclesiastical hierarchy, but made it national, freeing it from foreign dictation. The English reformation was the joint work of people and sovereign.

JOHN CALVIN.

John Calvin.—The career of Calvin offers many points of contrast with the career of Luther. Luther was a pioneer, as has been shown; forced into a position of leadership, every step of his spiritual progress experimental and unforeseen. It might be said of him that he drilled his battalions under fire. With Calvin the case was very different. Educated for the law, which he studied at Paris and at Lyons, he came gradually under the influence of Lutheran opinions, which had begun to spread themselves in France, and worked out his scheme of doctrine in detail before his actual work as a leader of reform was begun. His "Institutes of the Christian Religion," which he composed in the quiet of his study, was a complete system of Augustinian theology, and became the handbook of the sect which he founded.

Reformation in Latin countries.

Called to Geneva in 1536, to assume the leadership of the reform movement in that city, Calvin ruled and molded the little commonwealth, which became a hive of industry and a model of sobriety under the guidance of his stern and puritanical spirit. The Genevan reform, the product of Calvin's legal mind, affording a complete system of material and spiritual life, commended itself to the most progressive peoples of Europe : to the Rhenish Germans, to the Dutch, to the Scotch, and eventually to a great portion of the English people. Its sterling qualities, as expressed in Congregationalism, determined the character of our New England civilization.

Geneva.

In France the logical side of Calvinism made it stronger with the middle and upper classes. Its followers, called Huguenots, counted in their numbers many of the great nobles of the realm. It gained ground against Lutheranism, no doubt because its French origin caused it to appeal more strongly to the French mind.

France.

In thus hastily reviewing the effects of the new doctrines upon the several nations of Europe, one fact stands out in bold relief : the political organization of each country, at the time of the Reformation, determines the manner in which the great religious question will be decided. In compact nations, with strong central governments, as in England, for example, it is evident that one party or the other, Catholic or Protestant, will ultimately prevail to the exclusion of its opponent. England, and France and Spain as well, must be wholly Protestant or wholly Catholic. In countries of the other class, like Germany, with its hundred principalities, or Switzerland, a loosely united group of cantons, the principle of state rights is certain to be the determining factor. This was in truth the basis of settlement in Germany and Switzerland. In Germany, at the Peace of Augsburg, 1555, each state was permitted to select its own religion,

General remarks.

,holic or Lutheran. In Switzerland, by the Peace of ᴗappel, 1531, each canton was at liberty to decide the religious question for itself. It is to be borne in mind that at this time, and for many generations to come, the idea that persons of different religions might live together harmoniously in the same state seems to have occurred to no one.

HENRY VIII AND HIS WIVES

	WIVES	CHILDREN
Henry VIII.	1. Catharine of Aragon, m. 1509; divorced 1533.	Mary, m. Philip II of Spain (no issue).
	2. Anne Boleyn, m. 1533; beheaded 1536.	Elizabeth (unmarried).
	3. Jane Seymour, m. 1536; died 1537.	Edward VI (no issue).
	4. Anne of Cleves, m. 1540; divorced 1540.	
	5. Catharine Howard, m. 1540; beheaded 1542	
	6. Catharine Parr, m. 1543; survived the king.	

SOURCE REVIEW

I.—The Act of Supremacy (26 Henry VIII, 1535).—"Albeit the King's majesty justly and rightfully is and ought to be the supreme head of the church of England, and so is recognized by the clergy of this realm in their convocations, yet, nevertheless, for corroboration and confirmation thereof, and for increase of virtue in Christ's religion within this realm of England, and to repress and extirpate all errors, heresies, and other enormities and abuses heretofore used in the same : Be it enacted by authority of this present Parliament, that the King our sovereign lord, his heirs and successors Kings of the realm, shall be taken, accepted, and reputed the only supreme head in earth of the Church of England, called *Anglicana Ecclesia;* and shall have and enjoy, annexed and united to the imperial crown of this realm, as well the title and style thereof, as all honors, dignities, preeminences, jurisdictions, privileges, authorities, immunities, profits, and commodities, to the said dignity of supreme head of the same church, belonging and appertaining.

"And that our said sovereign lord, his heirs and successors Kings of this realm, shall have full power and authority from time to time to visit, repress, redress, reform, order, correct, restrain, and amend all such errors, heresies, abuses, offenses, contempts, and enormities, whatsoever they may be, which by any manner spiritual authority ought or may lawfully be reformed, repressed, ordered, redressed, corrected, restrained, or amended, most to the pleasure of Almighty God, the increase of virtue in Christ's religion, and for the conservation of the peace, unity, and tranquillity of this realm ; and usage, custom, foreign laws, foreign authority, prescription, or any other thing or things to the contrary hereof notwithstanding."

II.—Ordinance Concerning the Times of Assembling at Church in Geneva (1547, period of Calvin's influence).—"That the temples be closed except during hours of service, in order that no one shall enter therein out of hours, impelled thereto by superstition ; and if anyone be found engaged in any special act of devotion therein or near by, he shall be admonished for it ; if it be found to be of a superstitious nature, for which simple correction is inadequate, then he shall be chastised."

REFERENCES

Seebohm : *Era of the Protestant Revolution,* pp. 167–199 ; Johnson : *Europe in the Sixteenth Century,* pp. 271–276 ; Green : *Short History of the English People,* pp. 331–348.

§ 10. THE COUNTER-REFORMATION

The revolts which had torn away one-half of Europe from Rome were not without their effect upon the internal organization of the Catholic church. An era of zeal and devotion succeeded to the indifference of the fifteenth century ; and this new life was felt in all departments of the church. To the popes of the Renaissance type, men who, like Leo X, were more interested in the patronage of art and letters

Effects of the Reformation upon the church.

and in the subtleties of Italian politics than in the vital needs of the church, succeeded a line of energetic popes, who applied themselves vigorously to the task of reorganization. This Catholic revival had all the enthusiasm of a popular movement. Rome rose from her slumbers and showed again the greatness of her resources, her spirit of sacrifice, her genius for organization. Ancient religious orders were reconstituted and new ones founded. The Inquisition was reorganized in countries where the government remained in Catholic control; the Congregation of the *Index* was established (1559) for the censorship of the press; and, in addition to these methods of defense against the new ideas, the Society of Jesus, powerful and aggressive, became, in the hands of the papacy, a potent instrument in winning back lost ground.

PAUL III., POPE OF THE COUNTER-REFORMATION AND OF THE COUNCIL OF TRENT.

Loyola was born in 1491, of noble Spanish family. He grew up in the court of Ferdinand, with a passion for arms and chivalry characteristic of his time and station. The fortune of war changed in a moment the current of his life. Wounded at the siege of Pampeluna in 1521, a military career became for him im-

Ignatius Loyola.

IGNATIUS LOYOLA

possible. Thus suddenly cut off from his earlier interests, his vigorous spirit sought employment in the activities of the mind. Cured of his wound, but with impaired health, Loyola lived some time with the hermits of Montserrat and made the pilgrimage to Jerusalem. Recognizing his lack of spiritual training, he commenced the study of theology at the University of Salamanca and continued his course at Paris. There, in association with other Spanish students, Lainez and Francis Xavier, he organized, in 1534, a new religious order, to which they gave a military name, the Company of Jesus. The keynote of their discipline was implicit obedience to the papal authority, so generally attacked in the decade just elapsed. They took vows of chastity, poverty, and obedience. Their organization complete, Loyola and his followers betook themselves to Rome and offered their services to the pope. In 1540 their project of association was confirmed by the Roman See.

It is interesting to note how the military instinct of Loyola, thwarted in its natural career, expressed itself in the organization of his spiritual army. Unquestioning obedience to the commander, the General of the Order, who, under the supervision of the pope, formulated at Rome the policy of the association, was the foundation principle of the new society. This, with care in the selection of its members, made the Society of Jesus the most effective instrument of control that Christendom has ever seen.

The contribution of the Society of Jesus toward the Counter-Reformation was threefold :

1. A ceaseless struggle against heresy,
Work of the Jesuits. a stiffening of the conservative element in localities invaded by the new ideas. It is largely due to the efforts of the Jesuits (as well as to the dissensions among the Protestants : Lutherans, Zwinglians, and Anabaptists) that Austria and South Germany, at one time largely Protestant, were won back to the

Catholic fold. Vienna, Ingoldstadt, and Cologne became centers of Jesuit influence.

2. By their close relations with the papacy, standing between it, as it were, and the mass of Catholic Christianity, they held the church aloof from all suggestions of doctrinal change and compromise, and preserved intact the main features of the ancient theology.

3. Recognizing that the Protestant ideas were largely the result of the educational tendencies of the Renaissance, the Jesuits sought to win back into the hands of the church the education of youth. In this they succeeded admirably. The Jesuit school system came to be one of the great formative agencies of modern times. The leading statesmen and writers of the three centuries following were educated in the Jesuit schools. "Let us have charge of the boys," they said, "and we shall be sure of the men."

The Emperor Charles V, struggling to reconcile the religious factions of Germany, sought, by means of a general council, to solve the problems of the church, as had been done in the time of Sigismund. By imperial order the council convened at Trent, in 1545. Its prime object, that of reconciliation, was not effected ; nor did the council settle down to work until after the Peace of Augsburg, when division was established, and reconciliation was no longer possible. Its real work was the careful formulation of Catholic doctrine ; so that, in the matter of doctrine, the ultimate effect of the Reformation was rather to strengthen than to modify the fundamental dogmas of the Catholic Church. The Trentine Council, however, while it established more firmly the doctrine of papal authority, removed, in a great degree, the old administrative and financial abuses, of which the fifteenth century had complained so bitterly. The commercialism of the medieval church, which reached its highest point of development in the traffic in indulgences and benefices,

The Council of Trent.

was allayed ; but too late for the unity of the Church ; for half of Europe was irretrievably lost to Rome.

SOURCE REVIEW

I.—The *Index* was a list of books, the possession or perusal of which was forbidden by the ecclesiastical authorities. That it was not without results is shown by the following testimony of contemporaries : A Dominican monk, Castiglione, writes, in 1581, "The Inquisitors frequently publish orders forbidding the sale of this or that work. The booksellers are no longer willing, therefore, to take the risk of importing books, while they are frequently prevented from selling those already in stock. There must be in Rome at present unsalable books to the amount of several thousand florins."

Josias Simler, in 1565: "A new index has appeared, wherein so many books are condemned that a number of professors in the Italian universities complain they cannot lecture, if the edict remains in force. Frankfort and Zürich and other German cities have written to the Senate of Venice, urging it not to accept an edict whereby the book trade will be ruined."

II.—**Loyola and His Work. Fròm Parkman's *The Jesuits in North America :*** "It was an evil day for new-born Protestantism when a French artilleryman fired a shot that struck down Ignatius Loyola in the breach of Pampeluna. A proud noble, an aspiring soldier, a graceful courtier, an ardent and daring gallant was metamorphosed by that stroke into the zealot, whose brain engendered and brought forth the mighty Society of Jesus. His story is a familiar one : how, in the solitude of his sick-room, a change came over him, upheaving, like an earthquake, all the forces of his nature ; how, in the cave of Manresa, the mysteries of Heaven were revealed to him ; how he passed from agonies to transports, from transports to the calm of a determined purpose. The soldier gave himself to a new warfare. In the forge of his great intellect, heated, but not disturbed by the intense fires of his zeal, was wrought the prodigious enginery whose power has been felt to the uttermost confines of the world.

"Loyola's training had been in courts and camps ; of books

he knew little or nothing.   He had lived in the unquestioning
faith of one born and bred in the very focus of Romanism ;
and thus, at the age of thirty, his conversion found him.   It
was a change of life and purpose, not of belief.   He presumed
not to inquire into the doctrines of the church.   It was for
him to enforce those doctrines, and to this end he turned all
the faculties of his potent intellect and all his deep knowledge of mankind.   He did not aim to build up barren communities of secluded monks, aspiring to Heaven through
prayer, penance, and meditation, but to subdue the world
to the dominion of the dogmas which had subdued him ; to
organize and discipline a mighty host, controlled by one purpose and one mind, fixed by a quenchless zeal or nerved by a
fixed resolve, yet impelled, restrained, and directed by a single
master hand.   The Jesuit is no dreamer : he is emphatically
a man of action ; action is the end of his existence.''

REFERENCES

Seebohm : *Era of the Protestant Revolution*, pp. 199–208 ;
Johnson : *Europe in the Sixteenth Century*, pp. 261–271.

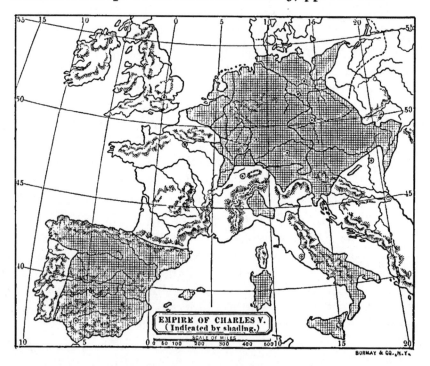

EMPIRE OF CHARLES V.
(Indicated by shading.)

SCALE OF MILES

BORMAY & CO., N.Y.

CHAPTER IV

Wars of Religion

§ 11. THE RELIGIOUS STRUGGLE IN GERMANY

THE Lutheran Reformation possesses one characteristic which distinguishes it from the religious revolts of the earlier period. The movements of Wyclif and Huss took on extravagant forms, developing into forms of social anarchy, and lost thereby the sympathy and support of the more influential classes. The same danger was present in Luther's case ; but the great reformer showed an ability closely akin to statesmanship in keeping clear of embarrassing entanglements. When Luther raised the banner of revolt all the elements of discontent in German life felt that their opportunity had come. The free imperial knights, a class of small lords, surviving from the Middle Ages, whose castles were little more than robbers' dens along the Rhine and other highways of commerce, cast in their lot with the new movement, hoping for the downfall of their natural enemies, the great princes. At the outset their spokesman, Ulrich von Hutten, materially advanced the Lutheran cause with his writings ; but when, in the Knights' War of 1522, the issue was joined between knights and princes, Luther did not permit his cause to be compromised by an alliance with the knights, as they had hoped, but held steadfast to his natural protectors, the princes, of whom Frederick the Wise was one.

The peasants, in their rising of 1525, looked to Luther for aid. Himself a peasant, they thought to find in him a friend. But in this they were disappointed. Luther recognized clearly that the success of his cause lay in a close alliance with the princes, whose protection, especially in

Luther and the peasants.

the case of Frederick the Wise, alone rendered the *Decree of Worms* inoperative. We may regret that he turned against the peasants with violence, publicly exhorting the princes to crush their rebellion ; but it is evident that an alliance with a social and agrarian revolution would have condemned the Lutheran movement in the eyes of the only people who were able to bring it to a successful issue, by holding off the imperial power, until the reform gathered strength to stand alone.

Charles V was prevented in various ways from making good the *Decree of Worms*. So great were the needs of his

The division of Germany.

immense empire that more than once he was obliged to seek the aid of Luther's protectors against his enemies. At the Diet of Spires, in 1526, when Charles was seeking aid against the French, it was left to each German state to take its own course in the matter of Lutheran teaching. Again at Spires, in 1529, when the Emperor was stronger at home and abroad, a decree was passed, re-enacting the *Decree of Worms,* whereupon the Lutheran princes protested, and earned thereby the name of " Protestants." The following year, the Diet being held at Augsburg, the Emperor came to enforce the ban against Luther and his followers. The leaders of the Protestants, John of Saxony (successor of Frederick the Wise) and Philip of Hesse, presented a conservative statement of the reformed belief, the *Augsburg Confession,* and there were hopes of compromise. But the Emperor was steadfast, and gave the Protestants only a few months for submission. Fearing a resort to force, the Protestant princes, on their way home, came together and formed the "League of Schmalkalden," for defense. Thus was Germany arrayed in two hostile bands.

While Luther lived civil war was averted. Luther had a horror of war and great respect for the civil power. To take up arms for the extension of religious principles seemed to him unjustifiable; it was even doubtful if religion might be defended by force against the ruling powers. Luther's last

The Schmalkaldic War.

MAURICE OF SAXONY.

days were embittered with the thought of the impending struggle.

Luther died in 1546. His death was a signal for the commencement of hostilities. The Schmalkaldic League was crippled by the defection of Maurice, Duke of Saxony, cousin and rival of the Elector, and the Protestants were easily overcome with Spanish soldiery, introduced by Charles V from his Italian garrisons. For once, however, Charles's judgment was at fault; his treatment of the Protestant leaders, John and Philip, who, condemned to death, were closely confined in foul dungeons, aroused such anger throughout Germany that Maurice was forced to break his pact with the Emperor, and seek to undo the mischief he had brought upon his kinsmen. Then, too, all Germany was enraged at the importation of Spanish troops, contrary to the provisions of the Emperor's election bond. The national pride revolted against Spanish methods put into use against German princes, and Germany made a Spanish province. Maurice of Saxony, turning to his natural allies, plotted against the Emperor, and entered into an alliance with Henry II, king of France, by which the Protestants were supplied with money, and Henry was permitted to take for his share the great frontier posts of the Empire—Metz, Toul, and Verdun.

CHARLES V. AT THE CLOSE OF HIS REIGN.

Charles, having no suspicion of Maurice's treachery,

was an easy victim. Caught in a defile of Tyrol, he was obliged to yield. The Convention of Passau, 1552, closed the war; but the peace of Augsburg, 1555, defined the status of Catholic and Protestant. It gave to the ruler of each state the power to define the religion of the land. To this religion all persons within the state must conform. Nonconformists were permitted to migrate elsewhere, and take their property with them. This treaty, although weak in many particulars (it made no provision for the growing sect of Calvinists), furnished a *modus vivendi* to Germany for sixty years.

Peace of Augsburg.

The Emperor Charles V, overwhelmed with the sudden collapse of his imperial power, and broken in health, abdicated, leaving Spain and the Netherlands to his son Philip, and to his brother Ferdinand, Austria and the Empire. Charles retired to the monastery of Yuste, in Spain, and there remained until his death in 1558; but not as a monk, for he kept in touch with the affairs of Europe and frequently advised his successors.

SOURCE REVIEW

I.—Regret of Charles V that he had dealt so mildly with the New Doctrines at the start.—Extract from his Abdication Speech at Brussels: "Soon came the death of my grandfather Maximilian, in my nineteenth year, and, although I was still young, they conferred upon me in his stead the imperial dignity. I had no inordinate ambition to rule a multitude of kingdoms, but merely sought to secure the welfare of Germany, to provide for the defense of Flanders, to consecrate my forces to the safety of Christianity against the Turk, and to labor for the extension of the Christian religion. But, although such zeal was mine, I was unable to show so much of it as I might have wished, on account of the troubles raised by the heresies of Luther and the other innovators of Germany, and on account of the serious war into which the hos-

tility and envy of neighboring princes had driven me.   .   .   .
(To his son, Philip) Above all, beware of the infection from
the sects of neighboring lands.   Extirpate at once the germs, if
they appear in your midst, for fear they may spread abroad
and utterly overthrow your state, and lest you may fall into
the direst calamities.''

II.—Charles V at the Monastery of Yuste.—''At the end of
his first year's residence the absence of all fatigue, the calm,
the solitude, the mildness of the air brought him an almost
embarrassing surprise, a return to health, something which
had not entered into his calculations, and which threatened to
seriously disturb his plans.   He did not dream of quitting the
monastery, to enter the world once more, but at one time he
formed the resolution, it is said, of undertaking a journey to
the Pyrenees.

''Thus his repose and his isolation were far from being absolute.   His sisters, Queen Mary of Hungary and Queen Eleanor,
the latter the widow of Francis I, came to visit him at Yuste.
Their sojourn at the monastery gave him great pleasure.   The
conversations of these three personages, at this solemn hour,
after a life so full of events, would furnish an interesting page
of history.   Two of them were endowed with superior intelligence.   As for Eleanor, she had neither the spirit nor the
courage of her sister.   It was her curious fate to marry the
military and political rival of her brother, and, being devoid
of interest and feeling in the affairs of state, she rejoined her
family after the death of the king, her husband.   These two
queens died in Spain, not at San Yuste, but during the period
of their brother's residence there.

''Charles V received ambassadors at the monastery, and
attended to his correspondence.   When, at the day's decline,
he was conducted to a terrace, built expressly that he might
enjoy the beauty of the surrounding country, it pleased him
better to breathe the temperate air, so beneficial to his health,
and to meditate on the letters, the audiences, and the various
occurrences of the day, than to admire the southern splendor
of the landscape and the distant outline of the mountains of
Estramadura.''—*Jules van Praet.*

REFERENCES

Seebohm : *Era of the Protestant Revolution,* pp. 162–166 ;
Johnson : *Europe in the Sixteenth Century,* pp. 220–252.

§ 12. RELIGIOUS WARS IN FRANCE

The attitude of the King of France toward the Reformation was largely determined by external politics. Francis

Francis I, 1515–1547.

I, in whose reign the Lutheran reformation was begun, was inclined to tolerate the new opinions, on account of his sympathy with literature and with the cul-
ture of the Renaissance. He even intervened to save from destruction his friends who were accused by the clerical authorities of leaning toward the new doctrines. As a consequence of this policy of indifference and toleration, Lutheran ideas rapidly gained ground in France. About 1529, however, the political necessities of the king brought about a change in his attitude toward the Protestants. Defeated by

FRANCIS I. OF FRANCE.

his great rival, Charles V, in a struggle for the possession of northern Italy, Francis formed an alliance with Pope Clement VII against the Emperor, one of the conditions of which was the extirpation of heresy in France. This change of policy, together with the extravagances of the reformers, who placarded the walls of Paris with insulting attacks upon the mass, turned the royal attitude from indifference into persecution.

In the meantime a new and aggressive element had

been added to the Lutheran influence in France.   Calvinism brought in the principle of religious association. Churches were organized after the democratic system of Geneva, and the forces of revolt, gathered together under able leadership, formed a threatening party in the state.   Henry II did not possess the literary tastes of his father ; he was only twenty-nine when he came to the throne, and he gave himself unreservedly into the hands of the conservative party.

Henry II,
1547-1559.

KING HENRY II OF FRANCE.

Several measures were taken against heretics. It is likely that the French king was concerting plans with Philip of Spain for a general reduction of the Protestants, when he was killed by the accidental thrust of a lance at a tournament, in 1559, and the crown was transferred to his son, Francis II, a youth of sixteen.

The death of Henry II was the beginning of a period of confusion and decline in the political life of France, which lasted forty years. Three children of Henry II and Catharine de Medicis his wife, all of them weak and degenerate men, wore in turn the crown of France : Francis II (1559–1560) whose chief interest in history is his marriage with Mary, Queen of Scots ; Charles IX (1560–1574), in whose reign occurred the massacre of St. Bartholomew ; and Henry III (1574–1589), last of the Valois, who spent his days and nights in frivolous rioting, while his kingdom fell into anarchy and ruin. During the reigns of these three kings a struggle was taking place behind the throne, a triangular contest, in which the following persons were engaged : the Queen Mother, ambitious of supreme control ; the family of Guise, able and aspiring men, leaders of the Catholic party, who hoped to establish their line upon the throne of France with the extinction of the sterile race of Valois ; finally, the Protestant nobles, led by the Admiral Coligny, whose candidate for the crown was the Protestant prince, allied to the family of Valois, Henry of Navarre.

Catharine de Medicis.

Early in the reign of Charles IX, when the direction of affairs was in the hands of the Queen Mother, attempts were made to reconcile the rival factions. A meeting was held at Poissy, in the presence of the king, at which the Protestants were permitted to present their views for joint discussion. Theodore Beza, a disciple of Calvin, a man of courtly training and the ablest of the Huguenot orators, spoke before Charles and Catharine. The tendency of the time was toward

Colloquy of Poissy (1561).

toleration. An Edict of January, 1562, permitted the Huguenots to assemble for worship in any place outside of walled towns.

The time had not yet come, however, when the minds of men were prepared to grasp the principle of religious toleration. Up to the nineteenth century it seemed impossible for men of different religious confessions to live together in the same community. The idea that religion

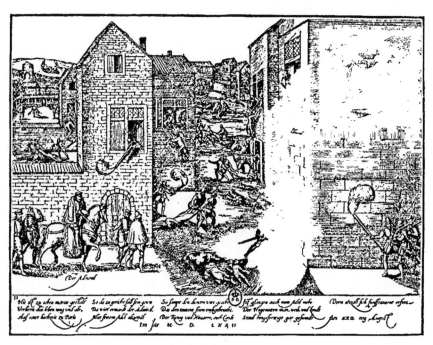

ST. BARTHOLOMEW.

On the left is represented the attempted assassination of Coligny, August 22d; on the right the murder of Coligny on the night of August 24, 1572.

is a personal thing, and can be separated from political and even from social life, was beyond the mental grasp of nearly all men of the sixteenth century. Chancellor l'Hôpital, who was a man far beyond his times, and was responsible for the edict of toleration of 1562, himself confessed that: "A Frenchman and an Englishman who are of the same religion have more affection for each other than citizens of the same city, or vassals of the same lord, who hold to different creeds."

The attempted adjustment of Catharine and l'Hôpital failed, and France was thrown into the horrors of civil war, which endured, with alternating periods

Civil War (1562-1598).

of treacherous peace, until the end of the century. In 1589 the assassination of Henry III. put an end to the house of Valois, and threw the succession, by right of blood, into the house of Bourbon, whose representative was Henry of Navarre. But because he was a Protestant, it took Henry of Navarre nine years to make good his claim against the opposition of the Catholics. Even then his success was the result of compromise, and a very serious one at that. Henry himself formally accepted the Catholic faith, and with this barrier removed France, exhausted with her forty years of civil war, was glad to allow his claims, and see the great house of Bourbon seated on the throne.

HENRY IV. OF FRANCE.
(Henry of Navarre.)

Thus the religious wars came to an end through the exhaustion of France, and the Edict of Nantes (1598), which fixed the conditions of final peace between Catholics and Protestants, is clearly a

Edict of Nantes.

compromise and temporary expedient. Since France was a compact nation, no such adjustment was possible as had been effected in Germany or in Switzerland ; but the Edict sought to apply the same principle, in so far as it was possible. The basis of the Edict was the recognition of the feudal unit of society. To each lord of a fief was given the right to celebrate, in his manor-house, for himself and

his retainers, the religion of his choice ; but in the city of
Paris, or elsewhere in the presence of the king, the rights
of the Catholic religion alone might be performed.   This
Edict is an evident makeshift, clearly violating the traditional spirit of French political development, which is
toward unity and a similarity of institutions throughout
France.   The Edict of Nantes contemplated a division of
France into an infinity of discordant units.   It is no
wonder, therefore, that, when the Bourbon power was well
established, King Louis XIV should restore the principle
of unity even at great economic loss to France, in the
exile of her most industrious citizens.   (Revocation of
Edict of Nantes, 1685.   See § 18.)

SOURCE REVIEW

I.—Extracts from the Edict of Nantes :

" VII.   It is permitted to all lords, gentlemen, and other
persons, natives and others as well, making profession of the
said religion called Reformed, having high justice or full
military tenure in our realm or in the countries of our sway,
be it as proprietor or in usufruct, in whole or in half, or for a
third part, to enjoy in their houses of said high justice or tenure as above mentioned, which they shall be required to name
before our bailiffs and seneschalls, each one in his jurisdiction,
as their principal domiciles, the exercise of the said religion,
as long as they there reside ; or in their absence their wives, or
indeed their family, or any part of the same."

" XIV.   (They are forbidden) ' as well from performing
any function of the said religion in our court or retinue, or
equally in our lands or territories beyond the mountains, or
in our city of Paris or within five leagues of said city ; at the
same time those of the said religion who live in the said lands
beyond the mountains or in our said city, and for five leagues
thereabouts, may not be investigated in their houses, nor con-
strained to do anything in respect to religion contrary to their
consciences, providing they comport themselves in other respects according to that which is contained in our present
Edict.' "

II.—French Kings of the Reformation Period.

Francis I = (1) Claude, daughter of Louis XII, his predecessor ;
1515-1547 | (2) Eleanor, sister of Charles V, 1530
         Henry II. = Catharine de' Medici
         1547-1559 |

Francis II,	Elizabeth,	Charles IX,	Henry III,	Francis	Margaret,
1559-1560,	m. Philip	1560-1574	1574-1589	duke of	m. Henry
m	II, K. of			Alençon,	of Na-
Mary Stuart	Spain.			died 1584	varre
					(Henry IV
					of France)

III.—Massacre of St. Bartholomew, August 24, 1572. Relation of Margaret, sister of the King : " King Charles, who was a prudent man and had been always very obedient to his mother, seeing the trend of affairs, took a sudden resolution to join the queen, his mother, and conform to her wishes, and protect himself against the Protestants by a closer union with the Catholics. Going to find the queen his mother, he sent for Monsieur de Guise and all the other Catholic princes and captains, and it was there resolved to cause, that night, the massacre of St. Bartholomew. And, quickly putting their hands to the task, the chains were stretched, the tocsin sounded, and each one rushed upon the quarter assigned to him, seeking the admiral and the other Huguenots as well. Monsieur de Guise went to the lodging of the Admiral, and Besme, a German gentleman, mounted to Coligny's chamber, and, after having stabbed him, cast his body through the window to Monsieur de Guise."

REFERENCES

Johnson: *Europe in the Sixteenth Century*, pp. 387-448 ; Adams : *European History*, 341-344 ; Myers: *Medieval and Modern History*, pp. 457-468.

§ 13. SPAIN AND THE NETHERLANDS

Philip II was the most powerful of the Catholic kings of the sixteenth century. If his territories were less in extent than those of his father, the Emperor Charles, they

were more absolutely his.   The title of Emperor was a fine
thing, but less productive of revenue than of embarrass-

Philip II of
Spain ments.   In some respects Philip was more
fortunate than his father. He was master of
Italy, where no one contested his sway.   The
old hostility of France, which had been the chief obstacle
in his father's path, no longer existed ; by the treaty of
Cateau-Cambrésis Philip was reconciled with Henry II of
France. Henry abandoned all claims upon Italy, and

gave to Philip his eldest daughter Elizabeth for a wife. Philip
exercised absolute power over
his lands, and his galleons
brought him wealth from
America.

Philip II looked upon himself as the lieutenant of God
upon earth for the extirpation
of heresy. He sought to establish a universal Catholic monarchy. From his somber palace of the Escorial, surrounded
by his advisers, he pulled the
wires of European diplomacy.

PHILIP II. OF SPAIN.

That he failed in his great un-
dertakings, that Spain touched the pinnacle of her greatness, and advanced far along the path of her decline within
the fifty-two years of his reign, is due to the fact that with
all his opportunities he was a man of small intelligence, of
narrow and bigoted views and misdirected energy. Suspicious of his agents, he reserved to himself the decision
of all points of policy, delaying action when haste was essential. " Time and I," he said, "are a match for any
other two ; " but it was not so.

The first task of Philip was to purge the Spanish kingdom of heretics. Comparatively few Spaniards were at-

tracted to the new doctrines; but about the year 1558 some few congregations of reformers were to be found in the larger towns of Spain. The dying Emperor, from his retreat at Yuste, mindful of his own experience in Germany, urged his son to spare no effort in rooting out the evil. Philip required no urging; with him it was a labor of love. He published an edict, condemning to the stake all who bought, sold, or read the prohibited books. The terrible instrument of the Inquisition brought to the stake all those suspected of heresy. The "*Auto da Fé*," or public burning of heretics, was for years the delight of Spanish audiences. Philip included an "*Auto da Fé*" in the fêtes he offered to his third bride, Elizabeth of France, on her arrival in Spain.

The purging of Spain.

In Philip's reign the Moriscoes, or "New Christians," as the descendants of the Moors who had accepted Christianity and remained in Spain were called, still inhabited the uplands of Granada, which they had converted into one of the most fertile parts of Spain. The fanaticism aroused by the persecution of Protestants proved their ruin. By irritating laws, suppressing their national songs and destroying their baths, the Moriscoes were driven into rebellion; they sought the aid of the Sultan of Turkey, but in vain. Overwhelmed with Spanish armies, by the Edict of 1570 they were scattered and removed to other parts of Spain, where they flourished as a result of their industrious habits, until in 1609 they were finally forced to leave the country, victims of Spanish hatred and fanaticism.

In 1580 the grandeur of Philip's reign reached its height. Through a vacancy in the succession to the throne of Portugal, Philip had added this realm to Spain, urging the claims of his first wife, Isabella of Portugal. His plans were far-reaching: he hoped to take England from Elizabeth; to aid the Catholics in France to overthrow their enemies, and thus, with

The Netherlands.

France and England at his back, to turn with a supreme effort upon Lutheran Germany. But an unreckoned factor came to ruin his prospects: the revolt of the Netherlands.

The Netherlands under Philip's rule contained two well-defined racial elements. The northern provinces (now Holland) were German, and lived from fishing and commerce; the southern provinces (now Belgium) were Flemish, and lived from agriculture and manufactures. The Dutch provinces had become Protestant; the Flemish remained Catholic. The new doctrines had been combated with vigor by Charles V and by Philip his son; but the Protestants increased in numbers in the North, and chose for their leader William of Orange, called the Silent, formerly governor of Holland under Charles V.

The conflict was fought with obstinacy on both sides. Philip sent the Duke of Alba into the Netherlands, and he established a reign of terror which endured from 1567 to 1573. Seeking to support the war in the Netherlands with taxes levied upon the people, Philip ruined the commerce of the country. Eighteen thousand persons were tried by his military tribunals and condemned to death. These atrocities drove the Flemish provinces to a union with Holland, and strengthened the Dutch in their faith and resistance. After 1573 a milder policy prevailed; but all in vain. In 1579 the Union of Utrecht proclaimed the independence of the seven provinces of the North; but it was twenty years before they obtained a recognition of their independence. The United Provinces were recognized in 1609 by the Archduke of Austria, to whom Philip had given the Netherlands at his death. The Peace of Westphalia, in 1648, ratified the concession, and made it a part of the public treaty law of Europe. The Flemish provinces remained under Spanish rule.

War for independence.

The intervention of Philip in England was equally disastrous. Rebuffed in his attempt to secure the hand of

The Invincible Armada.

Elizabeth, after the death of Queen Mary his second wife, and Elizabeth's half-sister, Philip supported the claims of
England.
Mary Stuart, widow of Francis II of France, Queen of Scotland and Catholic candidate for the throne of England. The execution of Mary of Scotland (1587) and the aid given by Elizabeth to the Dutch served Philip as a pretext for the invasion of England. An immense fleet was prepared and sent against the coasts of England under the command of the Duke of Medina-Sidonia. So proud were the Spaniards of their fleet, so confident were they in its success, that they named it the "Invincible Armada." It was dispersed by tempests in the Channel, and the ships of Elizabeth completed its ruin. When Philip heard of the disaster, in which his hopes of universal Catholic dominion were wrecked, he merely remarked to Medina-Sidonia : "I did not send you to combat the elements."

Everywhere Philip's plans miscarried. In France the success of Henry of Navarre broke the alliance formed with
Decline of Spain.
Henry II. Philip's armed intervention in France was in vain ; his forces were defeated at Fontaine-Française, and he was forced to sign the treaty of Vervins, leaving Henry IV to reign in peace and to give religious protection to the hated Protestants. In that year Philip II died (1598).

At the end of his reign Spain was bankrupt. To the surprise of his contemporaries the sovereign of the American mines had exhausted his resources. Spain had lost, since the discovery of America, the taste and habit of labor. The expulsion of the Moors and Jews had robbed her of her skilled laborers and her enterprising merchants. At a time when other nations were laying the foundation of the commercial and industrial life of the new time, Spain still lived on the results of her plunder of both Indies. Five-sixths of her home trade and nine-tenths of her Indian trade was monopolized by foreigners. Her copper and her leather, her chief products, were exported for manufacture. Spain failed to seize upon the spirit of the times and rapidly declined, so that, from a world power, she has become one of the least of European states.

SOURCE REVIEW

Why William was called the Silent.—Before the struggle with Spain was begun the Prince of Orange was present at the court of Henry II of France on a diplomatic errand. While hunting with the king in the forest of Vincennes that monarch unfolded to his guest a plan for the general extirpation of Protestants. "For the furtherance of the scheme in the Netherlands, it was understood that the Spanish regiments would be exceedingly efficient. The prince, although horror-struck and indignant at the royal revelations, held his peace and kept his countenance. The king was not aware that, in opening the delicate negotiation to the prince, he had given a warning of inestimable value to the man who had been born to resist the machinations of Philip and of Alba. William of Orange earned the title of "the Silent" from the manner in which he received these communications of Henry without revealing to the monarch, by word or look, the enormous blunder which he had committed. His purpose was fixed from that hour."—Motley: *The Rise of the Dutch Republic.*

REFERENCES

Johnson: *Europe in the Sixteenth Century*, pp. 315–386; Myers: *Mediæval and Modern History*, pp. 437-456.

CHAPTER V

Commerce

§ 14. STRUGGLE FOR THE INDIAN TRADE

THE goods brought from the East to Venice were sold in Venice to traders from the North and West. The Vene-

Distribution of Eastern goods. tians did not attempt to distribute their wares over the continent; it was left for the merchants of Europe to come to Venice, buy the goods, and carry them away. In the fifteenth century a constantly increasing amount of Eastern products, in

particular the spices, pepper, cinnamon, and cloves, was consumed in the countries north of the Alps, and it became a very profitable business for the merchants of the South German cities, especially those situated between the Alpine passes leading from Italy and the head-waters of the Rhine and Danube, to en-

OFFICE AND WAREHOUSE OF AN AUGSBURG MERCHANT—1495.

gage in the business of bringing goods from Venice and distributing them to the lower Rhenish countries and northeastern Germany. The goods were brought through

78

the mountains by wagon, or on the backs of packhorses and even of men.

It was along these routes of trade that the ideas of the Renaissance came into Germany, and established themselves amidst the patrician population of the wealthy German towns, such as Augsburg, Nuremberg, and Ratisbon. It was in these towns that accumulated wealth gave rise to art : painting and engraving, wrought-iron-work and jewelry of high artistic merit, and the wonderful development of the Gothic style of architecture, perpetuated in the cathedrals of Rhenish Germany.

This high development of German trade was overthrown, together with the commercial supremacy of Venice, of which it was a part, by the discovery *The ocean route.* of the ocean route to the Indies by Vasco da Gama in 1497. The advantage of the ocean route was so great that the spice trade was transferred at once to Lisbon. Although the distance was greater by the Cape of Good Hope route than by way of Egypt, yet there was no transshipment between the East and Lisbon, while by the Egyptian route at least three transshipments were necessary, and a caravan journey from the Red Sea to the Nile. But a still more serious obstacle was the heavy duties laid upon goods in transit by the Sultan of Egypt. In vain the Venetian ambassadors at Cairo urged a reduction of the duties, hoping thereby to compete successfully with the Portuguese. The Sultan was too stupid to see the point, and at length the whole matter of competition was summarily solved by the Portuguese, who seized the entrance to the Red Sea from the South, and cut off the water carriage of Indian goods to Egypt. Venice was left to handle only such goods as she might collect about the basin of the Mediterranean. The great spice trade went to Lisbon.

The Portuguese pursued the same policy as the Venetians in regard to distribution. They brought the goods

to Lisbon, where they stored them in the royal ware-
houses. The trade was a government monopoly, and only
such persons as obtained a royal privilege
were permitted to engage in it. Dutch, English, and German traders bought the India
wares in Lisbon, and took them to Antwerp, London, and
other North Sea and Baltic ports for distribution. The

The
Portuguese
trade.

merchant fleet of
Portugal set sail
from Lisbon bound
for the Indies, con-
voyed by ships of
war, once a year, in
February or March.
The voyage lasted
about eighteen
months, and al-
though, owing to
imperfect charts
and clumsy ships,
the losses were
great, still the prof-
its were immense.

The year 1542
marks the zenith of
Portu-
guese
power.

The Portu-
guese colonial
empire.

OCEAN SHIP OF THE FIFTEENTH CENTURY.

For sixty years the
King of Portugal
was the supreme ruler of the southern coasts of Asia. In
the West as well Portugal was powerful in trade. From
the coast of Africa came ivory, cotton, gold-dust, and
slaves; sugar from the Canaries and wine from Madeira.
In 1500 Cabral discovered the Brazils, named from the
dye-wood, which was the first product; later found to be a

magnificent empire, successor to the glories of the mother country.

The Portuguese colonial empire, so brilliantly and rapidly acquired, lasted little more than half a century. In 1580 the union of Pórtugal with Spain brought disaster to the colonies. Philip lived in his dream of Catholic restoration, and his wars with the Dutch had the effect, not only of wasting the resources of Portugal, but of driving the Dutch into the Indian seas, with the consequent loss of Portuguese possessions. Only a few small stations remained of their former great Indian empire. The policy of Spain had sapped the strength and vigor of Portugal.

The Dutch policy in the East differed materially from that of Portugal. Instead of a government monopoly, as at Lisbon, the Dutch trade was controlled by companies, privately organized, and chartered by the States General. The Dutch East India Company was chartered in 1602, absorbing some earlier and smaller companies. It was empowered to make peace and war with Eastern princes, to establish forts, and appoint administrative and judicial officers. Its headquarters were at Batavia, on the island of Java. The eastern dominion of Holland was divided into administrative departments: Java, Amboina, Ternate, Macassar.

Rise of Dutch colonial power.

In conformity with the ideas of the day, the Dutch sought to establish a strict monopoly in spices. The nutmeg was permitted to be grown only in Banda, the clove in Amboina. Elsewhere the trees were rooted out and destroyed. A small product at a high price was thought to be more profitable and more easily controlled than a larger supply at a smaller price.

The colonial possessions of the Dutch in the West were of less importance. Their attempt to find a northwest passage to the Indies resulted in the settlement of Man-

7

hattan.[1] In 1612 a fort was built on the gold coast of Upper Guiana, and in 1621 a West India company was formed after the model of the great East India Company.

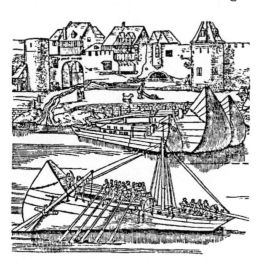

Various possessions were acquired in Africa and Brazil, but New Amsterdam, the main settlement in the West, was lost to the English in 1664. Altogether the western ventures were not profitable, and after an unprofitable career the company was disbanded in 1790. The Dutch colonial empire was more enduring

RHINE SHIPPING, SIXTEENTH CENTURY.

than the Portuguese; but what it had won from Portugal, Holland was forced to surrender in part to England, retaining, however, to this day, great and wealthy possessions in the Far East.

SOURCE REVIEW

Calecut and the Indian Trade; Trade Routes with the West, as they existed before the opening of the Cape Route by Vasco da Gama.—From the *First Voyage* of Vasco da Gama: "From this country of Calecut, or Upper India,[2] come the spices which are consumed in the East and the West, in Portugal, as in all other countries of the world, as also precious

---

[1] Manhattan Island, now New York, was settled in 1615, six years after Hendrik Hudson's voyage up the North River (Hudson), in search of a northwest passage.

[2] The India of to-day was called "Upper India," while the term "Lower India" was applied to the country of the famous "Prester John," the Christian sovereign of Abyssinia.

stones of every description. The following spices are to be found in this city of Calecut, being its own produce : much ginger and pepper and cinnamon, although the last is not of so fine a quality as that brought from an island called Çillan (Ceylon), which is eight days' journey from Calecut. Calecut is the market for all this cinnamon. Cloves are brought to this city from an island called Malequa (Malacca). The Mecca vessels carry these spices from here to a city in Mecca (Arabia) called Judea (Jidda), and from the said island to Judea is a voyage of fifty days' sailing before the wind, for the vessels of this country cannot tack. At Judea they discharge their cargoes, paying customs duties to the Grand Sultan (of Egypt). The merchandise is then transshipped to smaller vessels, which carry it through the Red Sea to a place close to Santa Catarina of Mount Sinai, called Tuuz (Suez ?), where customs duties are paid once more. From that place the merchants carry the spices on the backs of camels, which they hire at the rate of four cruzados[1] each, to Quayro (Cairo), a journey occupying ten days. At Quayro duties are again paid. On this road to Quayro they are frequently robbed by thieves who are in that country, such as the Bedouins and others.

"At Quayro the spices are embarked on the River Nile, which rises in Prester John's country in Lower India, and descending that river for two days they reach a place called Roxette (Rosetta), where duties have to be paid once more. There they are placed on camels, and are conveyed in one day to a city called Alexandria, which is a seaport. This city is visited by the galleys of Venice and Genoa, in search of these spices, which yield the Grand Sultan a revenue of 600,000 cruzados in customs duties."

§ 15. ENGLISH AND FRENCH COLONIZATION

Nearly one hundred years elapsed after the discovery of the ocean route to the Indies, before English mariners found their way about the southern cape of Africa. The struggle against the naval power of Spain developed the English into a nation of sailors. In 1582 an English cap-

---

[1] A *cruzado* was a gold coin of Portugal, worth about $2.25

tain, Stephens by name, sailed to India. In 1593 the capture of a Portuguese ship laden with precious oriental
wares stimulated the cupidity of English
merchants. On the last day of the year 1600
the East India Company was formed, "The
Company of Merchants of London trading into the East
Indies." In 1601 the first expedition, consisting of five
ships under Captain Lancaster, was sent out, with bullion,
broadcloth, tin, cutlery, and glass. The voyage was suc-

The English in India.

EARLY ENGLISH SAILORS.

cessful, but it failed
to arouse enthusi-
asm in England,
and for many years
the volume of trade
with India was
small. Factories,
however, were es-
tablished at various
places in India, and
Bombay, a part of
the marriage por-
tion brought to
Charles II by Cath-
arine of Portugal,

was given by the king to the Company, and a mint established there in 1668.

In the eighteenth century the East India Company,
which had been organized as a chartered trading company,
developed into a huge system of territorial government, the
ruler of vast territories and of millions of people. Since
the death of Aurungzebe, in 1707, the Indian empire of the
Moguls had fallen into pieces, and the numerous little
states into which it was resolved formed an easy prey for a
foreign power desirous of extending its authority. Both
France and England strove to improve this opportunity,
and the second half of the eighteenth century is full of the

struggles of these powers for the possession of India.   It is
a noteworthy feature of this conflict, that, although it was
waged between French and English, yet the penalty was
paid by the native princes, who became involved as allies
of one or the other of the rival powers, and eventually lost
their territories to the stranger.   Through the able general-
ship of Lord Clive, who showed great skill in converting
the native levies into able soldiery (Sepoys), the East India
Company extended its possessions and drove the French

EAST INDIA HOUSE.   LONDON, 1803.

out of India, as the English were, at the same time, driving
the French out of Canada.   In 1765 Lord Clive was governor
of Bengal, and in the same year received from the Great
Mogul at Delhi a recognition of English sovereignty over
northern India.

So long as the strict monopoly of the East India Company continued, the English trade with India was not
remarkable.   It formed in 1780 only one thirty-second
part of the foreign trade of the kingdom ; but while the
finances of the Company languished, its officials returned

home with enormous fortunes. The opportunity for plunder was perhaps the greatest that the modern world

Trade versus plunder.

has afforded. For two thousand years a stream of gold and silver had been flowing from Europe eastward in exchange for Oriental products. It was this stream of wealth, hoarded after the manner of the East, and passed from hand to hand by succession or conquest, that filled the treasure-chambers of Asian monarchs. Not until the times of Lord Clive and his successor, Warren Hastings, was it returned to the channels of western trade.

In 1784 the power of the East India Company was restricted by the establishment of a board of control. In 1813 the India trade was partially opened to private enterprise, with a marked result in the increase of trade. Upon the renewal of its charter in 1833 the Company was compelled to abandon entirely its trading, and in 1858 the Queen assumed the government of India.

In the sixteenth century the maritime nations of Europe began to turn their attention to the unknown possibilities

Western discoveries and colonization.

of the Western Hemisphere. Spain, by right of discovery and of her supremacy on the seas, was first in the field. She seized at once upon those portions of America which seemed most prolific in the precious metals. With the discovery of silver-mines in Mexico in 1532, and later in Peru, began the flow of precious metals into Spain. Her colonial policy, however, was merely one of exploitation. Comparatively few Spaniards went to make their permanent homes in America, and of the few that went many mixed with the natives, and produced a race inferior in ability and enterprise to the European. The same may be said of the Portuguese in Brazil.

It was not until the end of the sixteenth century that Englishmen, stimulated to maritime effort by the hostility of Spain, turned their attention to the West. The bold seamen of the age of Elizabeth, of whom Francis Drake was typical, bold pirates and sea-rovers, sailed about the world, plundering Spanish galleons and settlements, bringing home cargoes of booty, with a present for the Queen. The first attempts at colonization failed, Sir Humphrey Gilbert in Newfoundland and Sir Walter Raleigh at Roanoke; but later efforts met with success, when a band of self-exiled men laid at Plymouth and at Charles-Town the foundation of New England. In the middle of the eighteenth century thirteen colonies stretched from North to South between the Allegheny Mountains and the sea. Their European population was intact and free from native mixture, preserving the characteristics of the race from which they sprang.

Holland was too small a country to furnish colonists for

French colonies. so great an enterprise, and her possessions were little more than trading stations. France, however, had high ambitions toward a western empire. Her mariners, attracted to the cod fisheries of the Newfoundland banks, established her power in the valley of the St. Lawrence. Daring explorers navigated the Great Lakes, and traced the Mississippi from its sources to the Gulf of Mexico, taking possession of the drainage area of the great river and its tributaries in the name of their king, Louis XIV. Thus, while the English were content with the Atlantic slope, the French had registered a claim, by right of discovery, to the country of the middle West. With the expansion of the English colonies came the inevitable struggle, and in this the French, although possessed of points of great strategic

SIR WALTER RALEIGH.

value, were handicapped with their lack of population in the West : sixty thousand against a million of American-English. "The French and Indian War," with its terminal Treaty of Paris in 1763, gave to the English the country of the St. Lawrence and the Lakes, and an outlet to the Mississippi on the West.

SOURCE REVIEW.

I. Magnitude of the Conquest of India.—"We have always thought it strange, that while the history of the Spanish empire in America is so familiarly known to all the nations of Europe, the great actions of Englishmen in the East should, even among themselves, excite little interest. Yet the victories of Cortes were gained over savages who had no letters, who were ignorant of the use of metals, who had not broken in a single animal to labor, who wielded no better weapons than those which could be made out of sticks, flints, and fish-bones, who regarded a horse-soldier as a monster, half man and half beast, who took a harquebusier for a sorcerer, able to scatter the thunder and lightning of the skies. The people of India, when we subdued them, were ten times as numerous as the vanished Americans, and were at the same time quite as highly civilized as the victorious Spaniards. They had reared cities larger and fairer than Saragossa and Toledo, and buildings more beautiful and costly than the Cathedral of Seville. They could show bankers richer than the richest firms of Barcelona or Cadiz, viceroys whose splendor far surpassed that of Ferdinand the Catholic, myriads of cavalry and long trains of artillery which would have astonished the Great Captain."—Macaulay.

II. After Clive's Conquest of a Native Prince.—"The shower of wealth now fell copiously on the Company and its servants. A sum of eight hundred pounds sterling, in coined silver, was sent down the river. The fleet which conveyed this treasure consisted of more than a hundred boats, and performed its triumphal voyage with flags flying and music playing. Calcutta, which but a few months before had been so desolate, was now more prosperous than ever. Trade revived, and the signs of affluence appeared in every English house. As to Clive, there was no limit to his acquisitions but his own moderation. The treasury of Bengal was thrown open to him. There were piled up, after the usage of Indian princes, immense masses of coin, among which might not seldom be detected the florins and byzants with which, before any European ship had turned the Cape of Good Hope, the Venetians purchased the stuffs and spices of the East. Clive walked between heaps of gold and silver, crowned with rubies and diamonds, and was at liberty to help himself."—Macaulay.

CHAPTER VI

The Supremacy of France

§ 16. GREAT MINISTERS OF FRANCE

WITH the coming of Henry IV to the throne and the ending of the religious wars, France entered upon a period of supremacy in Europe. Her great rivals were no longer powerful : Spain was falling into decay ; in Germany religious differences were for more than two centuries a bar to national unity. For two hundred years the history of France is the history of the continent of Europe. Not only was she paramount in politics, but her decision was final also in the spheres of literature, of science, and of art. The courts of Europe reflected the fashions of the Bourbons.

The Bourbons.

This was due not wholly to the greatness of Henry IV and his successors. Only one of the successors of Henry IV was a man of strong personality, Louis XIV. It was due rather to a succession of great ministers, men of vast creative genius and administrative ability : Sully, Richelieu, Mazarin, and Colbert.

The brief reign of Henry IV was a period of recuperation for France. After a half century of civil war the whole fabric of society had fallen in anarchy. Having made good his claim as king of France, and brought the great nobles to his side by threats or gifts, Henry's next task was to bring about the economic recovery of his realm. In this he was aided by his minister, the Duke of Sully.

Sully.

Sully wisely held that agriculture was the basis of France's prosperity. The chief object of his policy was to

90

protect the peasants who tilled the soil, and who, as subject to the taille, or land-tax, were the chief contributors to the king's treasury. During the civil wars this class was crushed under intolerable taxes, and in many instances its rights in the land were usurped by nobles, so that a considerable body of land was cut off from taxation. The aim of Sully was to lessen the burdens of agriculture, and restore their property to the peasants. This he accomplished by economy in the public expenditures; by limiting the demands of the nobles upon their tenants; by the introduction of new lines of agriculture, such as silk-growing; and by an extension of the area of cultivation, draining marshes under government direction. The grain trade was freed from restrictions, and the grower allowed to sell in the best market, even outside the kingdom. The result was an increase in the production of grain and a greater profit to the producer. The king advised his nobles to return to their estates and see that they were properly culti-vated. "Agriculture and stock-

THE DUKE OF SULLY.

raising," said Sully, "are the two breasts of France; the true mines and treasures of Peru."

Sully was no special friend of manufacture, but the king had a wider vision. He encouraged the production of articles of luxury—silk, glass, linen, and metal goods—and laid the foundation of the specialties of French manufacture. Commerce received its share of attention; roads were improved, post-routes established, and canals built. Colonization received an impulse; in 1608 Champlain founded Quebec.

With the assassination of Henry IV, by the fanatic

Ravaillac, the crown passed to his infant son, Louis XIII.
The mother of Louis, Marie de Medicis, who became regent,

Richelieu.

lacked political ability, and France seemed about to relapse into anarchy. Religious discords came again to the front, and the regent, in her helplessness, called together the Estates General. The three estates could come to no agreement, and their powerlessness had the effect of discrediting this national parliament. It was never again assembled until the eve of the great revolution in 1789. The salvation of the house of Bourbon came, not through representative government, but

RICHELIEU.

with the introduction into public affairs of Cardinal Richelieu, who became chief minister of the king in 1624, and continued to direct the royal policy until his death in 1642.

The internal policy of Richelieu, as he announced it to Louis XIII, was " to effect the ruin of the Huguenot party, to abase the pride of the nobles, and to bring all subject to the king's obedience." To the accomplishment of these ends he set his inflexible will. Although Richelieu was never a personal favorite of the king, yet Louis XIII, fortunately for himself and for France, possessed enough intelligence to enable him to appreciate the value of Richelieu's aid.

The Huguenots constituted in France a state within a state. The success of their intrigues would have resulted in the disruption of the realm. Certain for-

The Huguenots.

tified places given them by the Edict of Nantes, as cities of refuge, were points of vantage, from which they defied the royal authority. Against the chief of these cities, the seaport of Rochelle, Richelieu turned his forces. After a desperate siege, in spite of English aid, the city was compelled to surrender. By the Edict of Alais, 1629, the Huguenots, while retaining liberty of conscience, secured them by the Edict of Nantes, were deprived of their strongholds, and reduced to the common condition of all subjects of the king.

The struggle with the nobles was long and desperate. Although Richelieu enjoyed the confidence and support of the king, he had to strive, nevertheless, against the influence of the king's immediate family. The queen-mother, and the queen, a Spanish princess, were with the nobles. Marie de Medicis summoned her son " to choose between his mother and a valet." Once the king vacillated and the enemies of Richelieu rejoiced. Richelieu prepared to leave Paris ; but the king summoned him to an audience, and restored him to his power. This was the famous " Day of Dupes." " Richelieu packed his boxes in the morning ; his enemies at night."

The nobles.

Richelieu conquered the nobles by enforcing against them the royal laws, repressing their disorders and checking their lawlessness, which arose from their pride of independence and belief in their superiority to the law. The great work of Richelieu, however, is his extension of the power of the royal government in the provinces. He sent into the provinces " *intendants*[1] of justice, peace, and finance," young and ambitious lawyers, eager to earn fame and nobility, devoted servants of the government of the king. These men, little by little, usurped the functions of the local grandees, who for generations had served, half independently, as royal governors. In this wise, and by the orderly arrangement of the central government at Paris, Richelieu built up a form of centralized control, such as

---

[1] The *intendant* was an officer of the king, sent into the province to attend to the judicial and financial interests of the crown. By faithful service he gained nobility.

Europe had never known since Roman times, a system so complete and automatic, that it served, in spite of abuses, and with weak kings at the helm of state, until the end of the eighteenth century.

Louis XIV, who succeeded his father, Louis XIII, in 1643, was five years of age. His mother, Anne of Austria, was appointed regent, and the minister of her choice was an Italian, Cardinal Mazarin, a pupil of Richelieu. In Mazarin's time the nobles rose against the royal power in the conspiracy of the "Fronde." The Queen and Mazarin were more than once obliged to flee

Mazarin.

MAZARIN.

from Paris. This last struggle against the royal authority filled France for two years with the horrors of civil war, and ended in the triumph of the centralized monarchy. At the death of Mazarin, in 1661, Louis XIV himself assumed the direction of affairs.

In Colbert Louis XIV found, at the beginning of his personal reign, a minister of finance of great ability. The finances of the country at the death of Mazarin were in great confusion. Corruption was the order of the day; nor had Mazarin been wholly free from suspicion. Of eighty-four millions collected in taxes in 1661 only twenty-three millions were turned into the royal treasury. Colbert attacked these abuses; new methods of collection increased the revenues of the state and lessened the burden of the people.

Colbert.

But Colbert's measures were not limited to reforms. He sought to bring about an age of prosperity through manufacture; and to secure the best results, he thought industry must be under government control. This theory of

" paternalism," a product of the ideas of government then prevailing, is in direct opposition to our present ideas of freedom in industry. By a series of protective tariffs, by the introduction of skilled workmen from abroad, by subsidies, and by minute government supervision of manufacture, intended to secure the best quality of product, Colbert built up French industry. Swedes and Germans established the iron industry ; Dutch weavers the manufacture of cloth ; the silk manufactures of Lyons became famous ; and English and Venetian lace-makers established their trade at Valenciennes. Colbert sought to develop foreign commerce by similar means. East and West India Companies were organized, and given a monopoly of trade.

SOURCE REVIEW

To be the chief servant of a king, and to endure his whims and uncurbed temper, must have called for great devotion and self-control. Henry IV often had occasion to repent his violent conduct toward his faithful minister, Sully. The following is one of the many instances of the kind related by Sully in his Memoirs : "I was still confined to the house by an unfortunate accident when the King came to me one day to confer with me about some affair of the heart, which I have forgotten. All I remember is that I was bold enough to represent to Henry that affairs of this kind, which so little suited with his age and dignity, were so many baneful wounds to his glory, and probably would end in something more fatal. My freedom, often graciously received, produced nothing this time but an extreme rage in Henry, and drew upon myself the most lively reproaches from him. He left my chamber in such wrath that he was heard to say aloud, and with great emotion : 'It is impossible to bear with this man any longer ; he is eternally contradicting me, and approves of nothing I propose ; but, by Heaven ! I will make him obey me—he shall not appear in my presence these fifteen days.' My disgrace appeared to all that were present as a thing absolutely resolved on. My servants were afflicted ; but many others, I believe, inwardly rejoiced at it.

"At seven the next morning the king came to the Arsenal with five or six persons, whom he brought with him in his coach. He would not allow my people to give me notice of his arrival, but walked up to my apartment and tapped at my closet door himself. Upon my asking, 'Who is there?' he replied, 'It is the king.' I knew his voice and was not a little surprised at this visit. 'Well, what are you doing here?' said he, entering with Roquelaure, De Vic, Zamet, La Varenne, and Erard the engineer ; for he had occasion to speak to me about the fortifications of Calais. I replied that I was writing letters, and preparing work for my secretaries. And, indeed, my table was all overspread with letters and statements of affairs, which I was to lay before the council that day. 'And how long have you been thus employed?' said his majesty. 'Ever since three o'clock,' I replied. 'Well, Roquelaure,' he said, turning to him, 'for how much money would you lead this life?' 'In truth, Sire, not for all your treasures,' replied Roquelaure. Henry made no answer, but, commanding every one to retire, he began to confer with me upon matters in which it was impossible for me to be of his opinion ; and this he readily perceived when I told him coldly that I had no advice to give ; that his majesty having, doubtless, taken his resolution after mature deliberation, all that remained to be done was to obey him, since he was displeased when my sentiments happened not to agree with his. 'Oh, oh !' said Henry, smiling, and giving me a little tap on the cheek, 'so you are on the reserve with me, and are angry at what happened yesterday ! However, I am so no longer with you ; come, come, embrace me, and live with me in the same familiarity as usual ; for I love you not the less for it ; on the contrary, from the moment that you cease to contend with me on occasions where I am convinced you cannot approve my conduct, I shall believe you no longer love me.'"

REFERENCES

Wakeman : *European History*, 1598–1715, pp. 15–38, 132–164, 184–205.

§ 17.   The Thirty Years' War (1618–1648)

The peace of Augsburg, 1555, sought to put an end to the religious struggles in Germany by fixing the territorial arrangement as it existed at the termination of hostilities in 1552, and permanently limiting the extension of either religion.   It made no provision for the growth or decline of the new faith.   Several of its clauses were certain to become subjects of disagreement.   One, called the "Ecclesiastical Reservation," provided that any dignitary of the Church, a bishop or an abbot, for example, who embraced the new doctrines should surrender the territory over which he had ruled as a spiritual prince.   This provision presented grave difficulties in the Rhine country, where the population became Protestant, and the bishops desired to convert their lands into temporal sovereignties.   At Cologne the Archbishop Elector, Gebhard Truchsess, was converted to Protestantism, and sought to retain his archbishopric.   Deposed by the pope, he was driven out by Spanish troops, and the affair resulted in much bitterness.

General causes of the war.

The secularizations were another bone of contention.   No Protestant prince was permitted to appropriate any portion of ecclesiastical property, as, for example, the lands of a monastery, which had not been secularized in 1552.   By this provision Protestant princes were obliged to tolerate the existence of little centers of Catholic influence in the midst of territories otherwise wholly Protestant.   Another weakness of the treaty was its failure to recognize Calvinism, a religion which was making great gains in South Germany and in the Rhine valley.   The Calvinists, having no legal status in the treaty, were willing to see it broken.

During the years immediately following the peace of Augsburg, when Protestantism was growing in Germany,

8

the Protestant princes treated the provisions of Augsburg, particularly in regard to secularizations, very lightly. When, however, on account of Jesuit effort and the dissensions among the Protestants themselves, the spread of the new doctrines ceased, and Catholicism began to gain ground, then the Catholic princes began to insist upon a literal interpretation of the clauses of the treaty. A struggle was inevitable, and the two parties began to prepare for it; the Protestants with the organization of the "Union," under the guidance of Christian of Anhalt; the Catholics with the "League," under the leadership of Maximilian of Bavaria.

Since the times of John Huss Bohemia had been a center of religious unrest. It had been retained in the church only by the concession of special privileges to the Bohemians in the exercise of their religion. The Austrian ruler of Bohemia, the Emperor Rudolph II, granted in 1609 a royal charter which gave to Bohemia a certain amount of national independence of Austria, and certain privileges, political and religious. Under the Emperor Matthias this charter was violated; the Archbishop of Prague, an Austrian official, suppressed and destroyed

MARTINITZ AND SLAWATA.

The war in Bohemia.

churches of the reformed faith. A riot followed ; a mob, led by Count Henry of Thurn, stormed the palace, threw Martinitz and Slawata, the imperial regents, from a window, and organized a revolutionary government. The Emperor Matthias died in March following, and the Bohemians refused to recognize his successor, Ferdinand of Styria. They proclaimed as king of Bohemia Frederick V, Elector-Palatine of the Rhine, who had recently married Elizabeth, daughter of the English king, James I.

But James I made no effort to aid his son-in-law. Even the " Union," ruled by Lutheran influences, held aloof (for Frederick was a Calvinist prince), and Frederick was left to meet the overwhelming forces of the Emperor. Bohemia was easily overrun, and the war carried into the Palatinate. The Bavarians, under Tilly, and Spanish troops from the Netherlands, ravaged the fair Rhenish country for three years. Frederick fled to England, and his electoral office was given to Maximilian of Bavaria. In this first struggle the Catholic powers had won an easy victory, and the Lutheran leaders of the " Union " were not grieved to see a Calvinist state despoiled.

The rapid invasion of North Germany by the imperial troops at length aroused the Protestant states to fear for their own safety. Christian of Denmark sought to stem the Catholic advance. The Emperor was without an army, but chance brought to his aid an able commander in the person of Wallenstein, a Bohemian nobleman. Wallenstein had distinguished himself in the Bohemian campaign against the Protestants, and was rewarded with confiscated estates and the title of Duke of Friedland. He offered to equip an army free of cost to the Emperor, providing for its subsistence and pay from the pillage of the enemies' country. Thus commissioned, he assembled an army of freebooters, mounted Croats from Hungary, foot-soldiers from Holland, the riff-raff of a generation of wars. This system

The Danish period.

of great mercenary armies, without patriotism, attended
with a camp-following of desperate men and women,
twice as numerous as the army itself, moving over the
country like a scourge, was the feature that made, the

LANDING OF GUSTAVUS ADOLPHUS.

Thirty Years' War the most destructive and terrible of
modern times. The Danish king was defeated and North
Germany overrun by Wallenstein. In the moment of
victory the Emperor issued an edict of restitution, demanding the restoration to the Catholic Church of all the
ecclesiastical property confiscated since the convention of
Passau.

Up to this time the Emperor had had his way; but now
a new defender of Protestantism appeared in the person
of the King of Sweden, Gustavus Adolphus,
the heroic character of the time. With his
strictly disciplined army, he crossed the Baltic and moved
through North Germany against the imperial forces, the
equal, if not the superior, of Wallenstein himself. Although prevented by the jealousy of the elector of Brandenburg from reaching Magdeburg in time to prevent the
pillage of the city, he defeated Tilly near Leipzig, and

Swedish period.

overcame Wallenstein at the battle of Lützen, where Gustavus himself was killed. The campaign of the Swedish king, heroic as it was, had little effect, except to break the forces of the Emperor. The war still continued, and the Elector of Saxony sought a separate peace and alliance with the Emperor.

The war dragged on. The Emperor was too feeble, the Protestant princes too selfish and disunited to give the final stroke. It was the intervention of a Catholic power, fighting upon the Protestant side, that broke the spell. The motive of Richelieu in intervening was to prevent the ultimate triumph of the house of Austria, the ancient enemy of

The intervention of France.

LÜTZEN, 1632   DEATH OF GUSTAVUS ADOLPHUS.

France, and to preserve the principle of disunion among the German states. Germany, welded into a Catholic empire under the absolute control of the Hapsburgs, would be a dangerous neighbor for France. The intervention took place in 1635.　First the Netherlands were invaded ; then the Swedish army, after the death of Gustavus Adolphus, passed under the leadership of France.　Richelieu died in 1642, but his foreign policy was carried on by Mazarin. French victories in Bavaria, the capture of Prague, and the threatened advance upon Vienna brought the Emperor Ferdinand II to terms.

A congress representing the powers of Europe met in 1645 in Westphalia : the Catholic delegates at Münster ; the Protestants at Osnabrück.　The negotia-

Peace of
Westphalia,

tions lasted three years.　The Spanish deputies withdrew, refusing to be a party to a general religious peace ; but signed the separate treaty of Münster, recognizing the independence of Holland.

The Peace of Westphalia regulated first of all the religious questions of Germany.　The principle of *cujus regio, eius religio* was maintained, each prince retaining the right to impose his own religion upon his subjects ; but dissenting subjects were given three years in which to migrate, and were allowed to retain possession of their goods. Ecclesiastical property, secularized before 1619 in the Palatinate, and before 1624 in the rest of Germany, might be held by Protestant princes.　Calvinists were admitted to the benefits of the Treaty of Augsburg, and given religious liberty in the meaning of that document.　Thus the religious question was settled, but at a fearful cost. The wealth and power of Germany were broken, whole districts were desolated, and cities lay in ruins.　In country places the arts of peace were forgotten, and wolves roamed over the ruins of former villages.

The power of the Emperor in Germany was reduced to a mere shadow.　He became little more than the president of the Diet, which held its regular meetings at Frankfort-on-the-Main.　Each of the 360 princes of Germany was made an absolute sovereign in his territories, with the right to make treaties and contract alliances with foreign states.

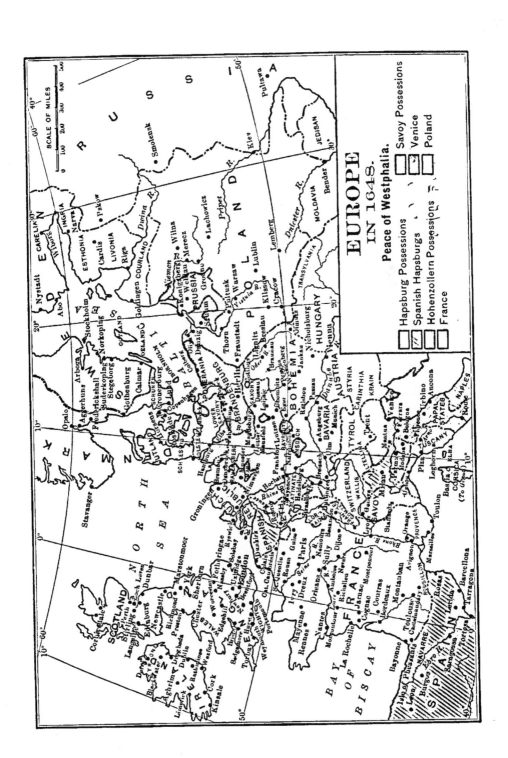

EUROPE
IN 1648.

Peace of Westphalia.

Hapsburg Possessions
Spanish Hapsburgs
Hohenzollern Possessions
France

Savoy Possessions
Venice
Poland

Thus the separatist principle triumphed completely in Germany, as a result of the religious struggle. Germany, desolated by war, became a patchwork of little states, and for two centuries ceased to contest with France the supremacy of Europe. The Treaty of Westphalia ends the period of Religious Wars, and effected the most important political rearrangement of Europe since the Treaty of Verdun (843).

SCENE IN THIRTY YEARS' WAR.

SOURCE REVIEW

I. Gustavus Adolphus.—Improvements in methods of warfare and in dicipline: "He was indisputably the greatest general of his age, and the bravest soldier in the army which he had formed. Familiar with the tactics of Greece and Rome, he had discovered a more effective system of warfare, which was adopted as a model by the most eminent commanders of subsequent times. He reduced the unwieldy squadrons of cavalry, and rendered their movements more light and rapid; and with the same view, he widened the intervals between his battalions. Instead of the usual array in a single line, he disposed his forces in two lines, that the second might advance in the event of the first giving away.

He made up for his want of cavalry by placing infantry among the horse; a practise which frequently decided the victory. Europe first learned from him the importance of infantry. All Germany was astonished at the strict discipline which, at the first, so creditably distinguished the Swedish armies within their territories; all disorders were punished with the utmost severity, particularly impiety, theft, gambling, and dueling. The Swedish articles of war enforced frugality. In the camp, the king's tent not excepted, neither silver nor gold was to be seen."—Schiller: *Thirty Years' War.*

II. The Scourge of Germany.—Military life of the time, described by Adam Junghaus, a contemporary: "Nothing is truer than this: that a soldier must have to eat and to drink, whether it is paid for by the sexton or the parson; for a lansquenet has neither house nor home, neither cow nor calf, and nobody will bring his food to him. Therefore he must pick it up wherever he can find it, and buy without money, whether the farmer likes it or not. To-day the brethren must suffer hunger and endure hard times; to-morrow they will have such abundance that they may clean their boots with wine and beer. Then their dogs will eat roast meat, and the girls and boys will have good positions: they will be housewives and butlers over other people's property. When the owner has been driven out with wife and child, then come the sad days for the chickens and the geese, the fat cows, the oxen, the swine, and the sheep. Money is divided up by the hatful, velvet, silks, and cloths measured with long spears; cows are killed for their hides, chests and boxes are broken into, and when all is plundered and nothing more is left then the house is set on fire.

"This is the kind of fire for a lansquenet, when fifty villages and hamlets are in flames. Then they go on further and begin again. That sort of thing makes fighting men gay, and it is a very desirable sort of life—except for those who pay the reckoning. It lures many a mother's son into the field, who never comes back home again, nor bothers his friends again; for the saying is: Lansquenets have crooked fingers and lame hands for work, but for pilfering and plunder the lame hands become straight and strong. That has been so before our time, and will be after we are gone. Whithersoever the fighting people go, they carry with them the keys to all apartments, their axes and clubs, and when there is a lack of stables for the horses, it makes no difference ; they stall their horses in churches and hermitages and in lordly halls. If dry wood is wanting for the fire, that is no matter, there are chairs, benches, plows, and everything the house contains. For green wood one need not go far ; just cut down the fruit trees that stand near by in the orchard ; for the saying is : While we live, let us live ; to-morrow we are away. Therefore, Master Host, cheer up. You have a guest or two, whom you will be glad to be rid of ; therefore bring out the best you have, and charge it up on the shutter. If the house burns, the chalk will burn too. That is the lansquenet's way : to have it charged, and ride away, and pay when we come back.''

REFERENCES

Adams : *European History*, pp. 344–355 ; Wakeman : *European History*, 1598–1715 ; Gardiner : *The Thirty Years' War*.

§ 18. AGE OF LOUIS XIV

When Louis XIV took up the reins of government at the death of Mazarin, 1661, the foundations were already laid for the erection of an absolute monarchy. The enemies of the royal power had been vanquished through the labors of Richelieu and his pupil. The Estates General, organ of popular representation, had been discarded in 1614, and was never called again during the long reigns of Louis XIV and his successor, Louis XV. When these kings wished to obtain popular sanction for their acts, they convoked the Assembly of Notables, whose members were carefully chosen by the king's agents. The Protestants had ceased to be dangerous since Richelieu had deprived them of their political privileges. The nobles were submissive ; their castles were

Inheritance of Louis XIV.

destroyed, their haughty spirit broken. Nothing was wanting but a strong personality, and that Louis XIV himself supplied. At the death of Mazarin he said to his chancellor : "I shall be for the future my own chief minister. I ask you and command you that no order shall be sealed except at my command ; and you, my secretary of state, and you, my superintendent of finance, I order you to sign nothing except with my consent."

Louis XIV entertained a high idea of his rights of sovereignty ; he thought he held his throne directly from God.

Louis XIV.

Theory of the divine right of kings. This opinion was perhaps not new; but it was in France, under Louis XIV, that it came to be erected into a principle, the vital principle of European monarchy in the seventeenth century. If the King of France was the chosen instrument of God, then the divine approval was given to the principle of absolute monarchy, and no other form of government possessed the divine sanction. This was the conclusion accepted by conservative society under the *Ancien Régime.*

Bossuet, the court preacher of Louis XIV, in a book written for the guidance of the son and heir of the king, says : "God is the true king ; he establishes the kings as his ministers and reigns through them over his people.— O, kings, you are yourselves gods, for you carry on your forehead the divine imprint. To speak against the king is a crime as great as blasphemy against God." Louis himself, in his memoirs, prepared for the instruction of the dauphin, betrays his conviction of the divine character of his office. "He who gave kings to the world desires that they should be respected as his lieutenants, reserving to himself the sole right of examining their conduct. It is his will that whosoever is born subject to the king should obey him without hesitation." That this theory of divine right was accepted by the contemporaries of the *Grand Monarche* is beyond doubt. One who was present at the death-bed of the king related as follows: "I watched the king while they bore to him the *viaticum*. I saw the great tears that fell from his eyes, evidence of a communion between their majesties divine and human." It was left for the eighteenth century to discover the hollowness of these pretensions, when the personality of the great Louis had departed, and in his place was found a man of evil life, indifferent to the sufferings of France, and powerless to aid her in her effort to adapt herself to the march of progress.

About the person of Louis XIV was assembled the most brilliant court that Europe had ever seen. All other courts of the century were feeble imitations of the household of the "King-Sun" ("*le roi soleil*"). The royal palaces of Paris were too narrow for his establishment. At Versailles he built an enormous residence, which, with its fountains and terraced gardens remains to-day one of the sights of Europe. This he made the royal residence; here he lived with oriental magnificence; here he finished the work which Richelieu had begun and Mazarin carried out against the nobles in the struggle of the Fronde. Insidiously Louis converted the nobility of France into a class of royal dependents. Lured to Versailles, their fortunes dissipated in the extravagances of court life, the nobles were driven to seek the generosity of the king. Pensions and appointments, civil and religious, were freely given, but only to those who acknowledged his authority with abject sub-

The court of Louis XIV.

THE RUINS.

ETHERINGTON.

VERSAILLES.

servience. His keen eye was everywhere. He observed, in his passage through the throng of courtiers at Versailles, the absence of those whose presence he desired. It was a demerit to miss the annual sojourn at court, a disgrace to stay away entirely. When an office was sought by his friends for such a one, the king replied with vigor: " I do not know him ;" or : " He is a man I never see ; " and this reply was final. To such a pass had been brought the proud nobility of France that princes of the royal blood competed for the privilege of presenting his garments to the king at the royal morning toilet. " The countenance of the King," said La Bruyère, " is the whole happiness of the courtier."

The Peace of Westphalia completed the supremacy of France. One other virile power remained on the continent of Europe ; but the ambitions of Sweden for the control of the Baltic led her to the North and East, away from the sphere of French control. Louis XIV sought the extension of the area and influence of France. Claiming the right of succession to the throne of Spain, by virtue of his marriage with the daughter of Philip IV of Spain, Louis plunged Europe into a general war, which lasted for fourteen years. By the terminal peace of Utrecht (1713), a great territorial adjustment like the Peace of Westphalia, Spain was shorn of her possessions in the Netherlands, which went to Austria ; and Louis's son, Philip of Anjou, was seated upon the throne of Spain as Philip V, founder of the Spanish Bourbons. Thus French influence prevailed in Spain.

Foreign policy of Louis XIV.

The revocation of the Edict of Nantes (1685) was the logical result of the French spirit of unity and centralization. " One faith, one law, one king," was the watchword of the Bourbon monarchy. Nevertheless, the revocation inflicted serious loss upon France. The Huguenots, who in the Valois period were for the most part turbulent nobles, had come to be, since the suppression of their political privileges, mainly artisans, merchants, and land-holders. In spite of the provision of the Edict of Revocation forbidding the emigration of Protestants, 300,000 left the realm and carried into Holland, to London and Berlin, the secrets of French manufactures and a hatred for their native country.

SOURCE REVIEW

The Toilette of the King.— A rigid etiquette ruled every hour of the king's day. From the moment of his awakening, and during the stages of his toilette, Louis XIV received successive deputations of princes, lords, and officials ; the proudest nobles were eager to perform the menial services of valet, and secure thereby admission to the intimate circle of the king. ''The honor of handing the king his shirt is reserved to the sons and grandsons of France ; in default of these, to the princes of the blood or those legitimated ; in their default, to the grand-chamberlain or to the first gentleman of the bed-chamber ; the latter case, it must be observed, being very rare, the princes being obliged to be present at the king's rising as well as the princesses at that of the queen. At last the shirt is presented and a valet carries off the old one ; the first valet of the wardrobe and the first *valet-de-chambre* hold the fresh one, each by a right and left arm respectively, while the two other valets, during this operation, extend his dressing-gown in front of the king to serve as a screen. The shirt is now on his back and the toilet commences. A *valet-de-chambre* supports a mirror before the king while two others on the two sides light it up, if occasion requires, with flambeaus. Valets of the wardrobe fetch the rest of the attire ; the grand master of the wardrobe puts the vest on and the doublet, attaches the blue ribbon, and clasps the sword around him ; then a valet assigned to the cravats brings several of these in a basket, while the master of the wardrobe arranges around the king's neck that which the king selects. After this a valet assigned to the handkerchiefs brings three of these on a silver salver, while the grand master of the wardrobe offers the salver to the king, who chooses one. Finally the master of the ward-robe hands to the king his hat, his gloves, and his cane. The king steps to the side of the bed, kneels on a cushion and says his prayers. This done, the king announces the order of the day and passes with the leading persons of his court into the cabinet, where he sometimes gives audience."—Taine : *Ancient Régime* (adapted from the *Memoirs of Saint-Simon*).

REFERENCES

Wakeman : *Europe, 1598-1715*, Chapter IX.; Adams : *The Growth of the French Nation*, Chapter XIII.

§ 19. THE REVOLUTION OF ENGLAND

The theory of the divine right of kings met with more opposition in England than in France. To be sure the Tudor kings, from Henry VII to Elizabeth, had ruled absolutely ; but their absolutism was permitted for at least two reasons : their reigns were full of danger from foreign foes, and England was in need of a strong hand in the period of religious wars ; again, the Tudor sovereigns, the Henrys and Elizabeth, were strong and vigorous characters, whose brilliant qualities won them popularity, and made them the champions of the English interests at home and abroad. For these reasons the constitutional limitations, so painfully and laboriously built up against personal and arbitrary government in earlier times, were, in the Tudor period, suffered to decline.

Absolutism and Parliament.

The Stuarts, who succeeded the Tudors at the death of Elizabeth in 1603, were of different stripe, either dull or frivolous ; nor were they able to associate themselves with the progressive elements of the English race. James I., the successor of Elizabeth, was narrow and pedantical, and gained for himself the title of the " Wisest Fool in Christendom." But he was filled with the idea of divine right, and resented any interference on the part of Parliament.

During the last years of Elizabeth's reign the Puritan or Calvinistic party was growing rapidly in England. The

The Puritans. Puritans were distinguished from the Anglicans, or Church of England people, by the austerity of their morals and their stern rules of life and conduct. Opposed to the king as the head of the Established Church, they stood for popular liberties and democratic ideas at variance with the Bourbon-Stuart theories of divine right. The Puritan party was strongly

CHARLES I., BY VANDYKE.

represented in the House of Commons, which, by virtue of England's increasing wealth, was coming to be much more powerful than ever before, its members constituting an aristocracy of wealth side by side with the feudal aristocracy of blood.

The struggle between the king and the middle classes broke forth during the reign of **Charles I.** Charles I., son and successor of James I. In 1628 Charles was compelled by need of funds to sign the " Petition of Right," which gave to Parliament the right to vote all taxes. This he violated in the following year, and upon the refusal of Parliament to grant him money, he dissolved that body and sought for eleven years to govern England without a Parliament. To aid him in securing a revenue, he revived an ancient tax, called " Ship-money," formerly levied upon the maritime counties of England for purposes of naval defence, and made it general for the realm. This was resisted by John Hampden as illegal, and, although he was defeated, his bold example strengthened the popular resistance to the arbitrary measures of the king.

In Scotland the efforts of Archbishop Laud to change

the forms of Presbyterian worship and introduce the English prayer-book led to civil war. Charles called Parliament in 1640, and strove by compromise to quiet the popular indignation. But the leaders of the popular party were not easily appeased ; a bill was voted condemning the general policy of the crown. The king demanded the arrest of the five principal signers of the bill, but they had escaped. Angry at this check to his authority, Charles left London, gathered his friends about him, and sought with warlike measures to coerce the Parliamentary faction.

The extreme Puritan party— the "Roundheads," they were called — took the field against the "Cavaliers," or partisans of the king. The Puritans soon found a leader of ability in Oliver Cromwell. Cromwell's troops, well drilled, prepared to "fight or pray," merited, with their heroic courage, the name

The "Great Rebellion."

OLIVER CROMWELL.

of "Ironsides." King Charles, defeated at Naseby, took refuge in Scotland, but was delivered to Parliament in 1647. Cromwell seized upon the king ; drove from ·Parliament a hundred members who opposed extreme measures, and with the consent of the remainder organized a special high court of justice, before which Charles was put to trial. Condemned to death as a tyrant and traitor, he was beheaded.

For four years England lived under the rule of the "Rump" Parliament. Cromwell and his "Ironsides" overran Ireland, and defeated Charles II, who, accepted by the Scots, invaded England with a strong army. In 1653 Cromwell and the army, dissatisfied with the "Rump" Parliament, dissolved it by force, and Cromwell assumed the title of Lord Protector. The Protectorate was a glorious period of English history; an alliance with Cromwell was eagerly sought by foreign princes, and at no time had England been so strong abroad.

The Commonwealth.

England would have been able, under the guidance of Cromwell, to dispute successfully with France the supremacy of Europe ; but the Lord Protector died in 1658, fully realizing that his death would be the end of his great work. His son Richard assumed without resistance the title of Protector, but he had no ability for public affairs, and abdicated after a brief experience of eight months. A period of struggle followed, ending in the restoration of the Stuart claimant, Charles II.

ENGLISH GENTLEMEN OF THE STUART PERIOD.

The Stuarts profited little by the lessons of adversity. Charles II brought back those extravagances of the court so distasteful to the middle class of Englishmen. His policy was subservient to the desires of the French king, Louis XIV, and he plotted to restore the Catholic faith ; yet so strong was the devotion of his subjects to the principle of legitimacy that he reigned for twenty-five years, and left the crown to his brother, James II (1685).

Restoration and Revolution

·James II emphasized in his reign the unpopular characteristics of his brother. He assumed the right to suspend Parliament, to modify its laws, and to interfere with the decisions of the courts. In his household he celebrated the rites of the Catholic Church with the pomp of Versailles. For three years England bore with this king, who represented the negation of all she had struggled to establish, but was looking forward to the eventual succession of Mary, eldest daughter of James, who was married to the Protestant prince, William of Orange, Stadtholder of Holland. When, however, in 1688, a son was born to James, English patience reached its limit, and William was invited to come and take possession of the government. He landed in November on the coast of England. Upon his banner were the words " *Pro religione et libertate ;* " his device : " *Je maintiendrai* " ("I shall maintain," *i.e.* the rights of the nation). James fled to the court of Louis XIV. Parliament declared the throne to be vacant, and promulgated a " Bill of Rights," affirming the ancient rights and liberties of England. The crown was offered to William and Mary, and they accepted it, under the constitutional limitations of the " Bill of Rights." Thus by the revolution of 1688 England overthrew the principle of divine right, weakly championed by the Stuarts, and established a constitutional monarchy, the gift of Parliament and the nation.

SOURCE REVIEW

Cromwell turns out the Rump Parliament.—" Wednesday, 20th April.—The Parliament sitting as usual, and being on debate upon the bill with the amendments, which it was thought would have been passed that day, the Lord General Cromwell came into the House, clad in plain black clothes, with grey worsted stockings, and sat down as he used to do in an ordinary place. After a while he rose up, put off his hat, and spake ; at the first and for a good while, he spake to the commendation of the Parliament, for their pains and care of the public good ; but afterwards he changed his style, told them of their injustice, delays of justice, self-interest, and other faults. Then he said : 'Perhaps you think this is not Parliamentary language : I confess it is not, neither are you to expect any such from me.' Then he put on his hat, went out of his place, and walked up and down the stage or floor in the midst of the House, with his hat on his head, and chid them soundly, looking sometimes, and pointing particularly upon some persons, as Sir R. Whitlock, one of the Commissioners for the Great Seal, Sir Henry Vane, to whom he gave very sharp language, though he named them not, but by his gestures it was well known that he meant them.   After this he said to Colonel Harrison (who was a member of the House): 'Call them in.'   Then Harrison went out, and presently brought in Lieutenant-Colonel Wortley (who commanded the General's own regiment of foot) with five or six files of musqueteers, about twenty or thirty, with their musquets.   Then the General, pointing to the Speaker in his chair, said to Harrison, ' Fetch him down.'   Harrison went to the Speaker, and spoke to him to come down, but the Speaker sat still, and said nothing.   'Take him down,' said the General ; then Harrison went and pulled the Speaker by the.gown, and he came down.   And it happened that day, that Algernon Sydney sat next to the Speaker on the right hand ; the General said to Harrison, ' Put him out.'   Harrison spake to Sydney to go out, but he said he would not go out, and sat still.   The General said again, ' Put him out.'   Then Harrison and Wortley put their hands upon Sydney's shoulders, as if they would force him to go out ; then he rose and went towards the door.   Then the General went to the table where the mace lay, which used to be carried before the Speaker, and said, 'Take away these baubles.'   So the soldiers took away the mace, and all the House went out; and at the going out, they say, the General said to young Sir Henry Vane, calling him by name, that he might have prevented this extraordinary course, but he was a juggler, and had not so much as common honesty.   All being gone out, the door of the House was locked, and the key with the mace was carried away, as I heard, by Colonel Otley."—*Sydney Papers.*

REFERENCES

Gardiner: *A Student's History of England.*   Part VI.; Myers: *Mediæval and Modern History,* pp. 504–539.

CHAPTER VII

The Eighteenth Century

§ 20. BENEVOLENT DESPOTISM

DURING the eighteenth century the personal governments of the Bourbons and Hapsburgs were moving to

Decline of personal government.

their decline. The growth of an intelligent middle class, alive to the advantages of trade and industry, accustomed to habits of thrift and economy, increased the dissatisfaction with the loose and extravagant methods of absolute monarchy. In France the reign of Louis XIV, with its expensive dynastic wars, left the country in a condition of financial ruin. His great-grandson and successor, Louis XV, lacked the stern and vigorous qualities of the *Grand Monarche;* in his feeble hands the system of Louis XIV displayed only its vices. Too indolent and self-indulgent to grapple with the problems of his time, he left the government to his mistresses and favorites, who squandered the resources of France in purposeless wars and in the support of a huge and insatiable aristocracy. Not that Louis XV did not recognize the drift of affairs ; he was philosopher enough for this, and the immense cynicism of his life is summed up in his remark that "France will last long enough for me."

For posterity, however, the weakness of his rule was an element of advantage. The severe system of repression, devised by Louis XIV, to cut off all freedom of thought and liberty of expression that might serve to weaken the absolute character of his authority, although it continued in form, was in reality but an empty shell in the reign of Louis XV. Under cover of strict censorship, the printing presses of France poured forth a stream of philosophy, attacking the principle of divine right; against the protests of the church, which stirred the government now and then into spasms of repression, the very foundations of the old system of theology were undermined. The king was too luxurious and too careless to intervene for the salvation of his system and his throne.

In one respect the foreign policy of Louis XV reversed the tradition of centuries. Peace was made with Austria, the ancient enemy and rival of France, and this unnatural alliance was cemented with the marriage of the Dauphin, afterward Louis XVI, with a daughter of the house of Hapsburg, Marie Antoinette.

Louis XVI.

In 1774, at the death of his grandfather, this young prince came to the throne. His ability was small, but his life was pure and he had the interests of France at heart. Far from being indifferent, like his grandfather, he took the affairs of his realm in hand, and sought to bring order out of the general financial confusion. He called to his aid men of pronounced liberal views: Turgot, an economist of the new school, and Necker, a Swiss financier. These men strove to curtail the privileges of the upper classes, by making all property alike subject to taxation; to modernize industry by the destruction of the gild system; and to cut down the expenses of the court. To this the king at first agreed; but he stood alone in his court and family. His brothers and his friends, his young and frivolous wife, all sought to dissuade him from a step which threatened their interests and pleasures. At last he yielded, dismissed his liberal ministers, and fell back into the old system of apathy and powerlessness. A strong king, conscious of the needs of the times, might perhaps have led France through a peaceful reconstruction of her political and social organization; but the task was too great for Louis XVI; it was left for the people to accomplish this for themselves amid the terrors of revolution.

In Austria a similar task was attempted by a man of more ability. Joseph II, Emperor and ruler of the possessions of the Hapsburgs, King of Hungary and of Bohemia, was a man of advanced ideas. Dissatisfied with the unwieldy character of his great patchwork empire, he wished to suppress the innumerable charters and privileges which his various possessions had inherited from the Middle Ages, and weld them all together into a unified and homogeneous Austrian state. The task was one of great difficulty. In the several states that one by one had come together under Hapsburg control were to be found the extremes of political and social development : Flanders, on the north and west of the Hapsburg lands, was a country of great industrial activity ; Hungary, on the south and east, was an agricultural state of the feudal type, where serfdom still existed in its medieval form.

Joseph II.

The Emperor's scheme of reorganization contemplated the general introduction of the German language, a uniform system of laws and administration, education under the supervision of the state, and the abolition of serfdom in Hungary and Bohemia. The inauguration of these reforms brought down upon Joseph a storm of opposition. The Flemish cities resisted a political rearrangement which deprived them of their city charters, dearly bought with blood and treasure ; the clergy were infuriated at the suppression of monasteries and the establishment of an imperial system of education beyond their control, and branded Joseph as an infidel ; the Hungarian lords bitterly resented the abolition of their feudal rights, and the absorption of the crown of Hungary into the Austrian state. The opposition evoked by the reform edicts on every side threatened to disrupt the Empire. Joseph was forced to yield, and abandon his efforts for reform ; obstacles of race and language and religious bigotry could not be legislated away by imperial edict. Some great upheaval of the middle

Joseph's projects of reorganization.

Joseph II Empereur des Romains.

classes was necessary. Only after the sword of Napoleon had swept from central Europe the vestiges of feudalism could the dreams of Joseph II be realized.

Not alone in France and Austria was tried the experiment of benevolent despotism. The second half of the

Other countries.

eighteenth century was a period of philosophic despots and experimenting ministers. In Spain, Aranda, minister of Charles III; in Portugal, Pombal, both thoroughly devoted to the principle of royal absolutism, were nevertheless believers in the modern doctrines of reform, and sought to overcome, with the reorganization of education and industry, the exhaustion and lethargy of their peoples. The influence of the Jesuits in education and government was an object of attack, and the pressure of the Catholic powers brought about the abolition of the order by Pope Clement XIV in 1773. In the Italian states as well, the impulse toward reform was felt. Naples enjoyed a period of enlightened rule under the Bourbon king, Ferdinand IV. His minister, Tanucci, deprived the barons of the feudal right of justice. In Tuscany, the Grand Duke Leopold, brother of Joseph II, projected the first uniform code of laws, and made of his little duchy the most modern state of Europe.

SOURCE REVIEW

I. Private Life of Louis XVI; his tastes and character.— "The only passion ever shown by Louis XVI was for hunting; he was so much occupied by it that when I went up into his private closets, at Versailles, after the tenth of August, I saw on the staircase six frames, in which were seen statements of all his hunts, both when dauphin and when king. In them was detailed the number, kind, and quality of the game he had killed at each hunting party, with recapitulations for every month, every season, and every year of his reign.

Above the king's library was a forge, two anvils, and a vast number of iron tools; various common locks, well made and perfect; some secret locks, and locks ornamented with gilt copper. It was there that Gamin taught the king the art of lock-making. 'The king was good, forbearing, timid, inquisitive, and addicted to sleep,' said Gamin to me; he was fond of lock-making to excess, and he concealed himself from the court and the queen to file and forge with me.

There were two men in Louis XVI—the man of knowledge and the man of will. The first of these possessed very extended and varied qualifications; his memory contained an infinite number of names and situations; he remembered quantities and numbers wonderfully. But on important affairs of state the king of will and command was nowhere to be found. Louis XVI was, upon the throne, exactly what those weak temperaments, whom nature has rendered incapable of an opinion, are in society. Although amid various counsels he often knew which was the best, he never had the resolution to say: 'I prefer the advice of such a person.' Herein lay the misfortunes of the state."—From Soulavie: *Memoirs of the Reign of Louis XVI.*

II. Joseph II at Paris, on a visit to his sister, Marie Antoinette.—"I was present at the queen's dinner almost every day. The Emperor would there speak much and fluently. He disguised none of his prejudices upon the subject of the etiquette and customs of the court of France, and even in the presence of the king aimed his sarcasms at them. The king smiled, but never made any answer; the queen appeared to feel pain from them.

"One day the queen was busied in signing warrants and orders for payment for her household, and was conversing with her secretary, who presented the papers one after another to be signed, and replaced them in his portfolio. While this was going forward the Emperor walked about the room; all at once he stopped, to censure the queen rather severely for signing all those papers without reading them, or, at least, without running her eye over them; and he spoke to her most judiciously upon the danger of signing her name inconsiderately."—Relation of Madame de Campan, First Lady of the Bedchamber to the Queen.

REFERENCES

Gardiner, B. M.: *The French Revolution*, pp. 17–32 ; Morse-Stephens : *The Revolution and Europe*, pp. 14–25.

§ 21. FREDERICK THE GREAT.

The eighteenth century witnessed the rise of Prussia, and her entrance into the circle of the Great Powers of Europe. The house of Hohenzollern took its origin on the borders of Switzerland. In 1275 Frederick of Hohenzollern was made Burgrave of Nuremberg. At the time of the Council of Constance the Emperor Sigismund conferred upon Frederick IV the Electorate of Brandenburg, a Slavic country, lying between the Elbe and the Oder, on the western boundary of Poland. In the following century Albert of Brandenburg, a brother of the Elector, was elected Grand Master of the religious order of the Teutonic Knights, who had founded in Prussia, on the shores of the Baltic, a German colony as an outpost against the pagan Slavs. During the early Reformation Albert became Lutheran, secularized the territory of the Knights, and was recognized by the King of Poland as Duke of Prussia, subject to the suzerainty of Poland. In 1618 the line of Albert became extinct, and the duchy of Prussia reverted to the Elector. Meanwhile the Hohenzollerns came into possession of a claim upon the territories of Cleves and Juliers, in the lower Rhine country, next to Holland.

Rise of Prussia.

At the close of the Thirty Years' War the Great Elector received, in the rearrangement of Europe at the Peace of Westphalia, East Pomerania and the secularized states of Magdeburg, Halberstadt, Minden, and Cammin. As a result of the decline of the imperial power and the freedom of action given to the German princes, Brandenburg became a

Frederick William, the "Great Elector."

sovereign state. The Great Elector was an autocrat in his possessions, a miniature Louis XIV. His rule was wise, tending toward the development of the resources of his people. In 1760 he freed the duchy of Prussia from Polish control. Thus, step by step, a fragmentary domain, scattered from the middle Baltic to the Rhine, was welded with the firm hand of an able and ambitious prince.

The subjects of the Great Elector were warlike. The situation of Brandenburg, compelling that state to defend itself against the Slavic nations of the East, tended to foster a military spirit. Of all the German states Brandenburg was best fitted, in the disruption of the Empire, to take the leadership of the Protestant states of the North against the Catholic primacy of the Hapsburgs. The struggle for the political supremacy of Germany between the two great houses of Hohenzollern and Hapsburg fills the history of Germany down to our time.

FREDERICK THE GREAT.

Frederick III, successor of the Great Elector, became Frederick I, King "of Prussia." Receiving permission of the Emperor, still his titular over-lord, to assume the royal title for his Prussian lands, his title was confirmed by the peace of Utrecht in 1713. The son of Frederick I, who came to the throne as Frederick William I, was a curious character, but of immense use for the future of Prussia. A coarse and brutal man, a tyrant in his family and with his subjects, his delight was in his army. His sole extrava-

Kingdom of Prussia.

gance was to recruit, at any expense, wherever they might be found, the largest and finest men for his regiments. To Frederick his son, whom he sought in vain to form after his own coarse model, he left a well-drilled army, one of the best in Europe, and a well-filled treasury, important instruments in the hands of the ablest statesman and general of his times.

Frederick II came to the throne (1740) with great ambitions. He desired to round out his scattered possessions into a compact kingdom; to cease to be, as Voltaire said of him, "King of the Borders." For the execution of his plans he possessed an army, a treasury, and a mind unfettered with scruples. Indifferent to the claims of justice, careless of good faith, and regardless of his obligations toward other princes, he was indomitable in adversity and moderate in the hour of triumph. An absolute sovereign, he left nothing to his ministers, but took upon himself the supervision of the minutest details.

Frederick the Great.

Fortune favored Frederick at the start. In the year of his succession to the throne, the Emperor Charles VI died and left an heiress, Maria Theresa, a girl of twenty-three. A dozen claimants sought the imperial crown, some with dynastic claims, as the Elector of Saxony and the Elector of Bavaria. Frederick II had no claim but that of the sword, but he was the first to move upon the threatened Empire with the invasion of Silesia, at the same time assuring Maria Theresa "of the purity of his intentions, and his desire ever to devote himself to the service of the house of Austria." He defeated the Austrians at Mollwitz; formed an alliance with the French, and recognized the Elector of Bavaria as Emperor with the title of Charles VII. The war was continued with varying success until the Peace of Aix-la-Chapelle, in 1748, closed hostilities for the time. Maria Theresa confirmed the Prussian title to Silesia; the Spanish Bourbons obtained

some Italian duchies ; but with these losses Maria Theresa
kept her Empire, overthrew the Bavarian claim, and

FRANCIS I, FOUNDER OF MODERN AUSTRIAN (HAPSBURG-LORRAINE)
DYNASTY.

secured the coronation of her husband, Francis of Lorraine, as Emperor Francis I.

But the energetic heiress of the house of Hapsburg was
not content to lose her province of Silesia without another
struggle. In 1756 hostilities were resumed. This time

the Franco-Austrian alliance of 1756 placed France upon the side of the Empress. Frederick turned to England, and concluded in the same year the treaty of Westminster with George II. Sweden and Russia fell upon the borders of eastern Prussia; six armies gathered in upon the Prussian king. Frederick had a moment of despair; the odds were too great. In spite of the brilliant victories of Rosbach and Leuthen, Berlin was pillaged by the Russians, and the Prussian lands laid waste. Chance turned the tide. Peter II, an ardent admirer of Frederick, succeeded Elizabeth in Russia, and withdrew his troops. France had lost her colonies to England, and was tired of the war. Maria Theresa was forced to abandon her hope of destroying Prussia, and the Peace of Hubertsburg (1763) left Silesia to the Hohenzollerns.

The Seven Years' War.

SOURCE REVIEW

I. Frederick William I and his Grenadiers. — To secure recruits for his three battalions of giants the king was willing to spend sums which were enormous for the times and for the meagre revenues of Prussia. James Kirkham, an Irish recruit, is said to have cost six thousand dollars. "In the town of Jülich there lived and worked a tall young carpenter. One day a well-dressed, positive-looking gentleman enters the shop; wants 'a stout chest, with a lock on it, for household purposes; must be of such and such dimensions, six feet six in length especially, and that is an indispensable point—in fact, it will be longer than yourself, I think, Mr. Carpenter; what is the cost; when can it be ready?' At the appointed day he reappears; the chest is ready; we hope, an unexceptionable article? 'Too short, as I dreaded,' says the positive gentleman. 'Nay, your Honor,' says the carpenter, 'I am certain that it is six feet six,' and he takes out his foot-rule. 'Pshaw, it was to be longer than yourself.' 'Well it is.' 'No, it isn't.' The carpenter, to end the matter gets into the chest, and will convince any and all mortals. No sooner is he in, rightly flat, than the positive gentleman, a Prussian recruiting officer in disguise, slams down the lid upon him, locks it, whistles in three stout fellows, who pick up the chest, walk gravely through the streets with it, open it in a safe place and find—horrible to relate, the poor carpenter dead ; choked by want of air in this frightful middle passage of his."—Carlyle, in his *Frederick the Great.*

II. "Sans-Souci," the favorite retreat of Frederick the Great at Potsdam.—"For the last forty years of his life, especially as years advanced, he spent most of his days and nights in this little Mansion ; which became more and more his favorite retreat, whenever the noises and scenic etiquettes were not inexorable.   'Sans-Souci,' which we may translate 'No-

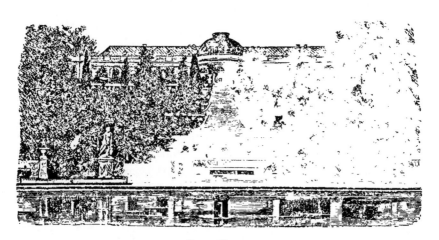

SANS-SOUCI.

Bother.'   A busy place this, too, but of the quiet kind ; and more a home to him than any of the three fine Palaces (ultimately four) which lay always waiting for him in the neighborhood.

"Certainly it is a significant feature of Friedrich ; and discloses the inborn proclivity he had to retirement, to study and reflection, as the chosen element of human life, why he fell upon so ambitious a title for his Royal Cottage.   The name, it appears, came by accident.   He had prepared his tomb, and various tombs in the skirts of this new Cottage ; looking at these, as the building of them went on, he was heard to say, one day : '*Qui, alors je serai sans souci* (Once there, one will be out of bother) !' A saying which was rumored of, and repeated in society, being by such a man. Out of which rumor in society, and the evidence of the Cottage Royal, there was gradually born, as Venus from the froth of the sea, this name : Sans-Souci : which Friedrich adopted." —Carlyle.

REFERENCES

Adams : *European History*, pp. 391–399 ; Hassall, *European History*, 1715–1789, pp. 241–279.

§ 22. SWEDEN AND RUSSIA

At the close of the Thirty Years' War (1648) Sweden had come to occupy a place among the great powers of Europe. She had conquered the southern **Height of the Swedish power.** and eastern shores of the Baltic, thereby shutting out her rivals, Russia and Poland, from access to the "Swedish Lake." Finland was also hers. This great advance of Sweden had been accomplished through a fortunate combination of circumstances: an able leader, in the person of Gustavus Adolphus; a well-disciplined army, filled with religious enthusiasm. These, together with the exhaustion of the continental powers, gave Sweden her opportunity ; but it was evident that her resources were too meagre to permit her to hold the place she had won.

Until the time of Peter the Great, Russia is not to be regarded as a European power. During the Middle Ages **Rise of Russia.** the Russian lands were for two centuries under the rule of the Mongols. Step by step the princes of Moscow absorbed the neighboring states ; in the fifteenth century Ivan the Great threw off the Mongol yoke. In 1613 the house of Rurik became extinct, and the dynasty of the Romanoffs was founded. Russia was still cut off from communication with the West ; Sweden kept her from the Baltic on the north ; the

Turks from the Black Sea on the south. The problem of Russia was to break through to the sea, and this was accomplished by Peter the Great.

Peter came to the throne at the age of seventeen. The empire to which he succeeded was of a medieval rather than of a modern character. The task of imposing his authority upon his turbulent nobles was a heroic one. He had no army; the imperial guard (the "Streltsi") had been accustomed to play the leading part in the revolutions of the palace. He had no fleet; no Russian Tsar before his time had seen the sea.

Peter the Great (1689-1725)

PETER THE GREAT.

Peter made a voyage across Germany and Holland to England. There he studied the industries of the country, labored as a carpenter in the ship-yards of Holland, and on his return to Russia brought with him sailors and shipbuilders, and began the construction of a fleet at Archangel, his only harbor, on the frozen coast of the White Sea. In 1703, while at war with Sweden, Peter laid in Swedish territory the foundations of his new capital, St. Petersburg, "a window to the west." Moscow, "the widow of the Tsar," mourned the change; but Peter wished Russia to leave her Oriental home; for his new work a new capital was necessary, at whose birth western influences had presided. Here it was easier for the Tsar to break with the old Muscovite traditions. He made his authority absolute over his nobles, the "boyards." He declared all land to be held from the Tsar; forced the nobles into his service, revoking the titles and lands of those who refused, making the imperial service the sole road to wealth and distinction. In this he was an apt pupil of the *Grand Monarche;* but his methods were those of the East ; the "knout" often reminded his noble servants that Peter was master in Russia.

Having made himself master of Russia, Peter set about to destroy the Oriental customs which prevailed in Russian society. In a few years he succeeded, with forceful measures, in giving to his court a superficial gloss of civilization. Long beards

Russian Society under Peter the Great.

and robes, after the Persian and Tartar style, were discouraged, and obstinate boyards were shaven by official barbers at the city gate. Struck with the elegance of the court of Versailles, which he visited in 1717, Peter sought to transform his Muscovite women into courtly dames, forbade the covering of their faces with veils, and compelled their attendance, under penalty of the knout, at the assemblies of the court.

CHARLES XII.

The extension of Russian Power to the Baltic was not

Charles XII of Sweden (1697-1718).

achieved except against the resistance of Sweden. In 1697 Charles XII came to the throne at the age of seventeen. Ignorant of the military genius of this young prince, the rivals of Sweden—Russia, Poland, and Denmark—formed an alliance for the overthrow of the Swedish power. But Charles XII was not dismayed. Attacking his enemies one by one, he forced Denmark to terms of peace, defeated the Russian army, and, entering Poland, drove Augustus II from the throne. Here his judgment failed. Lingering for several years in Saxony, Charles gave to Peter an opportunity of reorganizing his army. Then, instead of turning again to the North, he was induced by a Cossack chieftain, Mazeppa, to undertake an expedition against Moscow. At Pultova he met again the army of Peter, and was defeated, lost his army, and fled, with a handful of companions, into Turkey. There he wasted time in seeking to induce the Sultan to renew the war against Russia. Meanwhile the situation in the north had changed ; Augustus had recovered the throne of Poland ; Prussia, England, and Holland had joined the combination against Sweden. Still Charles fought on, until he met his death at the age of thirty-eight, seeking the subjection of Norway. With his death the power of Sweden rapidly declined. Her Baltic provinces were lost to Brandenburg and Russia.

A weak state, lying between the rising powers of Russia and Prussia, Poland had little chance of preserving her nationality. The arrogance of her nobles and the faults of her constitution prevented her accomplishing the transition from a medieval to a modern state. Poland was a monarchy of twelve millions of people, ruled by a hundred thousand nobles, who lived from the labor of a degraded peasantry. There was no middle class, commerce being in the hands of the Jews, who possessed no political rights. The king was elected, and a figurehead ; a curious feature of the constitution was the *liberum veto,* which gave the power to any member of the Diet to annul legislation. This alone was sufficient to make government impossible ; and the nobles were too selfish and stupid to permit a change.

On account of the jealousy of the nobles, it was customary to elect a foreign prince as king. In 1697 the Elector of Saxony was chosen as Augustus II. Deposed by Charles XII of Sweden, he regained his throne, and was succeeded by his son, Augustus III. In 1763 Augustus III died, and Frederick the Great and Catharine of Russia pressed the claims of Poniatowski, a Polish nobleman. His election brought anarchy into Poland, as the great enemies of Poland intended it should, and paved the way for intervention. But Austria could not be disregarded, and in the first partition of 1772 she had her share of the spoil. The share of Prussia was the smallest; but it was of great value, since it connected the Prussian lands with Brandenburg.

The succeeding partitions of Poland took place during the French Revolution. In 1793 Poniatowski sought to revise the Polish constitution and abolish the *liberum veto*. This aroused the fears of Catharine of Russia, lest Poland should become a virile state. She intervened, championing the interests of the conservative nobles against such a radical reform. The liberals appealed to Prussia; but Frederick William II, refusing his aid, threw an army into Poland, and shared with Catharine the spoliation of Polish territories. Russia's share again was greater; but Prussia got, among other bits, the cities of Danzig and Thurn. Austria was busy fighting France, and had no share.

Second partition, 1793.

The Polish patriot, Kosciuszko, refused to submit to the spoliation of his country, and raised the standard of national revolt; but his act was disavowed by Poniatowski, and Poland, divided against herself, could offer no front against her despoilers. A great Russian army entered Poland, and took the capital, Warsaw. Poniatowski was removed, and abdicated in November. Thus Poland for the third time fell defenceless into the hands of royal and imperial robbers. This time Austria was at hand, and received her portion, Galicia. Poland became extinct, easily crushed, at a time when France was holding her own against all Europe. The reason was that the people of Poland, kept down by arrogant nobles, were serfs, and had no appreciation of liberty, and no national pride.

Third partition, 1795.

SOURCE REVIEW

I. Peter the Great as a Social Reformer.—"Peter settled
the question of dress in his usual radical fashion.   He would
have no more beards, and everybody must wear European costume, either French or Hungarian.   His ukase on the subject
was published on the 29th of August, 1699, and patterns of the
regulation garments were exposed on the streets.   The poorer
classes were granted a temporary delay, so that they might
wear out their old clothes, but after 1705 every soul was to
appear in the new uniform, under pain of fines, and even of
severer difficulties.

"The reform, thus violently imposed, met with desperate
opposition, especially among the lower classes.   The poor
Moujik, forcibly deprived of the beard which had kept his
cheeks warm in 40 degrees of cold, begged that it might be
laid with him in his coffin, so that after his death he might
appear decently in the presence of St. Nicholas.

"But all this was nothing to Peter.   In 1704, at an inspec-
tion of officials of all classes, held as he was passing through
Moscow, he caused Ivan Naoumof, who had failed to use his
razors, to be flogged.   In 1706, soldiers were posted at all
the church doors in Astrakhan, with orders to fall upon
recalcitrant worshippers, and pull out their beards by main
force.   The Tsar also took upon himself to shorten the
women's garments, and any skirts which exceeded the regulation length were publicly torn up, without the slight-
est regard for decency.   Peter had a special and a kind of
personal hatred for beards.   To him they typified all the
ideas, traditions, and prejudices he was resolved to overcome."
—Waliszewski : *Peter the Great.*

II. Mazeppa and the Cossacks of the Ukraine. — "The
Cossacks had originally the privilege of electing a prince
under the name of general ; but they were soon deprived of
that right, and their general was nominated by the court of
Moscow.

"The person who then filled that station was a Polish gentleman, named Mazeppa.   He had been educated as a page
to John Casimir, and had received some tincture of polite

learning in his court. An intimacy which he had in his youth with the lady of a Polish gentleman having been discovered, the husband caused him to be whipped with rods, to be bound stark naked upon a wild horse, and turned adrift in that condition. The horse, which was brought out of the Ukraine, returned to his own country, and carried Mazeppa with him, half dead with hunger and fatigue. Some of the country people gave him assistance, and he lived among them for a long time, signalizing himself in several excursions against the Tartars. The superiority of his knowledge gained him great respect among the Cossacks, and, his reputation greatly increasing, the Tsar found it necessary to make him prince of the Ukraine.

"Being one day at table with the Tsar at Moscow, the emperor proposed to him the task of disciplining the Cossacks, and rendering them more docile and dependent. Mazeppa replied that the situation of the Ukraine and the genius of the nation were insuperable obstacles to such a scheme. The Tsar, who began to be overheated with wine and had not, when sober, always the command of his passions, called him a traitor and threatened to have him impaled.

"Mazeppa, on his return to the Ukraine, formed the design of a revolt, the execution of which was greatly facilitated by the Swedish army, which soon afterward appeared on the frontiers. He resolved to make himself independent, and erect the Ukraine, with some other ruins of the Russian empire, into a powerful kingdom. Brave, enterprising, and indefatigable, he entered secretly into a league with the king of Sweden, to accelerate the ruin of the Tsar, and to convert it to his own advantage."—Voltaire : *History of Charles XII.*

REFERENCES

Adams: *European History,* pp. 386–392 ; Wakeman : *European History,* 1598–1715, pp. 296–308.

§ 23.   THE FRENCH PHILOSOPHERS

Nothing is better calculated to show the vast gulf that lay between the seventeenth and the eighteenth century, between the age of Louis XIV and the age of Louis XV, than the respective attitudes of these monarchs toward liberty of thought and expression. In the reign of Louis XIV everything was made to conform closely to the ideas and desires of the king. In literature, as elsewhere, emphasis was laid upon elegance of form. It is no wonder, therefore, that verse was the approved method of literary expression, or that the age produced great stylists, like Racine and Corneille. Such writers, taking their themes from the times of Greece and Rome, did not affront the government with the discussion of vital questions.

The spirit of inquiry.

The reign of Louis XV, on the contrary, was a time of indifference, so far as the government was concerned; but in the field of thought and of literature it was a period of immense activity. Philosophy no longer confined itself to the abstruse problems of pure metaphysics, but became practical, dealing with the problems of the day. This is the distinctive feature of eighteenth century philosophy, due to the weakening of the principle of authority, both in Church and State. All things were open to analysis; the worldly lives of the clergy, the skepticism of many of its members; the abuse of despotism and the scandals of the court delivered religion as well as royalty to the discussions of the philosophers.

The inspiration for the French philosophical movement of the eighteenth century came from England. The events of the Revolution of 1688, depriving monarchy of its divine sanction, gave rise to a school of practical philosophers, who sought to explain and justify the new theories of civil government, which had found their expression in the Bill of Rights. John Locke (1632-1704) carried rational inquiry into the examination of many phases of human existence, and exercised great influence upon French thought. He may be called the "Father of Eighteenth Century Philosophy."

Montesquieu.

About the middle of the century Montesquieu (1689–1755), a French judge, pursuing his inquiries into the comparative excellence of the various forms of government, published his "*Spirit of the Laws*," in which he held the view that no form of government possessed any special sanction, but that the kind of government best suited to a country was that which was determined by the peculiar conditions of the country itself—geographical, racial, and otherwise. Some countries, especially in Asia, were better suited with a despotic government ; others with a limited monarchy ; others, again, with a republic. Simi-

VOLTAIRE.

larly with religion : he undertook to show that while Christianity was undoubtedly a better form of religion for Europe, yet in Asia and Africa different conditions had produced Mohammedanism, a religion better suited, be thought, to its surroundings.

The effect of this work, of which twenty-two editions appeared during the century, may be imagined. The seventeenth century had proclaimed that one single way was possible in all departments of human life and effort. That way had received divine sanction : in government, the monarchy ; in religion, the Church. No question of different surroundings was possible ; there must be one law, one set of institutions for the whole world. The eighteenth century opened the whole subject to discussion, and later attempts to restore the reign of authority were feeble and unavailing, as we shall learn.

Voltaire lived four years in England, studied Locke and Newton, and imbibed a love for English institutions. This he expressed in his "*Letters on the English*," which, although condemned by the French censors, was extensively read.   But Voltaire was not a practical philosopher.

Voltaire (1694–1778).

Aside from his activity as a writer of plays, his life was largely spent in an attack upon the Church, the "Infamous," as he termed it in his bitterness.   A Deist himself—that is to say, a believer in a Supreme Power—he attacked with keen invective all forms of revealed religion, Protestant as well as Catholic.   More than any other man he influenced the spirit of his time.   Voltairian skepticism became the fashion, even in the clergy; no salon was complete without a "philosopher" of this type.

This is but a single phase of Voltaire's life, but the most important for the future.   He was, apart from his destructive philosophy, the literary arbiter of his time. From his retreat at Fernay, on the borders of Switzerland, where he passed his later years, his influence reached throughout Europe.   Frederick the Great, Catharine II of Russia, the kings and princes of Europe, were flattered to receive letters from Voltaire.   His crusade against intolerance and superstition, although conceived with a violence which mars it for our taste, gave, nevertheless, to human thought a liberty which it had never known. Voltaire was, according to Cardinal de Bernis, "the great man of his century."

In strong contrast with Voltaire stands his great contemporary, Rousseau.   Voltaire was an aristocrat by birth and taste; Rousseau was the son of a Genevan artisan, and had all his life the instincts of a vagabond.   Yet it is doubtful if any man has so largely influenced modern society and in so many ways.   His "Emile" sketched a new system of education, inculcating simplicity and common sense in the training of children; his novel of the "Nouvelle Héloïse," was one of the first efforts to portray in fiction the artistic possibilities of the life of the middle classes.   Hitherto

Rousseau (1670–1741).

fiction had dealt by preference with the splendor of courts.

The most important book of Rousseau, however, measured in its effect upon his century, was the "*Social Contract.*" Here political society is described as the result of a contract freely made between the people and their king. For the better conduct of human affairs the people delegate to a ruler the functions of government. If the ruler fail in his duty the contract is broken, and the people regain their right to give to another the task of governing them. This, it will be observed, is a direct denial of the theory of the divine right of kings. Supreme power,

ROUSSEAU

instead of coming from above, comes from the people beneath ; the king, far from being a vicar of God, holding the nation as a divine gift, becomes a mere agent of the people, chosen for the execution of a common task, and removable at the will of his master, the people. These ideas of Rousseau, appealing strongly to the masses, became the program of the radical party in the Revolution.

SOURCE REVIEW

How Physical Conditions Determine the Form of Government; from the *Spirit of the Laws.* — " In Asia they have always had great empires; in Europe these could never subsist. Asia has larger plains; it is cut up into much more extensive divisions by mountains and seas: and as it lies more to the south, its springs are more easily dried up; the mountains are less covered with snow; and the rivers, not being so large, form more contracted barriers.

" Power in Asia ought then to be always despotic; for if

their slavery were not severe they would soon make a division inconsistent with the nature of the country.

"In Europe the natural division forms many nations of a moderate extent, in which the ruling by laws is not incompatible with the maintenance of the state; on the contrary, it is so favorable to it that without this the state would fall into decay, and become the prey of its neighbors.

"It is this which has formed the genius for liberty that renders every part extremely difficult to be subdued and subjected to a foreign power, otherwise than by the laws and the advantage of commerce.

"On the contrary, there reigns in Asia a servile spirit, which they have never been able to shake off, and it is impossible to find in all the histories of that country a single passage that discovers a freedom of spirit; we shall never see anything there but the excess of slavery."

REFERENCES

Gardiner: *The French Revolution*, pp. 13–17; Adams: *European History*, pp. 427–428; Morse-Stephens: *The Revolution and Europe*, pp. 8–10.

CHAPTER VIII

The French Revolution

§ 24. THE MEETING OF THE ESTATES GENERAL

The French Revolution is not to be regarded as the result of a sudden impulse, a volcanic outburst of popular exasperation. In its more important phases it is the result of a half century of deliberation. The reconstruction of French society which resulted from the Revolution had been worked out in detail by thoughtful men, before a step was taken toward the overthrow of the government of Louis XVI.

Causes of the Revolution.

The immediate cause of the Revolution was the financial crisis. The extravagance of Louis XIV, the indifference of Louis XV, had exhausted the resources of the government. Debt piled upon debt, until credit was gone. The efforts of Louis XVI to reorganize the financial system with the aid of Turgot and Necker have been related. The court favorites, who followed Necker in the ministry, completed the ruin of the treasury; the nation was bankrupt. Driven to a last extremity, the king had recourse to an expedient which marked the absolute failure of the royal resources. For one hundred and seventy-five years, since the firm establishment of Bourbon rule, the Estates General had never been called in France. Its summons in 1789 was a confession that the system of Louis XIV had broken down.

It would be a mistake, however, to suppose that the men who came together as delegates to the Estates General had in mind only the reorganization of the finances. The philosophical discussions of the times had given their

141

demands a wider scope. They came together to give France a constitution which should express the eighteenth century ideas of government and society.

The evils from which France was suffering at the end of the eighteenth century may be summed up in one word —privilege: the privilege of the king; the

State of France in 1789.

privileges of the nobles; the privileges of the clergy. These constitute the spirit of the *ancien régime*. At an earlier time these privileges were not without justification. When the clergy were burdened with the general superintendence of education and the care of the poor and suffering, as was the case in the Middle Ages: when the nobles were the bulwark of defence against the enemy, and guaranteed the safety of the peasant while he tilled the soil; then it was not unjust that these upper classes should have a part of the produce of the labor which they made possible through their guardianship and protection. And did not the king, so long as he was regarded as the representive of God on earth, possess the land and the people ? And what he refrained from taking himself was in his benevolence left to others.

But the eighteenth century changed all this. The function of the clergy, if in some respects as great, was in material things less evident ; and there were many, such as the Voltairians, who doubted altogether its efficiency. The nobles had no longer any place in the system. The protection which it was formerly their business to supply was now afforded by the state, through taxation. As for the king, the theory of his divine commission had been called into question by the political philosophy of which Montesquieu and Rousseau were representatives.

But if the king, the nobles, and the clergy had lost their special usefulness, they had preserved their privileges. The taxes of the realm went into the king's privy purse. From this fund he drew what he chose, being responsible to no man. What he left went for the purposes of administration. This was the king's privilege. The clergy were free from taxes. To be sure, they gave, as a body, a sum of money to the king at intervals, called the *don gratuit;* but it was a small contribution compared with the value of their estates, which constituted one-fourth of France. The nobles were exempt from the chief direct tax, the *taille,* and were permitted to make their own assessments for the remainder. None but a noble could hold a commissioned office in the army. The chief privileges then of the clergy and nobility were a whole or partial exemption from taxes, and the possession of the great offices of honor and value. From the peasants on their estates the nobles not only exacted rent, but a host of ancient feudal dues, for which they rendered no equivalent, squandering at Versailles the money wrung from toil.

The royal edict for the convocation of the Estates General was sent to the provincial governors for publication, January 24, 1789. Elections were held in each judicial district between the 7th of February and the 5th of May. In each district the electors chose delegates to the Estates General, and at the same time, in accordance with ancient usage, drew up a statement of grievances, and suggestions for the removal of the same. These statements, or " *Cahiers,*" as they were called, were to be taken by the deputies to the Estates General, and there condensed into three great " *Cahiers,*" one for each of the three estates, the Clergy, the Nobles, and the Third Estate, which made up the Estates General. Many of these Cahiers are preserved, and from them we learn that the people of France had thought deeply over the proposed changes; that the clergy and nobles were convinced of the necessity of giving up their privileges, and that the plan of reform, which the Revolution brought about, had been already worked out, in its main features, by the people. The

The Cahiers.

king and his advisers looked to the Estates General for a solution of the financial difficulties of the crown; but the people instructed their deputies to sit at Versailles until France had been given a constitution in harmony with her needs and wishes.

The deputies of the three orders came together at Versailles on the 5th of May. They were addressed by the king and his minister and left to their own devices. The vital question of the day was whether they should sit as one chamber, or as three. In accordance with the decree of convocation, the delegates of the Third Estate were equal in number

MIRABEAU.

to the combined delegates of the Clergy and Nobility. Sitting in one chamber, the Third Estate, with what help it might get from the liberals of the other orders, might expect a majority for its plans. Sitting as three chambers, the Third Estate, in spite of its larger representation, would be always outvoted, two to one. Under the leadership of Mirabeau the Third Estate took the name of the National Assembly, and refused to recognize the separate existence of the other orders. The king sought at first to use force, and closed the hall in which the representatives of the people held their sittings. Nothing daunted, they adjourned to a neighboring tennis court, and took an oath not to separate until they had given France a constitution. In spite of the king's commands, the Third Estate persevered in this policy of obstruction, and after two months' patient waiting, won; the king yielded; at his command the Clergy and the Nobles joined the Third Estate, and the National Assembly was organized into one chamber.

Meeting of the Estates General.

OATH OF THE TENNIS COURT, JUNE 20, 1789

SOURCE REVIEW

I. Among the many pamphlets which flooded Paris on the eve of the meeting of the Estates General was one by the Abbé Siéyès, entitled "What is the Third Estate?" In his discussion he attempts to show that the privileged orders are worse than useless to the state, and that the Third Estate is really the sum and substance of the nation. This idea, it is evident, lies at the root of the policy of the Third Estate, in the early days of the meeting of the Estates General, when they declared themselves the National Assembly. Siéyès says: "Who then shall dare to say that the Third Estate has not within itself all that is necessary for the formation of a complete nation? It is the strong and robust man who has one arm still shackled. If the privileged order should be abolished the nation would be nothing less, but something more. Therefore, what is the Third Estate? Everything, but an everything shackled and oppressed. What would it be without this privileged order? Everything, but an everything free and flourishing. Nothing can succeed without it; everything would be infinitely better without the others.

"The Third Estate embraces then all that which belongs to the nation, and all that which is not the Third Estate cannot be regarded as being of the nation. What is the Third Estate? It is the whole."

II. Extracts from a *Cahier*.—The Nobility of Blois demand as follows:

"That the Estates General about to assemble shall be permanent and shall not be dissolved until the constitution be established; but in case the labors connected with the establishment of the constitution be prolonged beyond the space of two years, the assembly shall be reorganized with new deputies freely and regularly elected."

[From this it will be seen that the people were looking forward to something more than the mere presentation of grievances. Again:]

"That a fundamental and constitutional law shall assure forever the periodical assembly of the Estates General at frequent intervals, in such a manner that they may assemble

11

and organize themselves at a fixed time and place, without the concurrence of any act emanating from the executive power.

"That the legislative power shall reside exclusively in the assembly of the nation, under the sanction of the king.

"That taxes may not be imposed without the consent of the nation."

[A study of the *cahiers* will show that the great reforms of the Revolution were in the minds of the people, and had been thoroughly discussed and formulated before the meeting of the Estates General.]

REFERENCES

Gardiner: *The French Revolution*, pp. 33–42; Morse Stephens: *The Revolution and Europe*, pp. 49–59.

§ 25.   THE GREAT REFORM OF 1791

The Estates General, converted by the act of the Third Estate into the National Assembly, began the work for which it was chosen : the political regeneration of France.   The king and the court party, who had expected no such result from the meeting of the Estates General, were at first inclined to resist ; but a popular uprising in Paris, resulting in the destruction of the Bastille, a royal fortress and prison for state offenders, betrayed too well the temper of the nation.

The National Assembly.

The first work of the National Assembly was destructive.   On the night of the 4th of August the Assembly voted to abolish all feudal rights.   This legislation was not forced upon the privileged classes by the Third Estate ; two great nobles, the Duc d'Aiguillon and the Duc de Noailles were the first to renounce their feudal privileges.   Members of the nobility and of the clergy hastened to follow this example.   The night has been called the "St. Bartholomew of Feudalism."

The Assembly, however, in spite of the enthusiasm of
the moment, went carefully to work. It divided feudal
dues into two classes : 1. Honorific or per-
Feudal dues. sonal dues, originally representing contributions exacted by the lord from his vassals in return for
protection. 2. Dues representing rent, paid to the lord
for his share in the common land, held jointly, according
to medieval custom. The Assembly cut away the first class
entirely. There was no longer any protection ; therefore

THE BASTILLE.

no reason for these dues. The second class, the rent dues,
were retained provisionally, until some plan could be devised, whereby the peasants might gradually buy out the
interest of the lord, and become actual owners of the land.
In many parts of the country, however, the peasantry rose
up against exacting landlords, burned their châteaux, and
drove them out of the country.

To destroy the old system was an easier matter than to

build up the new. Nevertheless, the Assembly faced its
task with courage, fortified with the extensive discussion
of the subject in the *cahiers*, and in the numerous pamphlets which had appeared in the period
just preceding the convening of the Estates
General. On August 26th the Assembly published a "Declaration of Rights of Man and of the Citizen," which, start-
ing with the statement that "men are born and remain
free and equal before the law," went on to secure to
Frenchmen those privileges of liberty and free speech
which are the foundations of modern political life, such
as the right of *habeas corpus* and of trial by jury.

The constitution.

MEDAL STRUCK TO COMMEMORATE THE FOURTH OF AUGUST.

The National Assembly, taking up the task of forming
a constitution, is called the Constitutional Assembly. At
this task it labored until its dissolution on the 30th of
September, 1791, when it had completed and presented to
its constituents the first written constitution of France.
It was accepted by the king, and went into operation.
This Constitution of 1791, as it was called, gave France a
limited monarchy. Conscious of what the nation had suffered from the absolutism of former kings, the Assembly
went to the other extreme, and reduced the royal power almost to nothing. Not alone was the king deprived of

the right of making laws, which his predecessors had done with a simple edict ; but he was even deprived of the right of vetoing legislation, when it came from the national parliament, the Legislative Assembly, as it was to be called. If the Legislative Assembly passed a bill three times against the royal disapproval, the bill became law.

Nor was the king free in the disposition of his ministers. They might be impeached before a special High Court, and, if successfully impeached, removed. This sudden reduction of the royal power was, perhaps, unwise. Not only did it startle Europe into an attitude of defence against French radical ideas, but it humiliated the king and alienated his sympathies from the reform. Although he accepted the constitution, he did so from fear, secretly intending to renounce his adherence when the opportunity came. He began to plot against France with his friends and relatives over the border, and did it so clumsily that he made the monarchy hateful to the people, and brought its ruin along with his own.

The Assembly was not satisfied with the reorganization of the state ; it also desired to reconstruct the church. The clergy. The church excited the apprehension of many thoughtful men, on account of the exceptional position in which it stood toward the state. It was, to a certain extent, a rival power, directed from Rome and owing its allegiance to the pope. The Assembly desired to nationalize the church, to make it a department of the state, to sweep away the whole system of tithes by which the church was supported, and to reduce the officers of the church to the status of government officials. This it proceeded to do in the " Civil Constitution of the Clergy," or law for the reorganization of the church. Clergymen were obliged to take an oath of allegiance to the Constitution. The property of the church was turned over to the nation, and the salaries of church officers fixed by schedule, and paid by the state. The enormous revenues

of the bishops were cut down, and the salaries of the par-
ish priests, a mere pittance before 1789, were raised.

In return for this obligation of the state to pay the salaries of the clergy, the Assembly voted to turn into the
public treasury the enormous vested wealth of
Finances.
the church, houses and lands, estimated at
one-fourth (by some, one-third) of the real estate of France,
and yielding an income of two hundred million of francs.
Recognizing the impossibility of selling outright so vast a
body of real estate at anything like its value, and being
in need of money, the Assembly conceived the idea of issu-

AN ASSIGNAT.

ing a paper currency,
called *assignats*, sup-
posed to represent the
land itself, and event-
ually to be turned in
for the purchase of
the property at a fixed
price. The scheme
seemed safe, and would
have been, if the issue
of *assignats* had been
limited to the value of
the church property ;
but as the Revolution
progressed the increasing need of money for public purposes, and the fatal ease with which it could be taken from
the printing-press, resulted in an overissue, which carried
the value of the *assignats* nearly to zero. The lands
themselves were largely bought by speculators, but eventually they were cut up, and came into the hands of the
people, adding to the number of small peasant proprietors,
who constitute the bone and sinew of the French nation.

SOURCE REVIEW

I. The Fourth of August; "Abolition of Feudalism."—
" A terrible report it was. Châteaux burning here and there ;
millers hung ; tax-gatherers drowned ; everywhere rioting and
nowhere peace. Among those who listened to the report was
the Vicomte de Noailles, a young man of thirty-three, who
had distinguished himself at the head of his regiment under
his cousin, Lafayette, in America. The Vicomte de Noailles
was the first to rush to the tribune. ' What is the cause of
the evil which is agitating the provinces ? ' he cried ; and
then he showed that it arose from the uncertainty under
which they dwelt, as to whether or not the old feudal bonds
under which they had so long lived and labored were to be
perpetuated or abolished, and concluded an impassioned
speech by proposing to abolish them at once. One after another the young liberal noblemen, and then certain deputies of
the Third Estate, followed him with fresh sacrifices. First the
old feudal rights were abolished ; then the rights of the dove-
cote and the game laws; then the old copyhold services ; then
the tithes paid to the Church, in spite of a protest from
Sieyès; then the rights of certain cities over their immediate
suburbs and rural districts were sacrificed ; and the contention
during that feverish night was rather to remember something
or other to sacrifice than to suggest the expediency of maintaining anything that was established. In its generosity the
Assembly gave away what did not belong to it. The old
dues paid to the pope were abolished, and it was even declared that Avignon, which had belonged to the pope since
the Middle Ages, should be united to France, if it liked ; and
the sitting closed with a unanimous decree that a statue
should be erected to Louis XVI, ' the restorer of French
liberty. ' "—Morse-Stephens: *History of the French Revolution.*

II. The *Emigrés*.—It was the misfortune of France that the
natural leaders, the men of political and social prominence,
whose interests and instincts would have served to moderate
the course of revolution, deserted their posts, and betook
themselves to the German and Italian frontiers, awaiting the
intervention of Europe. Meanwhile France was left in the

hands of a set of new men, inexperienced in public affairs and often without any personal stake in the great political game which they sought to direct. Chancellor Pasquier, in his *Memoirs*, thus writes of the Emigration : "It has oftentimes been asked how so extraordinary a resolution came to be taken ; how it had entered into the minds of men gifted with a certain amount of sense that there was any advantage to be derived from abandoning all posts where they could still exercise power ; of giving over to the enemy the regiments they commanded, the localities over which they had control ; of delivering up completely to the teachings of the opposite party the peasantry, over whom, in a goodly number of provinces, a valuable influence might be exerted, and among whom they still had many friends ; and all this, to return for the purpose of conquering, at the sword's point, positions, a number of which at least could be held without a fight."

REFERENCES

Morse-Stephens: *The Revolution and Europe,* pp. 60–123 ; Gardiner: *The French Revolution,* pp. 49–86.

§ 26. THE JACOBIN REVOLUTION

If the Revolution had ceased with the great reforms of 1791, history would have been spared one of its most

Why the Revolution went on.

tragic episodes. Why it did not stop is a question of much difficulty, which cannot be answered with a word. In all revolutions—political, social, and religious—there is a tendency toward extravagance : begun by radicals, the movement passes into the hands of fanatics. It has been noted in the case of Martin Luther that his reform owed its success largely to the ability of its leader to keep it from degenerating into extravagance and anarchy.

The French revolution was the end of a long period of social oppression. The distinction between nobles and bourgeois, and between bourgeois and proletariat arrayed the classes in hatred against one another. The reforms

of 1791 were a triumph for the bourgeoisie, for it had reduced the distinctions between that class and the nobility;
and it was felt by the extreme social reformers that the
work of leveling ought to go on, until all distinctions of
wealth and social degree had been removed between the
bourgeoisie and proletariat. A reign of "liberty, equality,
fraternity," in the literal sense of the words, was their demand.

Under more favorable circumstances the bourgeoisie

TRIAL OF THE DEPOSED KING, CHARGED WITH TREASON.

would have held their own and prevented the Revolution
from passing into the hands of the social theorists; but
unfortunately, the very foundation of the structure of 1791
was unsound. The king himself was out of sympathy with
the government. Putting himself into correspondence with
his friends outside of France, he conspired to overthrow
the constitutional monarchy with the aid of foreign bayonets. The treachery of the king, when it became known,
broke down the monarchy, gave strength to the demands
of the masses, and eventually brought about the execution

of King Louis XVI and his wife Marie Antoinette. Without a king the monarchy could exist no longer ; the Constitution of 1791 was no longer valid. The conservative institutions of the Estates General had failed through the defection of the king, and a Constitutional Convention was called to devise a new form of government for France.

The Convention, called for the purpose of giving France a new constitution, actually governed the country for three years. The monarchists, who had guided the Revolution at its start, lost control, and the power passed into the hands of a group of ambitious lawyers, Rousseauans and social reformers, whose strength consisted largely in the fact that they were leaders of the Jacobin Club. This club, organized as a place of social gathering for the provincial deputies, took its name from its place of meeting—the abandoned monastery of the Jacobin monks. It became the most powerful organization in France, with affiliated branches all through the provinces. At its daily meeting the policy of the government was made the subject of debate, until the club had determined its lines of action ; and then its members, who were for the most part members of the Convention, went to the sessions of that body, prepared to act as a unit in the support of the Jacobin policy. Even when numerically in the minority, their unity and formulated plan of action gave the Jacobins control of the Convention ; and with their affiliated clubs they were able to control the elections in the provinces.

The Convention 1792-1795.

Under Jacobin pressure the Convention evolved one of the most absolute and forceful governments that Europe has ever seen. A committee was appointed, the "Committee of Public Safety," and into the hands of this committee the Convention confided its administrative powers. France, decentralized by the Constitution of 1791, became again centralized as never before, under the absolute rule of this committee.

The Reign of Terror.

At its head were Robespierre, Couthon, and St. Just. Eight other members divided among them the various departments of government : the army, the navy, finance, and the like. All measures were reported to the Convention, and received its sanction.

The chief business of the government of the "Terror" was to defend France against her enemies. The states of Europe, terrified at the execution of Louis XVI, and fearing the extension of republican ideas into their own territories, took up arms against France. In addition to this, parts of the west and south of France, faithful to the king and church, rose in rebellion, so that the Convention had domestic as well as foreign foes to fight. But the spirit of France in this hour of danger was wonderful. The country, which under Bourbon rule seemed bankrupt, was able, in a time of national inspiration, to find men and supplies for such a war as Europe had never witnessed. The task was enormous ; the armies had to be organized and equipped under fire ; but in spite of all these difficulties the

ROBESPIERRE.

French republican troops defeated the united armies of Europe, and not only drove the invaders out of France, but carried the war into the enemies' country and moved the boundaries of France to the Rhine.

While her armies were defending France on the border it was necessary to keep down the disaffected ones at home. This was accomplished by the system of "Terror." All persons of aristocratic birth, or who were otherwise open to suspicion, when not provided with "cards of civism," issued by the courts, and establishing for the bearer a character of patriotism, were " suspects." They might at any time be arrested and carried before the " Revolution-ary Tribunals," courts especially created for the trial of suspected persons. Indeed, there were committees, called " Revolutionary Committees," composed of approved patriots, whose business it was to watch suspects, and report their shortcomings. To be brought before a " Revolutionary Tribunal " in those times of mutual distrust and danger, was serious, indeed. The usual forms of trial were suspended ; the jury had a right to declare itself satisfied and reject further evidence. Human life was cheap, and the guillotine near at hand. So complete was the system of Terror that, when the wagons passed through the street with their freight of human victims bound for the guillotine, passers-by and the people at the windows were afraid to raise their eyes, lest an involuntary expression of pity might be detected by the lynx-eyed partisans of the Convention.

System of the "Terror."

The method by which the Convention got its supplies was in harmony with the arbitrary character of its rule. All food-supplies and other military necessities were requisitioned and paid for in assignats. The assignats were produced at the cost of ink and paper, and their circulation at par was enforced under penalty of death. All persons were required to turn in their gold and silver to the government and receive assignats in exchange. In order to prevent commodities rising to high prices in exchange for assignats the " Law of the Maximum " was enacted, whereby a maximum price was fixed for articles of prime necessity. Such goods might not be sold for more than this price, under penalty of death. To prevent the withdrawal of goods from sale, it was further enacted that every merchant or warehouseman must post an inventory of all articles held by him ; and all stock not so posted was subject to confiscation, one half its value going to the informer. By such measures as these all the resources of France were put into the hands of the government of the Terror, and used in the defeat of Europe and the subjection of domestic rebels.

Thus a handful of men governed France with methods of terror, while the nation obeyed in fear and trembling.

Why the Terror was endured. The only place of safety for one who had the misfortune to be of aristocratic birth, and was too patriotic to desert his country in her need, was with the army at the front. But France endured the Terror, because it was accomplishing that which was of more importance than all the rest—it was rescuing the country from the danger of foreign and domestic enemies. Before we condemn utterly Robespierre and the men of the Terror, let us remember their position. The times were not ordinary times, and called for desperate measures. Some system of repression was necessary to keep down the enemies of the Republic, who were everywhere, both in and out of France, ready to deliver France to the English or the Austrians. It was necessary for the Committee to hold them down with one hand, while with the other it fought the armies of Europe.

As soon as the danger passed, and the threat of invasion was gone, the Terror fell, and the men who had organized it, Robespierre and the rest, went to the block. Patriots or fiends, deserving well or ill of their country, they fell victims to their own ruthless system. Of the Committee of Public Safety one alone was saved from death or exile : Carnot, who had the army in his charge, for he " had organized victory."

SOURCE REVIEW

Execution of the King.—On the 10th of August, 1792, King Louis XVI, who had become hateful to the people on account of his intrigues with the enemies of France, was driven from his residence of the Tuileries by a mob, and conducted for safe-keeping to one of the city prisons. Papers found in the king's apartments established beyond doubt the fact of his guilt. He was deposed, accused of treason, and tried before the Legislature. Being found guilty, he was condemned to death, and decapitated January 21, 1793. The Queen, Marie Antoinette, was executed on the 16th of October following ; the young Dauphin, only son of the royal pair, was given over to the care of a shoemaker, Simon, and succumbed, it is supposed, to brutal treatment. The following is Carlyle's account of the execution : "He mounts the scaffold, not without delay ; he is in a puce coat, breeches of gray, white stockings. He strips off the coat ; stands disclosed in a sleeve-waistcoat of white flannel. The executioners approach to bind him : he spurns, resists ; Abbé Edgeworth has to remind him how the Saviour, in whom men trust, submitted to be bound. His hands are tied, his head bare ; the fatal moment is come. He advances to the edge of the Scaffold, 'his face very red,' and says : 'Frenchmen, I die innocent : it is from the Scaffold and near appearing before God that I tell you so. I pardon my enemies ; I desire that France '—A general on horseback, Santerre or another, prances up with uplifted hand : 'Tambours !' The drums drown the voice. 'Executioners, do your duty !' The executioners seize the hapless Louis, and bind him to their plank. Abbé Edgeworth, stooping, bespeaks him : 'Son of Saint Louis, ascend to Heaven.' The Axe clanks down; a King's Life is shorn away."—*The French Revolution.*

CHAPTER IX

Napoleon Bonaparte

§ 27. BONAPARTE, GENERAL OF THE DIRECTORY

THE fall of the Terror was followed by the government of the Directory. The Convention, freed from the influence of the Jacobins, set itself to perform the task for which it had been chosen, the making of a constitution. Its final work was the Constitution of 1795. This provided for a legislature of two chambers, the "Ancients" and the "Five Hundred." The executive power was confided to a "Directory" of five members, elected by the legislature, and having in turn the right of appointing ministers, generals, and other officers of administration.

The Directory.

The last days of the Convention were filled with struggle. The fall of the Jacobins brought back a host of moderates and royalists, who sought by violence to obtain control of the government. It was in the suppression of one of these insurrections, the royalist uprising of the 13th Vendémiaire, that public attention was first called to Napoleon Bonaparte. Barras, to whom the defence of the Convention was entrusted, summoned to his assistance this young general, then in Paris protesting against his recall from the army of Italy on account of his supposed Jacobin sympathies. This was Bonaparte's opportunity, and he improved it. The rioters advanced upon the palace of the Tuileries, the seat of the Convention, expecting a feeble resistance; but Bonaparte placed his cannon to control the streets leading up to the Tuileries, and cut down the

The 13th Vendémiaire.

rioters and national guardsmen as they advanced. By these means he saved the Convention, and commended himself to the Directory, about to assume the reins of government.

The military successes of the Convention had driven to terms of peace all the enemies of France, except Austria and England. Against these powers the

The Army of Italy.

Directory was obliged to carry on the war, and Austria was selected for the first attack. The plan of the campaign of 1796 against Austria divided the French forces into three armies, two operating against the Rhenish borders of Austria, the third to strike at her

JOSEPHINE.

possessions and allies in Italy. The Army of Italy was placed under command of Bonaparte. This rapid promotion was due to Barras, who had been chosen one of the first five directors; to the reputation young Bonaparte had gained from the affair of Vendémiaire; and also, it is said, to a masterly plan of the Italian campaign, which Bonaparte had submitted to the Minister of War. On the eve of his departure for Italy, Bonaparte married Josephine Tascher de la Pagerie, widow of General Beauharnais, a clever creole woman of West Indian origin, who moved in the influential circles of the Directory, and was in a position to aid her husband through her influence with politicians.

When Bonaparte arrived at the headquarters of the Army of Italy, his youth (he was only twenty-seven) and his inexperience aroused the jealousy of his fellow-officers, many of whom were soldiers of experience in the armies of the Revolution. By the firmness of his character, and by the evident wisdom of his commands, he succeeded in

BONAPARTE IN EGYPT.

establishing his authority. The common soldiers he gained by his care for their welfare, and by the stirring promise of his proclamations.

Advancing into Italy, Bonaparte defeated the Austrians and their Italian allies at every point. The petty sovereigns of Italy, and the pope as well, cut off from Austrian protection, were glad to purchase peace at Bonaparte's price ; and this was put so high, that the commander of the Army of Italy was able to pay the expenses of his campaign, and sent home to the Directory a neat balance out of the plunder of Italian treasuries.

The Italian Campaign.

Three armies sent by Austria into the plains of Lombardy were defeated in turn by Bonaparte, and in the spring of 1796 he began his march northward against Vienna. The Austrians, fearing for their capital, sued for peace, and it was accorded to them in the treaty of Campo-Formio. By this treaty the Emperor, Francis I, recognized the natural boundaries of France as the Alps and the Rhine. Its most important feature, however, was the constitution of Italy. Lombardy and the Duchy of Modena, together with some parts of the Papal States, were formed into the Cisalpine Republic, with a constitution modeled after that of France. This was the beginning of that breaking down of the feudal states of Italy by Napoleon Bonaparte, which paved the way for the eventual creation of the modern Kingdom of Italy. On the other hand, liberty lost one of its earliest strongholds. Venice, a republic from medieval times, lost its independence, and was given to Austria in exchange for Lombardy.

Bonaparte, returning to Paris from his Italian victories, was the man of the hour. His immense popularity excited the apprehension of the Directors, and well it might, as future events proved. But Bonaparte's hour had not yet arrived. He applied himself to the preparation of an expedition, ostensibly against England, the remaining enemy of France ; but when the expedition sailed from Toulon its destination was found to be Egypt. The Directory was only too glad, no doubt, to send him on a distant and doubtful expedition. The reason for the Egyptian expedition is a matter of doubt. Was Bonaparte willing that France should learn, by his absence, how necessary he was to her existence ? Was it his plan to strike at England through her Eastern possession, or did he really seek to establish an Eastern empire on the ruins of the empire of Alexander, and hope to turn back upon Europe from the East, as he once said, at the head of an insuperable army of Asiatics, drilled by him to a point of efficiency?

The Egyptian expedition.

The Toulon squadron escaped the English fleet, which was cruising in the Mediterranean, and reached Alexandria. The conquest of Egypt was rapidly accomplished. Beneath the Pyramids Bonaparte defeated the Mameluke cavalry and occupied Cairo. Meanwhile Nelson, with the English fleet, had found and destroyed the French squadron, in the " Battle of the Nile," and the retreat from Egypt was cut off.

Bonaparte organized a government at Cairo and sought to rouse a national spirit among the Egyptians, who for generations had been subject to the Turks and their Mameluke soldiery. Hearing that a Turkish army was advancing against him by land, Bonaparte crossed into Syria, and met and defeated the Turkish forces at Mount Tabor. Returning to Egypt, he found his government disorganized, and learned that another Turkish army had been landed by the British fleet at the mouth of the Nile. Again he defeated the Mamelukes at Cairo, and, marching down the Nile, drove the Turkish army into the sea ; but at this moment he received the first news that had come to him from Europe. He determined to return at once to France, and embarked with a few friends, leaving Kléber in command in Egypt.

Expedition into Syria.

Bonaparte's ship escaped the English fleet, and he landed on the coast of France, October 9, 1799.

Meanwhile matters had gone ill with the Directory. Russia had joined with Austria, war had been renewed, and all that Bonaparte had gained for France was lost. The French were driven from Italy, and the treaty of Campo-Formio was a dead letter. When Bonaparte reached Paris men of all parties sought his aid. But he held himself aloof, and with his friends planned the event which was to raise him to the height of power. The four years of the Directory, with its plots and counter-plots, its scandals and financial difficulties, had discredited its rule. The absence of Bonaparte had proved his worth to France. Surrounded by enemies, she once more sought a strong hand at the helm.

The 18th Brumaire.

On the 18th Brumaire, Year VIII, the two chambers of the legislature were removed to St. Cloud, under

MEDAL OF THE THREE CONSULS.

the pretext that their sojourn in Paris was accompanied with danger; and they were then surrounded by troops devoted to Bonaparte. Of the Directors, two were unwilling to yield, and they were guarded in their palace of the Luxemburg. On the morning of the 19th Brumaire, Bonaparte entered the chambers, escorted by soldiers. The Ancients yielded quietly, but the popular body, the Five Hundred, was less docile, and resisting deputies were expelled with force. That evening thirty deputies organized a government, and supplanted the Directory with a provisional executive, consisting of three Consuls. A committee was appointed to draw up a new constitution. This was the

Constitution of the Year VIII, organizing the Consulate. The executive consisted of three Consuls; of these Bonaparte was First Consul, with the powers of a king.

SOURCE REVIEW

I. The Revolutionary Calendar.—In 1793 the Revolutionists, desiring to efface all memories of the olden time, adopted a new calendar. It was dated back to September 22, 1792, when the Republican Era began, with the proclamation of the Republic. There were twelve months of thirty days each, each month divided into three decades of ten days each, with every tenth day a holiday. This left five days over (and on leap-year six). These were special holidays (*"Sans-Culottides"*). The new names of the months were invented by a poet of the time and are very beautiful and expressive. They are: *Vendémiaire* (September 22d–October 22d), *Brumaire, Frimaire; Nivôse, Pluviôse, Ventôse; Germinal, Floréal, Prairial; Messidor, Thermidor, Fructidor.* The years were indicated with Roman numerals; and this usage continued until the Empire. (For "Table of Concordance of the Republican and Gregorian Calendars," see Morse Stephens: *The Revolution and Europe*, p. 374.)

II. Address to the Army of Italy, at the beginning of the Campaign of 1796.—"Soldiers, you are naked and ill-fed! Government owes you much and can give you nothing. The patience and courage you have shown in the midst of these rocks are admirable, but they gain you no renown; no glory results to you from your endurance. It is my design to lead you into the most fertile plains of the world. Rich provinces and great cities will be in your power; there you will find honor, glory, and wealth. Soldiers of Italy! will you be wanting in courage or perseverance?"

III. Picture of Napoleon in Italy, after the successes of his first campaign, as seen by Miot de Melito.—"I found myself in his presence a few moments after he had alighted. I was strangely surprised at his appearance. Nothing could be further from the picture which I had formed of him. I saw, in the midst of a numerous staff, a man below the medium height and extremely thin. His powdered hair, which was cut in a peculiar, square fashion below the ears, fell down to his shoulders. He had on a straight coat, closely buttoned up, decorated with a very narrow gold embroidery, and wore a tri-colored plume in his hat. At first glance the face did not seem to me a fine one, but the striking features, a quick and searching eye, and abrupt, animated gestures proclaimed an ardent soul, while the broad, serious forehead showed a deep thinker.

"I found Bonaparte at the magnificent residence of Montebello in the midst of a brilliant court rather than the headquarters of an army. Severe etiquette was already maintained in his presence. His aides-de-camp and officers were no longer received at his table, and he exercised great care in the choice of those whom he did admit, it being considered a rare honor, obtained only with difficulty. He dined, so to speak, in public, and during the meal the inhabitants of the country were admitted to the dining-room and allowed to feast their eyes upon him. He showed himself, however, in no way embarrassed or confused by this exhibition of esteem, and received them as if he had always been accustomed to such tributes."

REFERENCES

Morse Stephens : *The Revolution and Europe*, pp. 173–211 ; Judson : *Europe in the Nineteenth Century*, pp. 45–58 ; Rose : *The Revolutionary and Napoleonic Era*, pp. 93–118.

§ 28. CONSULATE AND EMPIRE

Bonaparte's first task, on assuming chief power in the Republic, was to chastise Austria. This he accomplished in the campaign of Marengo. Again he de-

The Consulate.

feated the Austrian armies in northern Italy, and forced the Emperor to the treaty of Lunéville, by which the conditions of Campo-Formio were re-established. A period of peace followed. Even England signed with her great adversary the Peace of Amiens, which lasted for fourteen months, an interval of peace in what has been called the "Second Hundred Years' War between France and England."

This year and more of peace was the only time of rest

NAPOLEON, EMPEROR.

France was to know under Napoleon Bonaparte. She quickly recovered from the wounds of war, and made rapid strides along the path of internal development, under the direction of the greatest administrator Europe had ever known. Many ideas of the early Revolution were realized by Bonaparte. A system of laws, adapted to modern needs, the Code Napoléon, was drawn up under his supervision ; the finances of the country were regulated; a system of public education, projected by the Convention, was perfected and put into operation ; the recognition of the pope was much appreciated by the people at large, who were still Catholic, in spite of the extravagances of the Jacobins. The Consulate was a confirmation of the conservative reforms, begun by the men of 1789. In 1802 Bonaparte was given the Consulate for life. The popular vote (plebiscite) upon the change stood 3,500,000 to 8,000.

In May, 1804, the Senate, which merely reflected the wishes of the Consul, offered him the title of Emperor. Emperor. 1804. This time a majority of three and one-half millions confirmed the offer. On the second of December Napoleon crowned himself in the presence of the pope. Five days later Francis II proclaimed himself Emperor of Austria, and the Holy Roman Empire was at an end.

Once an emperor, Napoleon surrounded himself with all the pomp of empire. He created a court with stately ceremonials and ancient customs, and gave to Paris the spectacle of royalty, the absence of which it had long regretted. Yet with all this splendor, which recalls the times of the Bourbons, it must be remembered that the empire of Napoleon was democratic. If his imperial will was made law by a subservient legislature, there was nevertheless a free field for ability. Any man, no matter what his birth, could hope to win the great prizes of the civil and of the military career. Three generations of nobility were no longer necessary to obtain a captain's commission ; there were no privileges of rank ; all was open to ability, and in this essential particular the aspirations of the men of 1789 were realized.

When Napoleon ascended the throne war with England was at hand. A great army was assembled at Boulogne, on the Channel, ready for the invasion of England. The combined French and Spanish fleets sought to draw away the English squadron from the Channel, to permit the transportation of the French army to the coast of England. But Nelson destroyed Napoleon's ships at Trafalgar, and the project of the invasion of England, if ever seriously entertained, was abandoned.

Wars of conquest.

Meanwhile Austria and Russia had joined with England. Napoleon swung his great Boulogne armament into central Austria, and with the victories of Ulm and Austerlitz forced the Peace of Pressburg (December 26, 1805), with great loss to Austria. Prussia, whose policy had been vacillating, was forced out of her position of neutrality by the war party, and defeated in the battles of Jena and Auerstädt. Berlin was occupied, and Napoleon advanced against his third great continental adversary, Russia, whom he forced, by the victory of Friedland, to the Peace of Tilsit (July 7, 1807). Thus in twenty months Napoleon had, by the rapidity of his movements and the excellence of his organization, defeated the great powers of central Europe. His ability as a strategist was great; but his successes were earned with hard work. His campaigns were planned ahead with infinite pains. In the great transcontinental swing from Boulogne to central Austria every move was worked out beforehand; every combination came to pass as planned. Napoleon's title to genius lay in his ability for continuous mental effort. All day and night he worked without rest, while his secretaries fainted at his side from exhaustion.

Although Napoleon had the Continent at his feet, he had no means at hand to coerce England. English fleets swept the Channel, and invasion was impossible. But on her commercial side England was vulnerable. She had become a vast workshop, and the Continent was her market.

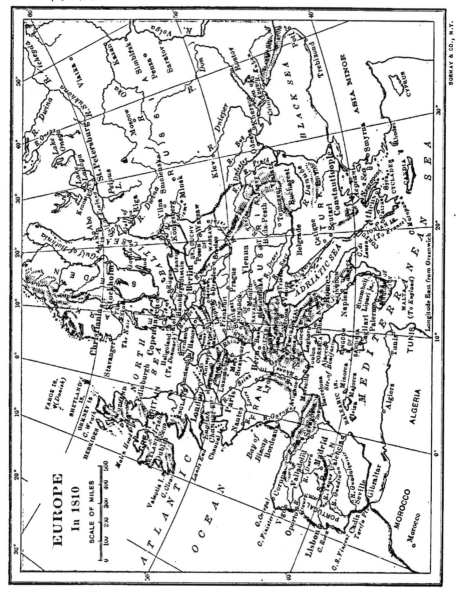

EUROPE
In 1810

SCALE OF MILES

0   100 200 300 400 500

ATLANTIC OCEAN

NORTH SEA

BALTIC SEA

R U S S I A

BLACK SEA

ASIA MINOR

MEDITERRANEAN SEA

ADRIATIC SEA

TURKEY

FRANCE

PORTUGAL

ALGERIA

MOROCCO

Longitude East from Greenwich

SORMAY & CO., N.Y.

Once this trade was cut off, and the looms and forges of England silenced, England would be ruined. For this pur-

The Continental system. pose the "Continental System" was devised; its aim was to close the markets of Europe to English goods. In order to accomplish this it was necessary for Napoleon to control the vast extent of sea-coast from the Baltic to the Adriatic, a herculean task, too great, perhaps, even for the ablest man in Europe. Everything in Napoleon's career, after the Peace of Tilsit, bears upon this problem. England recognized that for her it was a life or death struggle. She spent her money freely in support of Austrian and Prussian armies. She sent an army under Wellington into Spain, to co-operate with the Spaniards, who opposed the introduction of the Napoleonic system into Spain.

Napoleon aimed wider than the mere subjection of England. He sought the consolidation of Europe under his control, a system of vassal and allied states centered about France, drawing their inspiration from his policy. He even contemplated a group of palaces on the Seine, where each subject prince should spend a portion of his time, in touch with the source of power. It was for this reason that he placed his brothers and marshals upon conquered thrones: Louis in Holland, Joseph first in Naples (succeeded there by Murat), then in Spain; and for Jerome he cut out the new kingdom of Westphalia from the petty German states across the Rhine. His stepson, Eugene Beauharnais, he placed as Viceroy on the throne of Italy, a kingdom created from the nucleus of the Cisalpine Republic.

It was a noble plan, this European empire. It meant the transmission of French intelligence and energy into the dark corners of Europe; it meant the gift to Europe of the benefits of the French Revolution. Everywhere the Napoleonic impulse touched, Europe was galvanized into life. In Italy, in Germany, it was the beginning of the new time.   Spain and Portugal, where the English in-fluence predominated and locked the Pyrenees against the beneficent influences of France, alone failed to catch the spirit of progress.

It was the policy of England to prevent a consolidation of the continental powers.   So long as they were occupied with jealousies and wars they left the field of industry and commerce to England.   If by union Napoleon should give peace and a high industrial development to the Continent, the supremacy of England would be gone.   More or less clearly England perceived this, and that her safety lay in the destruction of Napoleon; and to this end she strained every effort.   She was aided by the natural aversion of the larger states to be swallowed up in the Napoleonic system.   Russia was the first to break away and open the Baltic ports to English goods. Napoleon protested, and when his protest remained un-heeded, marshaled his hosts to strike at Russia and close the gap in the system of exclusion.

Fall of Napoleon.

Six hundred thousand men of all nations moved east-ward; 315,000 crossed the River Niemen for the March to Moscow, the traditionary and religious cen-ter of Russia.   Moscow was reached without difficulty, but was burned by the Russians before the eyes of Napoleon as he arrived.   Winter ap-proached, and retreat was inevitable.   Napoleon had relied upon the possession of Moscow, to dictate terms of peace; but Moscow was in his hands, in ashes, and Russia had no vulnerable spot to strike.   The retreat was terrible, with hunger, cold, and the pursuit by the enemy.   Of the 155,000 Frenchmen who entered Russia, not more than 25,000 recrossed the Niemen.

The Expedition to Moscow. 1812.

The blow was fatal to the Empire.   As Napoleon turned westward central Europe rose behind him.   In 1813 he lost the battle of Leipzig; in 1814 the Allies invaded France. Napoleon's military skill was as great as ever, but his

troops were gone.   Step by step he was beaten back, until
in March Paris capitulated, and, abandoned by his general-
als, the Emperor abdicated on the sixth of April (1814),
and was sent into exile on the island of Elba.

NAPOLEON'S TOMB, HÔTEL DES INVALIDES, PARIS.

SOURCE REVIEW

I. Napoleon and his Brothers.

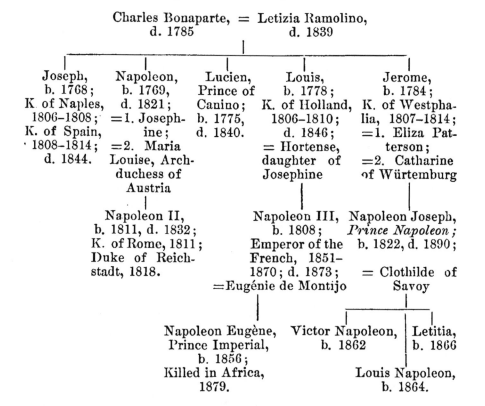

Charles Bonaparte, = Letizia Ramolino,
d. 1785   d. 1839

Joseph, b. 1768; K. of Naples, 1806–1808; K. of Spain, 1808–1814; d. 1844.

Napoleon, b. 1769, d. 1821; =1. Josephine; =2. Maria Louise, Archduchess of Austria

Lucien, Prince of Canino; b. 1775, d. 1840.

Louis, b. 1778; K. of Holland, 1806–1810; d. 1846; = Hortense, daughter of Josephine

Jerome, b. 1784; K. of Westphalia, 1807–1814; =1. Eliza Patterson; =2. Catharine of Würtemburg

Napoleon II, b. 1811, d. 1832; K. of Rome, 1811; Duke of Reichstadt, 1818.

Napoleon III, b. 1808; Emperor of the French, 1851–1870; d. 1873; =Eugénie de Montijo

Napoleon Joseph, *Prince Napoleon;* b. 1822, d. 1890; = Clothilde of Savoy

Napoleon Eugène, Prince Imperial, b. 1856; Killed in Africa, 1879.

Victor Napoleon, b. 1862

Letitia, b. 1866

Louis Napoleon, b. 1864.

II. Portrait of Napoleon, by Mme. de Remusat, at one time lady-in-waiting to Josephine.—"Napoleon Bonaparte is of low stature, and rather ill proportioned; his bust is too long, and so shortens the rest of his figure. He has thin chestnut hair, his eyes are grayish-blue, and his skin, which was yellow while he was slight, became in later years a dead white without any color. His forehead, the setting of his eye, the line of his nose — all that is beautiful, and reminds one of an antique medallion. His mouth, which is thin-lipped, becomes agreeable when he laughs; the teeth are regular. His chin is short, and his jaws heavy and square. He has well-formed hands and feet; I mention them particularly, because he thought a good deal of them.

"He has a slight stoop. His eyes are dull, giving to his

face when in repose a melancholy and meditative expression. When he is excited with anger his looks are fierce and menacing. Laughter becomes him ; it makes him look more youthful and less formidable. It is difficult not to like him when he laughs, his countenance improves so much. He was always simple in his dress, and generally wore the uniform of his own guard. He was cleanly rather from habit than from a liking for cleanliness; he bathed often, sometimes in the middle of the night, because he thought the practice good for his health. But, apart from this, the precipitation with which he did everything did not admit of his clothes being put on carefully ; and on gala days and full dress occasions his servants were obliged to consult together as to when they might snatch a moment to dress him.''

III. Habits of Work.—Meneval, private secretary of Napoleon, gives the following account of the Emperor's methods : ''His activity grew in proportion to the obstacles put in his way, and he sorely taxed my strength, which was by no means equal to my zeal. To give an idea of his prodigious activity, it is necessary to acquaint the reader with the new order of things which Napoleon had established in the dispatch of his numerous affairs. The Emperor used to have me waked in the night. When, by chance, he had got to the study before me, I used to find him walking up and down with his hands behind his back, or helping himself from his snuff-box. His ideas developed as he dictated, with an abundance and a clearness which showed that his intention was firmly riveted to the subject with which he was dealing ; they sprang from his head even as Minerva sprang, fully armed, from the head of Jupiter. When the work was finished, and sometimes in the midst of it, he would send for sherbet and ices. Thereupon he would return to bed, if only to sleep an hour, and could resume his slumber as though it had never been interrupted.

''Napoleon used to explain the clearness of his mind and his faculty of being able to prolong his work to extreme limits, by saying that the various subjects were arranged in his head as though in a cupboard. 'When I want to interrupt one piece of work,' he used to say, 'I close the drawer in which it is, and I open another. The two pieces of business never get mixed up together, and never trouble or tire me. When I want to go to sleep I close up all the drawers, and then I am ready to go off to sleep."

IV. Financial Improvement of the Peasantry in the Time of Napoleon.—"Before 1789, out of a hundred francs of net revenue, the peasant gave fourteen to his lord, fourteen to the clergy, fifty-three to the state, and kept only eighteen or nineteen for himself. Since 1800, from a hundred francs income, he pays nothing to the lord or to the church, and he pays to the state, the department, and the commune but twenty-one francs, leaving seventy-nine in his pocket."—Taine.

REFERENCES

Morse Stephens: *The Revolution and Europe*, pp. 212–335 ; Rose: *Revolutionary and Napoleonic Era*, pp. 119–292.

CHAPTER X

The Restoration

§ 29. THE CONGRESS OF VIENNA

THE fall of Napoleon placed the destinies of Europe in the hands of the Allies. Russia, Prussia, Austria, and England assembled to "divide among themselves the spoils of the vanquished." The immediate task was to provide a government for France. By the terms of the Treaty of Paris, France was reduced to her old boundaries of 1792. The Allies affected to believe that they were welcome in France as deliverers of the land from the grasp of Napoleon. They insisted that Napoleon should renounce for himself and his descendants the thrones of France and Italy; and the Bourbon claimant, the elder of the two brothers of Louis XVI, was seated on the throne as Louis XVIII. But the new king came to the throne as a constitutional monarch, thanks to the liberal spirit of the

Louis XVIII and the Charter.

LOUIS XVIII.

Tsar Alexander, who insisted that France be permitted to retain her "institutions, at once strong and liberal, with which she cannot dispense in the advanced stage of civilization to which she has attained." Louis XVIII gave to the French a constitution, the "Charter of 1814." It differed from the earlier constitutions of France in the fact that, instead of being the work of the people, it was the gift of a king.   Thus the returning Bourbons clung, even in a modified form, to the principle of divine right.   The Charter, in the form of government which it provided, introduced into France, with some limitations, the English parliamentary system ; but, what is of more importance, it secured to the French the rights and liberties of the citizen—in a word, that civil status established by the conservative revolution of 1789.

If the Allies were unable to undo the real work of the Revolution in France, they undertook the difficult task of preventing the spread of liberal ideas elsewhere.   On the first of November, 1814, their deputies met at Vienna.   Their task was the reconstruction of Europe ; the undoing, in so far as possible, of the results of the Revolution ; the restoration of the conditions of 1789.

Congress of Vienna.

TALLEYRAND.

Through the diplomatic ability of Count Talleyrand, the representative of Louis XVIII, France succeeded in securing her admission as one of the great Powers, and, as a fifth important member of the Congress, gave in many instances the deciding vote.

The chief difference of opinion between the Powers arose from a secret agreement between Russia and Prussia, whereby Russia was to acquire the whole of Poland, and Prussia was to be recompensed with the gift of Saxony, which was to be punished for its adherence to Napoleon after the other German states had dropped away.   Talleyrand perceived at once that England would view with distrust an extension of the influence of Russia to the westward, and that Austria would never sanction such an addition to Prussian territories as would make Prussia the leading

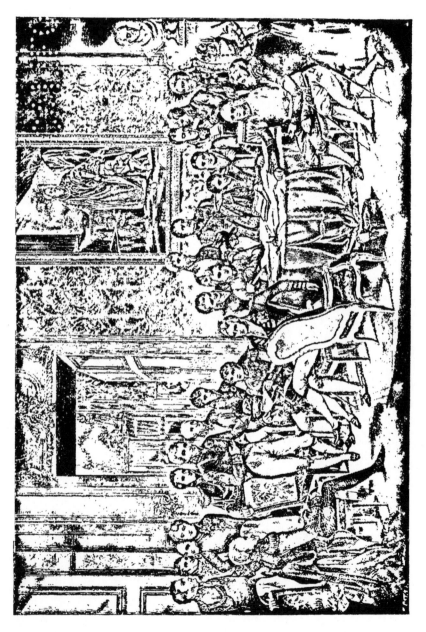

CONGRESS OF VIENNA.

power in Germany. He therefore set about the formation of an alliance of England, Austria, and France, to oppose the plans of Russia and Prussia. The Tsar gave up with great reluctance his designs upon Poland, and Prussia, in the place of Saxony, was given territory on the west bank of the Rhine, including Cologne, Treves, and Aix-la-Chapelle. It is notable that, within a few months after the occupation of Paris by the Allies, France should come forward again as the determining factor in European politics. Much was due to the diplomatic skill of Talleyrand ; but it may be questioned whether it was not a misfortune for France that the most vigorous of the German states should have been made the guardian of the Rhine against the French. The creation of Rhenish Prussia was the beginning of the struggle between Prussia and France, a struggle which ended in the discomfiture of France in 1871.

The Congress of Vienna discouraged the idea of Italian unity, which had been fostered by Napoleon. Here the principle of legitimacy was applied to effect the reorganization of the former Italian states. The Bourbon king, Ferdinand IV, was restored in Naples, and a score of petty dukes and princes came into their own throughout central Italy. Thus over a disunited Italy the influence of Austria was restored, and for fifty years this baneful interference held back the development of the peninsula. In Spain the Bourbon king, Ferdinand VII, was restored ; the Catholic provinces of Belgium and Protestant Holland were united in the Kingdom of the Netherlands, under the former Stadthalter, William I.

Other changes.

England's territorial recompense was not great, considering the immense pecuniary sacrifices she had made for the destruction of the Napoleonic system. Ceylon and the Cape of Good Hope she retained from Holland. Her reward, however, was greatest of all. The Continent, disunited and given over to internal strife, too much occu-

13

pied with political wrangling to permit the rise of a commercial and colonial policy, was her market for the greater part of the century. England was much impressed, however, as a result of her recent experience, with the danger of an exclusively European market. Her efforts were turned toward the establishment of trade relations with the Americas, and her championship of the independence of the South American Republics, which were seeking to cut adrift from the mother country, Spain, was an outgrowth of this policy.

The deliberations of the Congress of Vienna were rudely interrupted by the return of Napoleon from Elba. In

The "Hundred Days."

spite of her sufferings in his wars, France was still enamored of the great Corsican. His democratic regime seemed the more attractive when contrasted with the aristocratic tendencies of the restored Bourbons. Louis XVIII was not popular, and it was his misfortune that his reign opened with the mutilation of France at the hands of the Allies. He naturally favored his friends of the *ancien régime* at the expense of the new men of the Empire. Returning nobles were given the military rank in the French army which they had acquired while fighting against France, and advanced over the veterans of the Empire.

When Napoleon heard of the dissatisfaction in France he felt that his opportunity had come. His stay at Elba was rendered difficult by the failure of the Allies to pay him the allowance agreed upon. Accordingly, on the 26th of February, Napoleon left the island, landed on the coast of France, and made his way northward, gathering force as he proceeded. As he approached Paris, Louis XVIII quitted the Tuileries and fled to Ghent in Flanders. Napoleon entered the palace, and the army and the populace declared for the Empire.

But the effort was in vain. The Allies were in arms, prepared for such an emergency. One great battle, Waterloo, decided the issue of the Hundred Days. Napoleon retired to Paris, sought to flee to America, and, failing in this, delivered himself over to an English captain of the war-ship *Bellerophon*. He was exiled to the island of St. Helena, off the coast of Africa, where he died in 1821.

SOURCE REVIEW

The association of the Great Powers for the purpose of preserving the peace of Europe and of suppressing liberal tendencies is commonly known as the "Holy Alliance." The text of the Holy Alliance was prepared by the Tsar Alexander, under the influence of the religious exaltation which characterized his later days, and was published with the signatures of the sovereigns of Russia, Austria, and Prussia. It sets forth a high ·ideal of political action, but it is difficult to see that it exerted any marked influence upon the policy of Prince Metternich and his associates; indeed, it was regarded rather humorously by the diplomats themselves. Metternich called

ALEXANDER I., TSAR.

it mere "verbiage," and even the Emperor Francis signed with some misgivings. It is safe to say that it was in no respect the political program of the Allies; but the name was striking, and it came to stand for the whole policy of the Congress of Vienna. The following is the opening paragraph of the treaty: "Their majesties, the Emperor of Austria, the King of Prussia, and the Emperor of Russia, in view of the great events which the last three years have brought to pass in Europe, and in view especially of the benefits which it has pleased Divine Providence to confer upon those states whose governments have placed their confidence and their hope in Him alone, having reached the profound conviction that the policy of the powers, in their mutual relations, ought to be guided by the sublime truths taught by the eternal religion of God our Saviour, solemnly declare that the present act has no other aim than to manifest to the world their unchangeable determination to adopt no other rule of conduct, either in the government of their respective countries or in their political relations with other governments, than the precepts of that holy religion, the precepts of justice, charity, and peace. These, far from being applicable exclusively to private life, ought on the contrary to control the resolutions of princes and to guide their steps as the sole means of establishing human institutions and of remedying their imperfections.''

REFERENCES

Alison Phillips: *Modern Europe*, pp. 14–56 ; Judson : *Europe in the Nineteenth Century*, pp. 72–79.

§ 30.   THE POLICY OF METTERNICH

Prince Metternich, prime minister of the Emperor of Austria, was the guiding spirit of the Restoration.   To

METTERNICH.

Prince Metternich and his policy. him has been ascribed the policy with which for thirty years the Allies sought to throttle the liberal sentiment of Europe.   The watchword of the system was ''legitimacy,'' its task to preserve intact the European status determined by the Congress of Vienna.   It was particularly opposed to the granting of constitutions by rulers, and deplored the fact that in France this had been found necessary.   The liberal elements of Europe writhed under the weight of this repressive policy ; but Metternich and his armies were ever on the alert to repress all signs of revolt. The history of Continental Europe to 1848 is the story of the gradual weakening of this repressive policy, and its final abandonment.

France, in spite of the limitations imposed upon her by the conquerors of Napoleon, was politically much in advance of the other nations of the Continent. Her Charter of 1814 assured to her individual liberty, and gave, in the parliamentary system which it introduced, a fair field for the attainment of political liberty. The parliamentary system, even in England, whence it came, had not in 1814 reached its full development. It divided the powers of government between two factors, the king and parliament; but it had not yet been determined that the powers of the king were wholly administrative, and that the full power of legislation was possessed by parliament. Indeed in France, under Louis XVIII, the Charter reserved to the king the right to initiate legislation. The legislature could consider only those measures presented to it by the king. This limitation of the right of popular legislation was resented by the French, and was the beginning of a struggle for control between the legislature and the king, which ended in the overthrow of the Bourbons.

France under
the Bourbons.

Louis XVIII died in 1824, and was succeeded by his brother, who came to the throne as Charles X. He was personally much less liberal than his brother. Standing for the principle of absolute monarchy, he represents the last struggle of the *ancien régime* against liberal ideas in France. His interests were with the "ultramontane" or Roman party. The wealthy middle class, which had been important in the Empire, was offended at seeing the court swarming with priests and nobles. A milliard of francs ($200,000,000) was voted to the emigrant nobles, whose lands had been confiscated and sold by the Revolution. As representing a concession to the nobility this measure was unpopular ; but it was wise, because it set at rest forever the question of the validity of titles to land acquired through the Revolutionary government.

In 1830 the opposition to the king organized itself. An address signed by 221 deputies of the lower house criti-

The Revolution of July.

cised the king's speech from the throne, saying : " Harmony no longer exists between the political views of your government and the desires of your subjects." The king dissolved the legislature, but a new election brought back the 221 signers of the address. The king decided upon a *coup d'état*. By virtue of Article 14 of the Charter, which gave the king the power to " make the regulations and ordinances necessary for the execution of the laws and for the security of the state," Charles published four ordinances : suspending the liberty of the press, dissolving the Chambers, limiting the right of franchise, and summoning a new legislature. Forty-four journalists protested against this arbitrary interpretation of the Charter. Their protest is interesting, as indicating the appearance of a new factor in politics—the press.

The king's act was answered with insurrection ; barricades were erected in the streets of Paris on July 27th. The royal troops were driven from the city, and a provisional government invited Louis Philippe, Duke of Orleans, the king's kinsman, to act as Lieutenant of the kingdom. Charles X abdicated in favor of his grandson, the Count de Chambord, and retired to England. August 7th the Chambers named Louis Philippe " King of the French." The Charter of 1814, shorn of the dangerous Article 14, was presented by the people to the new king and by him accepted.

All over Europe, where the Bourbons were reseated on their thrones, the people were not long in finding the dif-

Spain.

ference between Napoleonic and Bourbon institutions. Eagerly as Spain had struggled to pull the English chestnuts out of the fire and repulse the mild régime of Joseph Bonaparte, six years of Ferdinand VII brought them to rebellion. The troops assembled at Cadiz for transport to America marched against Madrid. Ferdinand was obliged to yield and re-establish the liberal constitution of 1812. But secretly he called upon the Allies, who assembled at Verona, and decided to send troops against the Spanish rebels. The position of the French king was embarrassing. Fearing to use his troops to put down a liberal government in a neighboring state, Louis was still more unwilling to permit a German or Russian army to pass through his kingdom on the way to Spain. Of the two evils he chose the former, and in April, 1823, a French army of 95,000 men marched to Madrid and restored to Ferdinand his absolute power. Thus was France made an instrument of despotism, much to the disgust of her people, and French troops were used to put down liberal ideas.

In Italy as well the Restoration brought revolution. Secret societies spread through the land ; in 1819 the Car-

Italy.

bonari numbered 60,000. In 1820 Naples revolted against the brutal government of Ferdinand IV, and forced the king to accept the Spanish constitution of 1812. A similar movement forced Charles Felix, King of Sardinia, to accept a similar constitution. But Austria was at hand, willing to make good her authority in Italy. At the mandate of the Allies she put down the liberals with troops and supplied the Neapolitan and Sardinian despots with foreign garrisons.

The Napoleonic régime affected Germany variously, but in one way or another it was the beginning of her modern

Germany.

life. Western Germany, from the Rhine to the Elbe, was directly affected by Napoleonic administration. The South German states—Bavaria, Würtemberg, and Baden—creations of the Napoleonic wars, were inspired with the liberalism of their French neighbor. Prussia, which had never known French administration, was nevertheless influenced by it. In her darkest hour, when Berlin was in the hands of the enemy, and Prussia stood upon the verge of extinction, began a nationalist reaction, which, headed by the noble figure of the Queen; Louisa, and voiced by men of letters and university societies, reorganized Prussia in a modern sense, adopting voluntarily some of those ideas which the Revolution had forced upon western Germany. The names of Stein, Hardenberg, and Scharnhorst are forever associated with the introduction of economic and political reforms into Prussia and the reorganization of the Prussian army.

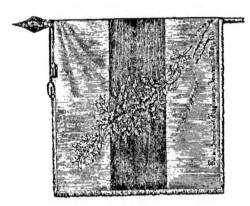

FLAG AND SWORD OF GERMAN
STUDENT SOCIETY.

The German states were formed by the Congress of Vienna into a loose German Confederation, under the presidency of Austria. Article XII of the constitution of the Confederation provided that each of the confederated states should have a constitution with representative government. But they were not accorded (except in Saxe-Weimar, and in a limited degree in Bavaria, Würtemberg, and Baden). In Prussia a powerful and ignorant nobility held fast to its privileges; in Austria the influence of Metternich prevailed. The liberals protested, particularly the student organizations, which had contributed so much to the Liberation movement of 1814. In March, 1819, a theological student, Sand by name, stabbed the writer Kotzebue, who was suspected of being a Russian agent. Metternich was roused ; he called the princes to a congress at Carlsbad. "Germany is seized with gangrene," he said, "and needs the hot iron." It was applied. A series of regulations, called the "Carlsbad decrees," were made for Germany. In each university a special commission was appointed to watch the students and to arrest dangerous individuals. A special commission sat at Mayence for the apprehension of suspected persons. Thus all Germany, like Italy, fell into the hands of the Austrians.

SOURCE REVIEW

One of the tasks of the Allies was to restore to their respective owners the art treasures which the victorious Napoleon had transferred from the museums and palaces of Europe to Paris. A memorial from all the artists resident at Rome claimed for the Eternal City the entire restoration of the immortal works of art which had once adorned it. The allied sovereigns acceded to the just demand, and Canova, impassioned for the arts and the city of his choice, hastened to Paris to superintend the removal. It was most effectually done. The bronze horses (from Venice) were restored to their old station in front of the church of St. Mark. The Transfiguration and the Last Communion of St. Jerome resumed their place in the halls of the Vatican; the Apollo and the Laocoon again adorned the precincts of St. Peter's; the Venus was enshrined again amidst beauty in the Tribune of Florence; and the Descent from the Cross, by Rubens, was restored to the devout worship of the Flemings in the Cathedral of Antwerp. The amount of curiosities and valuable articles of all kinds—statues, paintings, antiquities, cameos, manuscripts, maps, gems, antiques, rarities—was immense. Among them were 127 paintings, many of them of the very highest value, taken from the palaces of Berlin and Potsdam alone; 187 statues, chiefly antique, taken from the same palaces during the same period; and 86 valuable manuscripts and documents seized in the city of Aix-la-Chapelle. The total articles reclaimed by the Prussians exceeded two thousand.—Adapted from Alison: *History of Europe.*

REFERENCES

Judson: *Europe in the Nineteenth Century,* pp. 80–90; Alison Phillips: Chapter V.

CHAPTER XI

France since 1830

§ 31. Reign of Louis Philippe

THE unnatural union of Belgium and Holland, which the Congress of Vienna had decreed, was broken at the

Separation of Belgium and Holland.

first shock of the Revolution of July. Brussels rose in revolt, and the Dutch officials were driven out of Flanders and Brabant. On the 18th of November a congress proclaimed the independence of Belgium. Circumstances were favorable for a union of Belgium with France. Language and interests were common; but the Powers hastily intervened to prevent such an extension of French influence. A conference of ambassadors assembled at London, to settle the fate of Belgium. The Belgians organized a constitutional monarchy, and offered the crown to the Duke of Nemours, second son of Louis Philippe; but the French king, newly seated on the throne, was unwilling to arouse the antagonism of Europe, and especially of England, and the Duke of Nemours was instructed to decline the honor. The second choice of the Belgians was Leopold of Saxe-Coburg-Gotha, a petty German prince, related to George IV, King of England. He was made king. The King of Holland refused to accept the decision of the London Conference regulating the frontiers of Belgium, and a French army, with the mandate of the Powers, wrested Antwerp from the Dutch. It was not until 1839 that King William of Holland recognized the independence of Belgium. Thus in liberal northwestern Europe, by the expulsion of the Bourbons from France, and the recognition of the Belgian insurgents, the system of the Congress of Vienna was falling to pieces.

The position of the new King of France, Louis Philippe, was one which called for much tact and diplomacy. The

The "Citizen King." king of a revolution, he owed his throne to a popular uprising, and to the hatred felt for the expelled Bourbons. It was necessary, then, that he should show his democratic principles in his disregard for the pomp of royalty. His predecessor, Charles X, was anointed at Rheims with the sacramental oil of Clovis; the coronation of Louis Philippe was conducted without religious forms.

The Citizen King walked in the streets of Paris, clad in the modest frock-coat and stove-pipe hat of the bourgeois, and sent his sons to the public schools. At the beginning of his reign he avoided the Tuileries, and remained at his family residence, the Palais Royal, receiving deputations from the communes and cities of France, and shaking hands with his subjects in true democratic style.

LOUIS PHILIPPE.

But the problem which faced the "King of the Barricades," as his legitimist enemies called him, was one of great difficulty. Like any man raised to a mighty throne, he desired to rule with force and dignity, and to secure the succession for his sons. His problem was to establish himself in France, and to win his reception among the crowned heads of Europe, many of whom looked with suspicion upon his revolutionary origin.

One of his embarrassments came from the impulse which the Revolution of July gave to liberal movements throughout Europe. Everywhere liberals rose in insur-

rection against the yoke of Metternich, and looked to
France for aid. France, the source of liberty, having
thrown off the Bourbon dominion, would, it
was thought, come again to the rescue of
Europe. In Italy, in the Rhenish states of
Germany, and in Poland the effect of the July Revolution
was felt.

Louis Philippe
and foreign
insurrections.

But Louis Philippe had no desire, by means of such
associations, to lay further emphasis upon his revolutionary origin. In France itself the difficulty of suppressing
the Republican factions kept him sufficiently employed.
The sole hope of the monarchy in France was to avoid a
policy of foreign interference, and to disarm the suspicions
of European courts by turning a deaf ear to the entreaties
of foreign revolutionists. In Italy the French Government
contented itself with demanding the withdrawal of Austrian troops from the Papal States, occupying Ancona
with French troops as a check to Austrian influence. In
Poland, when French public opinion clamored for intervention, Louis Philippe co-operated with England in a protest to the Tsar Nicholas against the revocation of the
liberties granted to Poland by the Congress of Vienna.
With these half measures the Bourgeois Monarchy grace-
fully withdrew from the leadership of liberal Europe.

The question of whether king or parliament should rule
the land was inherited by the monarchy of Louis Philippe
from the Bourbon régime, along with the
Charter of 1814. Two great political parties were developed, representing the oppos-
ing views ; one, under the leadership of Guizot (whose literary works have outlived his political fame), sustained the
view that it was the king's prerogative to choose his ministers and formulate his policy independent of the desires
of the majority in the legislature. The other party, headed
by Thiers (whose great labors for France were just beginning), maintained that the king should choose his minis-

Parliamentary
struggle.

try in accordance with the will of the legislature, and leave his ministers to govern without personal interference. Its motto was: " The king reigns, but does not govern." Louis Philippe naturally inclined toward the policy of Guizot, and, after a period of parliamentary struggle, a temporary but fatal peace was obtained by the Guizot ministry, which inaugurated a system of electoral corruption, buying up the votes of deputies with offices and other executive favors and thereby gaining a majority in the legislature. Thus a deceptive calm was secured; but the liberal opposition, overcome in the legislature, was driven to other methods of appeal to the people, and the outcome was fatal to the monarchy.

The keynote of the foreign policy of Louis Philippe was the alliance with

The Spanish marriages. England. The interchange of goods and capital, resulting from this era of good-feeling between the two countries, was aiding the economic development of France and building

GUIZOT.

up the wealth of the middle class. The Spanish marriage, the result of the Citizen King's desire to establish his dynasty firmly in Europe, led to a rupture of these cordial relations, and to a weakening of the king's support. Queen Isabella of Spain and her younger sister, Louisa, were of marriageable age. Louis Philippe would have sought the hand of Isabella for his son, but England objected to so close a union of France and Spain as disturbing the " Balance of Power " in Europe. In 1845, however, it was settled that Isabella should marry a Bourbon prince, and that after an heir had been born to the Spanish throne, the Princess Louisa might be married to the Duke of Montpensier, a younger son of Louis Philippe. But through the excessive zeal of the French minister at Madrid the two marriages were celebrated simultaneously. The English Government regarded the affair as a breach of faith, and declared the good understanding between England and France at an end ; whereby Louis Philippe lost his great liberal ally, and injured the business interests of his middle-class supporters at home.

SOURCE REVIEW

I. Personality of Louis Philippe.—"Louis Philippe, born in 1773, was the son of that notorious 'Egalité' who, during the revolution, had ended his checkered career under the guillotine. His grandmother was the noble Elizabeth Charlotte, a native of the Palatinate, who had the misfortune to be the wife of the effeminate Duke of Orleans, brother of Louis XIV. Louis Philippe was a Bourbon, like King Charles ; but the opposition of several members of this Orleans branch of the royal house had caused it to be regarded as a separate family. From his youth up he had displayed a great deal of popular spirit and common sense. Seemingly created by nature and career to be a citizen king, he had long since, as early as 1814, determined to accept the throne in case it were offered him." —Müller : *Political History of Recent Times.*

II. The System of Guizot, against which the efforts of the Liberals were directed.—"The population of France was then 34,000,000, and the privilege of the political franchise was vested exclusively in those who paid in direct taxes a sum not less than forty dollars. The class numbered little more than 200,000. The government had 130,000 places at its disposal, and the use which was made of these during the eighteen years of Louis Philippe's reign was productive of corruption more widespread and shameless than France had known since the first revolution. In the scarcely exaggerated language used by M. de Lamartine, 'the government had succeeded in making a nation of citizens a vile band of beggars.' It was obvious to all who desired the regeneration of France that reform must begin with the representation of the people. To this end the liberals directed much effort. Reform banquets, attended by thousands of people, were held in all the chief towns, and the pressure of a peaceful public opinion was employed to obtain the remedy of a great wrong.''—Mackenzie : *The Nineteenth Century.*

REFERENCES

Alison Phillips : *Modern Europe,* pp. 186–198 ; Judson : *Europe in the Nineteenth Century,* pp. 90–96 ; Lebon : *Modern France,* Chapter IX.

§ 32.   REVOLUTION OF 1848 AND SECOND EMPIRE

Several causes brought about the fall of the Bourgeois Monarchy and the Revolution of 1848 :

Causes of Revolution of 1848.

1. The failure of the foreign policy of Louis Philippe, and especially the rupture with England, regretted by the moneyed classes.

2. The Liberal protests against the methods of the Guizot ministry, the corruption of the franchise. Since by these methods the Liberals lost their representation in the legislature, they inaugurated a campaign of banquets, at which the king and Guizot were criticized, and toasts were offered to the " Spirit of 1789."

3. Another and most important cause was the growth of a socialist movement, which took a strong hold upon the artisan population of Paris and of other industrial centers. The relations of labor and capital, of which we hear so much in our time, were coming to the front as public questions. France alone of Continental nations had advanced to a point where, the equality and rights of the citizen before the law having been established, she could turn her attention to the solution of the social questions. At this time socialism seemed to Frenchmen the natural remedy for social inequality. Louis Blanc, a socialist philosopher, developed a scheme of production, according to

which the state should assume control of all manufactures, and assure to each laborer the certainty of employment.

The Liberal reformers planned a great banquet in one of the wards of Paris, to voice the opposition to the policy of Guizot. The government forbade the meeting, and the revolt which ensued, although it seemed at first a mere demonstration, spread like wildfire through the inflammable and dissatisfied population of Paris. On the 23d and 24th of February the streets were full of fighting. Louis Philippe dismissed Guizot ; but the concession came too late. Convinced of his unpopularity, and wishing to preserve the throne for his family, the king abdicated in favor of his grandson, the Count of Paris ; but the Chamber of Deputies, invaded by a mob, crying "Down with Royalty!" yielded to the popular demand and appointed a provisional government. Meanwhile the followers of Louis Blanc at the City Hall proclaimed the Republic.

Revolution of February.

A struggle ensued between these two factions. The followers of Blanc desired to introduce at once state socialism, and workshops were established in Paris for the unemployed ; but the socialists were in the minority, and the deputies, who came in from all parts of France, in response to a summons for a Constitutional Convention, to devise a new government for the nation, had little sympathy with the socialist demands. They were republican, but not socialistic, and they decreed : "France shall be constituted a republic." "The French Republic is democratic. Its principles are Liberty, Equality, Fraternity ; its foundations : the family, rights of property, public order."

The President of the Second Republic was elected by universal suffrage. Among the candidates was Louis Bonaparte, head of his house, and heir to the claims of Napoleon. The third son of Louis Bonaparte, brother of Napoleon and for a time King of Holland (1806–1810), he had come to

Louis Bonaparte, Prince-President.

be the representative of the Bonaparte party by the death of Napoleon's son, the "King of Rome" (1832), and of his own two elder brothers. Educated in Switzerland, Louis Bonaparte had made himself known to the French already by two ineffectual and absurd attempts to enter France and assert his imperial claims during the reign of Louis Philippe. After the first attempt he had been shipped off to America; but the second attempt led to his imprisonment in the fortress of Ham, whence he made his escape into Germany. After the fall of the "July Monarchy," Bonaparte came to Paris and was elected a delegate to the Constitutional Convention. As candidate for the presidency he received, thanks to his name, 5,400,000 votes, against 1,118,107 for General Cavaignac. He took his seat with these words: "I shall regard as enemies of the Republic all those who seek to change by illegal methods that which France as a whole has established."

NAPOLEON III.

The insurrection of the socialists in February had inspired in France a profound fear of social revolution.

The great coup d'etat. The result was that the elections returned as deputies to the new legislature a majority of monarchists (500 out of 750). By them the suffrage was restricted, taking away the votes of millions of laborers. This decreased the probability of Bonaparte's re-election in 1856 (the presidential term was seven years), and drove him to an act of violence. With the army at his back, he dissolved the legislature by force, and gave to the country a new constitution, modeled after that of the Consulate. The nation approved the President's act with 7,400,000 votes out of eight millions, and the Prince-

14

President was installed for ten years.   Resistance in Paris
and elsewhere was put down with an iron hand.   (December 1–4, 1851.)

The next step came soon.   In November, 1852, the
Senate decreed the Empire, and its decree was ratified
with a plebiscite.   Louis Bonaparte was pro-
The Second Empire. claimed Emperor with the title of Napoleon
III.   The Emperor did not seek, like Louis Philippe, to
ally himself with the dynasties of Europe, but married in
the following year Eugénie de Montijo, a Spanish Countess.   One child was born, the Prince Imperial, in 1856.

The second empire was, until its close, a period of
prosperity for France.   While parliamentary liberties were
restricted by the autocratic policy of the Emperor, yet
France regained to a certain extent her voice in European
affairs.   The revolution of 1848 had swept away Metternich and his policy, and the field was open for a master in
diplomacy.   Napoleon III did not rise to this level, but
his earlier efforts won him some renown.   In 1854 France,
England, and Sardinia joined forces to defend Turkey
against Russia.   The Crimean War, with its siege of Se-
bastopol, brought the Emperor some credit.   In 1859 he
aided Italy in throwing off the Austrian yoke, completing
the task his uncle had begun in the union of Italy, and received in return Savoy and Nice, added to the Empire.
His later projects were less successful.   The attempt to
establish the Austrian Archduke Maximilian as Emperor
of Mexico failed, owing to the hostile attitude of the
United States.

Meanwhile the ambitious plans of Napoleon III brought
him in contact with the rising power of Prussia, which in
1866 had defeated Austria and won the
Fall of the Empire. leadership of Germany.   In diplomacy Napoleon was no match for Bismarck, and his failing health
threw the decision of affairs more and more into the hands
of the Empress and her clerical advisers, who bitterly op-

posed the growing Protestant power of Prussia. Fooled
and humiliated by Bismarck in his effort to secure Luxem-

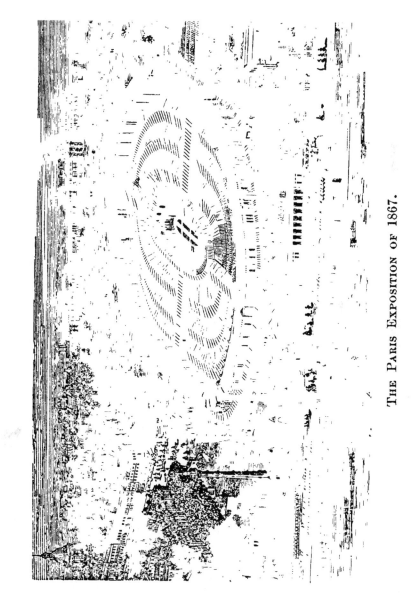

THE PARIS EXPOSITION OF 1867.

burg for France, the Emperor was spurred to a vigorous
protest against the project of seating a prince of the house
of Hohenzollern upon the vacant throne of Spain. The

candidate, Prince Leopold, was withdrawn, but the imperial government sought to soothe its wounded dignity by insisting upon a pledge from the King of Prussia that Prince Leopold should never again become a candidate. This was refused, and France declared war.

Under the stress of war the Second Empire collapsed. The French army was found to be unfit for service, although on paper it seemed large and powerful. Austria, the natural enemy of Prussia, and Italy, the beneficiary of France, refused a French alliance. Alone the French had to meet the army of von Moltke, the ablest military force the world had ever seen. The result was immediate; war was declared July 14, 1870; September 2d Napoleon capitulated at Sedan, and the Second Empire was at an end.

SOURCE REVIEW

I. Organization of the workshops established in Paris. — " These workshops were established in the outskirts of Paris. A person who wished to take advantage of the offers of the government took from the person with whom he lodged a certificate that he was an inhabitant of the Department of the Seine. This certificate he carried to the officials of his ward, and obtained an order of admission to a work-shop. If he was received and employed there, he obtained an order on his ward for forty sous. If he was not received, after having applied at all of them, and found them all full, he received an order for thirty sous. Thirty sous is not high pay ; but it.was to be had for doing nothing ; and hopes of advancement were held out. Besides this, bread was distributed to their families in proportion to the number of children. We have before us a list of those who had been enrolled on May 19th, and it amounts to 87,942. A month later it amounted to 150,000—representing, at four to a family, 600,-000 persons—more than half the population of Paris. To suppose that such an army as this could be regularly organized, fed, and paid for months in idleness, and then quietly disbanded, was a folly of which the Provisional Government

AFTER SEDAN.

was not long guilty. They soon saw that the monster which they had created could not be subdued, if it could be subdued at all, by any means short of civil war."—Senior : *Journals kept in France and Italy, 1848-1852.*

The result was the terrible " Days of June " (June 23-26), which followed the closing of the workshops by the government, in which 12,000 persons lost their lives. At the crisis of a political revolution the conditions were particularly unfavorable for an industrial experiment of such magnitude.

II. Sedan ; Fall of the Empire.—" That night—the night of September 1st—an aide-de-camp of the Emperor carried this note to the camp of the King of Prussia : ' *Monsieur Mon Frère.* —Not having been able to die in the midst of my troops, it only remains for me to place my sword in the hands of your majesty. I am your majesty's good brother, Napoleon.' With Napoleon III fell not only his own reputation as a ruler, but the glory of his uncle and the prestige of his name. The fallen Emperor and Bismarck met in a little house on the banks of the Meuse. Chairs were brought out, and they talked in the open air. It was a glorious autumn morning. The Emperor looked careworn, as well he might. He wished to see the King of Prussia before the articles of capitulation were drawn up ; but King William declined the interview. When the capitulation was signed, however, he drove over to visit the captive emperor at a château where the latter had taken refuge. The interview was private ; only the two sovereigns were present. The French Emperor afterward expressed to the Crown Prince of Prussia his deep sense of the courtesy shown him. The next day he proceeded to the beautiful palace at Cassel called Williamshöhe." — Latimer : *France in the Nineteenth Century.*

The Emperor afterward removed to England, and died at Chiselhurst, January 9, 1873.

REFERENCES

Alison Phillips : *Modern Europe,* pp. 232-272 ; Judson : *Europe in the Nineteenth Century,* pp. 137-144 ; Lebon : *Modern France,* Chapters XII, XIII.

§ 33.   THE THIRD REPUBLIC

The disaster of Sedan caused the fall of the Empire. The "Revolution of September 4," at Paris, drove the Empress out of France, and established the "Government of National Defense." Its representative, Jules Favre, sought to negotiate with Bismarck, but unwilling to meet the German demands for the cession of Alsace and Lorraine, the Government of National Defense resolved to continue the war. The seat of government was established at Tours, and as the Germans drew their lines about Paris, Gambetta, the

head and soul of the French resistance, escaped from Paris in a balloon, and joined his colleagues at Tours. In spite of desperate effort the undisciplined French troops made little headway against the German army, and the surrender of Bazaine at Metz with 120,000 men was followed by the capitulation of Paris on January 28, 1871.

GAMBETTA.

All hope being lost, an armistice was signed on the following day, and in February a National Assembly was convoked at Bordeaux, to discuss the terms of peace. Thiers was chosen to represent the French side, and he signed with Bismarck, at Versailles, the preliminaries of peace, which were formally ratified on May 10th, at Frankfort-on-the-Main. France lost Alsace and part of Lorraine, a loss of 1,500,000 citizens. She also engaged to pay a war indemnity of five milliards of francs (a billion of dollars), and to permit the occupation of French territory by German troops pending the payment of the indemnity.

But France had not yet touched the depth of her humiliation. The withdrawal of the German troops was followed by a local insurrection, more destructive of the city than the German bombardment.   A body of desperate

The Commune. men, socialists and revolutionists by trade, many of them foreigners, professing to fear a return of monarchy, organized an insurrectionary government (the "Commune") in Paris, and refused to recognize the National Assembly, which had changed its seat from Bordeaux to Versailles.   It was only after days of fierce fighting that the troops of the National Assembly overcame the *Communards,* and then not until in its mad rage the Parisian mob had destroyed with fire some of the finest buildings of the city, monuments of art, such as the Palace of the Tuileries and the Hôtel de Ville (City Hall).   Thousands of the *Communards* were killed and exiled, and their trials went on until 1876.

The National Assembly, "awaiting the nation's decision as to the eventual form of government," named Thiers "head of the executive power" avoiding

Government of Thiers (1871-1873). the use of the word "Republic."   Indeed the deputies of the people, in the years immediately following the fall of the Empire, were not in favor of republican government.   It was only the struggle between the royalists and the Bonapartists that made the republic possible as a compromise.   This is the leading fact in the history of the Third Republic.   The Republic was a temporary makeshift, until the royalists or Bonapartists could develop, either of them, a preponderance of strength. Meanwhile these parties have lost their strength, and the Republic, originally a compromise, has survived and won popular esteem.

Meanwhile Thiers had taken the title of "President of the Republic."   Originally an Orleanist, he became convinced that the Republic was best for France.   Fearing lest he should make it permanent, the royalists and imperialists joined together to secure the defeat of Thiers' policy, and brought about his resignation.   Marshal Mac-

Mahon, a man of high character, personally a royalist, was elected by the conservative majority.   At the beginning of his presidency an effort was made to unite the royalist parties (Bourbon and Orleanist) and give France a king.   The Orleanist pretendant, the Count of Paris, grandson of Louis Philippe, visited the Count of Chambord, the Bourbon heir, at his residence of Frohsdorf in Austria.   The Count of Chambord, "Henry V," as he was pleased to call himself, was childless, and the Count of Paris was willing to be chosen as his successor, thereby uniting the two lines.   But the

Presidency of Mac-Mahon (1873-1879).

MacMahon.

royal claimants could not agree upon the flag of the combined monarchy.   "Henry V," declared himself bound to retain the white flag of the Bourbons, "received as a sacred deposit from the old king, my grandfather, dying in exile," and to reject the tricolor, "symbol of revolution."   The Orleanists had accepted the tricolor in 1830, and it was generally recognized that France would accept no monarch who brought back the symbol of the Bourbons.   This failure to adjust the royalist pretensions made the formal acceptance of the Republic inevitable.   The National Assembly proceeded to the enactment of a series of constitutional laws, which form the body of the Constitution of 1875.

The President of the Republic is elected by a joint session of the legislative bodies, the Senate and the Chamber of Deputies, and holds office for seven years. He is permitted, in case of a legislative deadlock, to dissolve, with the consent of the Senate, the Chamber of Deputies.

Constitution of 1875.

The legislative power belongs to the Senate and the Chamber of Deputies. The Chamber of Deputies is chosen by universal suffrage. Members are elected for four years, and all are elected at one time. The Senate, as originally constituted, consisted of seventy-five life members, elected by the National Assembly from its own members. The remaining 225 members are chosen by indirect suffrage, the lectoral college of each department being made up of local governing bodies within the department, such as city councils and the like. Senators serve for nine years, and one-third of the Senate is renewed every three years. By an amendment of 1884 no more life Senators are to be chosen.

All public acts of the President of the Republic are performed through ministers, who are responsible to the Chambers for the policy of the government. This ministerial responsibility makes the Chambers (and practically the Chamber of Deputies, because in France the Senate has drifted into the background) the prime factor in governing the country. Each deputy has the right of Interpellation ; that is, he may, after due notice, call upon the ministry to explain or defend, before the Chamber, its policy or action in any matter. If the explanation is unsatisfactory to the Chamber, a resolution may be passed, expressing the Chamber's lack of confidence in the ministry, whereupon the ministry resigns, and the President has the task of forming a new ministry that will be satisfactory to the Chamber. In this manner the Chamber of Deputies controls the policy and acts of the government, and may be said to govern France.

As a result of the war of 1870, and the consequent loss of territory and prestige, France has lost her position of political superiority in Europe. If her intel-

France of to-day.

lectual superiority is no longer evident, it is due to no decline in the arts and sciences in France, but to the fact that other nations have advanced, and that intelligence and intellectual activity are now generally disseminated throughout Europe. Her colonial extension, which is, in modern times, so large an element of national progress, is hampered by the fact that the population of France does not increase, and there is no surplus of population for colonial settlement. But France is rich, and in no country are there more facilities for the enjoyment of life, or a greater degree of thrift and industry. Whatever the future position of France in Europe, she is entitled to the distinction of having been for two centuries the laboratory of ideas for Europe.

SOURCE REVIEW

I. The Commune.—Hopeless of maintaining their hold upon Paris against the troops of the French Government, the *Communards* in their rage sought to destroy the city. " On the 12th of May, in accordance with a public decree, they had destroyed the private residence of M. Thiers, with all its pictures and books ; on the 16th the magnificent column erected in the Place Vendôme in memory of Napoleon I, and crowned with his statue, was undermined on one side and then pulled to the ground by means of ropes and utterly destroyed ; and now on the 24th, in the last effort of despairing rage, bands of men and women, still more frantic and eager for blood than were those of the Reign of Terror, rushed through the doomed city. Early in the morning the Tuileries, the Hôtel de Ville, the Ministry of Finance, the Palais d'Orsay, and other public and private buildings were seen to be on fire. The Louvre, too, with all its inestimable treasures, was in flames, and was saved with the utmost difficulty. If the Commune was to perish, it had clearly resolved that the city was to perish with it. Men and women marched about in bands with petroleum, and aided the spread of the conflagration by firing the city in different places."—Martin : *Popular History of France.*

II. Last Chance of the Bourbons.—"Now was formed and matured a deliberate project to overthrow the young republic, and set up monarchy in its place. All circumstances combined to favor its success. The Orleanist princes agreed to waive their claims, and the Count of Paris was persuaded to pay a visit to the Count of Chambord at his retreat at Frohsdorf, to acknowledge the elder Bourbon's right to the throne, and to abandon his own pretensions. The Assembly was carefully canvassed, and it was found that a majority could be relied upon to proclaim, at the ripe moment, Chambord as king, with the title of Henry V. The Republic was now, in the early autumn of 1873, in the most serious and real peril. It needed but a word from the Bourbon pretender to overthrow it, and replace it by the throne of the Capets and the Valois. Happily, the old leaven of Bourbon bigotry existed in ' Henry V. ' He could concede the point of reigning with parliamentary institutions, but he would not accept the tricolor as the flag of the restored monarchy. He insisted upon returning to France under the white banner of his ancestors. To him the throne was not worth a piece of cloth. To his obstinacy in clinging to this trifle of symbolism the Republic owed its salvation.. The scheme to restore the monarchy thus fell through. The result was that the two wings of monarchists flew apart again, and the republicans, being now united and patient under the splendid leadership of Gambetta, once more began to wax in strength."—Towle : *Modern France.*

REFERENCES

Alison Phillips : *Modern History,* pp. 472-485 ; Judson : *Europe in the Nineteenth Century,* pp. 176-189 ; Lebon: *Modern France,* Chapters XIV, XV.

CHAPTER XII

The German Empire

§ 34. DEVELOPMENT OF PRUSSIA

ALTHOUGH Prussia, unlike the Rhenish states of Germany, did not pass under French domination, yet she was revolutionized by the crisis brought upon her by the wars of Napoleon. The system of Frederick the Great, although effective when vitalized by his genius, fell to pieces in the weak hands of his successors. Prussia was an absolute monarchy; the people were without voice in the government. Society was divided into hereditary castes: nobles, citizens, and peasants. All civil and military offices were reserved for the nobles; and the peasants lived in a condition of feudal subjection to the great landowners, who exercised over them the medieval rights of justice and control.

King Frederick William III was in no sense a reformer. It was with much hesitation, and against the advice of his nobles and officials, that he was induced to take the first steps toward reform. Curiously enough, the men who laid the foundations of modern Prussia were not Prussians. Baron Stein, the first of the great trio of reformers, was from Rhenish Germany; Hardenberg and Schornhorst were Hanoverians. All came from parts of Germany that had been subjected to French influences.

The Prussian reformers were not the result of the political philosophy of the eighteenth century. There was no impulse in Prussia, as in France, to transfer the source of power from the monarch to the people; no declaration of rights, after the manner of the Revolution of 1789. The

STEIN.

principle of despotic power remained unimpaired, and the reforms were, like those attempted by Joseph II of Aus-

Character of the reforms.

tria, a gift of the king to the people ; and had for their object, not the concession of certain rights to the citizens of Prussia, but the reorganization of a broken-down régime, with a view of making the subjects of the king more able to contribute to the needs of the state.

The most fundamental of these reforms was the edict of 1807, which broke down the social organization of castes. Up to this time the individual was bound to remain in the social group into which he had been born ; but by this edict nobles were permitted to enter into busi-

Industrial reforms. ness or professional careers, and the line of division between burgher and peasant was no longer hard and fixed. In 1818 followed a law giving full liberty of change of residence and in the selection of a pursuit. " No man," the edict ran, " shall be restricted in the enjoyment of his civil rights and liberty, further than is necessary for the general welfare of the state." A decree of 1810 abolished the monopoly of gild organizations. Any person paying the license fee was permitted to follow his occupation anywhere in the kingdom.

Although the people were given no voice in the gov-ernment of the kingdom, the king gave to his subjects a

City administration. measure of local self-government in the ad-ministration of city affairs. In each city a council was created, the members of which were elected by inhabitants owning property or enjoying an income suffi-cient to endow them with the right of citizenship. This council was unsalaried ; but supervised the affairs of the city, in connection with elected officers, who devoted their whole time to the city administration, and were paid. The council controlled the city expenditures and imposed the taxes. This union of responsible citizens, serving for honor and for the common interest, with paid officials, supervised by them, has made the Prussian cities the best governed in the world.

The Prussian peasantry was of two classes : those who were tenants on crown lands, and were free from the

Emancipation of the peasantry. burdens of serfdom ; and those on the private estates of the nobles, who were still attached to the soil and still subject to the degrading conditions of medieval land tenure. The introduction of Napoleonic reforms on both sides of Prussia, particularly the emancipation of the Polish serfs in 1807, forced the Prussian Government to take steps toward the improvement of the condition of its peasantry. In 1807 "hereditary subjection" was abolished throughout the kingdom, and all persons were declared to be personally free. On crown lands peasants were given full ownership on payment of an annual sum to the crown. The same principle of instalments was applied in 1811 to the estates of nobles, except that here the peasants were obliged to give up one-third of their holdings to the landlords, retaining two-thirds for themselves. In this manner the question of joint feudal ownership was settled, and each given the right of ownership in the modern sense.

The reorganization of the army was the most complete of the Prussian reforms, and one which was full of consequences for the future of Europe. Rejecting the old system of hireling troops, the new army was built up on universal military service. "All the inhabitants of the state

HARDENBERG.

are by birth its defenders." All able-bodied men were to become soldiers. The principle was most democratic, because it placed the military burden upon all classes alike. The period of service was fixed at three years, and the men who had been retired from the active army were kept in readiness by a short annual term of service in the reserve.

The adoption of universal military service was a turning-point in the history of Prussia. It gave her a national army, full of patriotism, and a nation of drilled reserves. It made her a military nation, because war was the business and the affair of all. The system has since been extended to all the great states of continental Europe. France, after her defeat in 1870, reorganized her army on the Prussian model. The advantages of the Prussian military system are evident ; its disadvantages are also great. While it permitted Prussia to rise to a position of the first military power in Europe, yet its adoption by the other states has fastened an immense burden upon the productive resources of Europe. Europe is a group of armed camps, each state straining, with limitless expenditures, to secure the highest efficiency in the art of war. The solution of this vexed problem of waste energy is one of the tasks of the twentieth century.

It will be evident, from the character of the reforms described, that Prussia, spurned by the heel of Napoleon, had roused herself from her antiquated despotism, and put herself into the path of modern progress. Some of her reforms were forced upon her by the spirit of the French Revolution ; others were of her own conception ; and of these the new municipal system and the military reorganization have contributed much to the substantial character of the modern German state.

SOURCE REVIEW

Fichte : philosopher and university professor, 1762-1814.— Touched by the sight of his country's humiliation under the flail of Napoleon, Fichte sought to rouse his countrymen to resistance. He is to be reckoned among those who, in the days of Germany's deepest humiliation, sounded the note of moral and political regeneration. · The following is an extract from the *Addresses to the German Nation*, uttered in the presence of the French conquerors : "In these addresses the memory of your forefathers speaks to you. Think that with my voice there are mingled the voices of your ancestors from the far-off ages of gray antiquity, of those who stemmed with their own bodies the tide of Roman domination over the world, who vindicated with their own blood the independence of these mountains, plains, and streams which under you have been suffered to fall a prey to the stranger. They call to you :—' Take ye our place ; hand down our memory to future ages, honorable and spotless as it has come down to you, as you have gloried in it and in your descent from us. Hitherto our struggle has been deemed noble, great, and wise ; we have been looked upon as the consecrated and inspired ones of a divine world-plan. Should our race perish with you, then will our honor be changed to dishonor, our wisdom into folly. For if Germany were ever to be subdued to the Empire, then had it been better to have fallen before the ancient Romans than before their modern descendants. We withstood those and triumphed ; these have scattered you like chaff before them. But as matters now are with you, seek not to conquer with bodily weapons, but stand firm and erect before them in spiritual dignity. Yours is the greater destiny—to form an empire of mind and reason ; to destroy the dominion of rude physical power as the ruler of the world. Do this and ye shall be worthy of descent from us.' "

REFERENCES

Morse Stephens : *The Revolution and Europe*, pp. 288–304 ; Rose : *Revolutionary and Napoleonic Era*, pp. 184-194.

§ 35. THE REVOLUTION OF 1848

The idea of German unity was growing during the first half of the nineteenth century. In the enthusiasm of the successful struggle against Napoleon came a reawakening of the German instinct, a new desire for welding the fragments, into which the triumph of the separatist principle had split the ancient German Empire. The Congress of Vienna, however, followed by the influence of Austria, succeeded in repressing all tendencies looking to change. The French Revolution of July passed over Germany without effect ; the policy of Metternich remained unbroken.

The eve of the revolution.

Meanwhile, among the educated classes there was growing a spirit of dissatisfaction with the system of repression,
combined with the desire for national unity and modern
institutions.   It expressed itself in the works of political
writers. Von Gagern, prime minister of Hesse-Darmstadt,
drew up a plan for establishing a central constitution, consisting of a president; a senate, representing the several
states; and a popular chamber, elected by the German nation.   It was at this time that the " German Rhine " and
the " Watch on the Rhine," expressions of the nationalist
spirit, became the popular songs of Germany. In 1847, the
Deutsche Zeitung, a nationalist newspaper, was founded
at Heidelberg by a professor of the local university, Ger-
vinus.   In the same year a meeting of German radicals
at Offenburg protested against the suppression of free
thought ; and a meeting of moderates at Heppenheim demanded the creation of a German parliament.

The outbreak of the Revolution of February in France
suddenly developed this general dissatisfaction into revolution. As the news came from Paris the
liberals organized meetings, demanded lib-
erty of the press and a representative system. Fifty-one
liberals met at Heidelberg and appointed a committee to
assemble, at Frankfort, a *Vor-Parlament,* or preliminary
parliament, which should make arrangements for the convening of a National Assembly and the organization of a
united Germany.

March days.

The smaller German states assented without difficulty ;
but the great military kingdoms, Austria, Prussia, and
Bavaria, were obstinate. In the meantime they were men-
aced with revolutions in their own capitals. On March
13th the Viennese rose and drove Metternich from his seat
of power. Metternich fled to England, and his imperial
master took refuge in the mountains of Tyrol. Prussia at
once caught the revolutionary spirit ; on the 15th of March
barricades began to appear in the streets of Berlin. There

was here no liberal organization, only a discontented multitude, moved by a vague democratic feeling, that rose against the king.

King Frederick William yielded before the storm, informed, no doubt, of the collapse of the government at Vienna. He addressed the people, and spoke in favor of a "constitutional organization of the German states," by an "agreement of the princes with the people." Robed in the colors of the Empire—red, black, and gold—he presented himself to his subjects, accepting the leadership of German unity. For Prussia he announced himself in favor of a constitutional system, and sanctioned the convocation of a Prussian National Assembly.

Meanwhile the great assembly of the German nation came together at Frankfort. The deputies represented the intellectual élite of Germany—lawyers, university professors and literary men, full of ideas, but without political experience. The old imperial supremacy of Austria was recognized in the appointment of the Archduke John of Austria as "Imperial Administrator." To him the Diet of the old Confederation transmitted its powers and was dissolved. The Assembly then proceeded to the creation of a constitution for united Germany. The university professors occupied the time with profound and scholarly debates. During the nine months of learned deliberation, Prussia and Austria had recovered from their fright, and were prepared to resist the popular movement, to which, in a moment of weakness and fear, they had yielded. The insurrection at Vienna had been quelled with troops ; at Berlin Frederick William felt strong enough to dissolve the Prussian National Assembly and proclaim a constitution of his own making. Thus when the Frankfort Assembly finally completed its constitution, in March, 1849, conditions were no longer favorable for its reception by the larger states.

The Assembly and the German people divided into two

The Frankfort parliament.

parties : one, the "Great Germany" party, wishing to include all German elements, reconciled themselves to the admission of Austria, with her majority of non-German peoples : the other, the "Little Germany" party, rejected Austria. This was the party which looked to Prussian leadership, and, after some very exciting contests, it prevailed in the Assembly by a vote of 261 to 224. By a vote of 290 the King of Prussia was declared Emperor of the Germans.

But Frederick William refused a popular crown, "a crown of mud and wood." "If anyone is to award the crown of the German nation, it is myself and my equals who should give it." His liberal sentiments of the March days had evaporated ; he would not be the Emperor of a Revolution. The advice of other German governments was asked. Twenty-eight states accepted the constitution, the hereditary empire, and the choice of the Assembly ; the larger states, Würtemberg, Bavaria, Saxony, and Hanover, however, rejected the election, jealous of Prussian control. Austria withdrew her deputies from the Assembly, and Frederick William, alarmed, definitely refused the imperial crown.

End of the assembly.

The Assembly, deserted by Prussia, struggled on, drifting into the hands of radicals. Revolutionary uprisings took place in Baden and elsewhere, but were quelled with force. In June the Assembly, reduced to 105 members, removed to Stuttgart. The government of Würtemberg finally closed the hall and scattered the delegates. The last stand of the radicals was taken in Baden, where the insurgents set up a provisional government. With Prussian aid they were conquered and dispersed. Many fled abroad, to Switzerland, France, and America. The republican party was exterminated in South Germany, the influence of Austria re-established, and the old Confederation restored.

SOURCE REVIEW

The King of Prussia and the Imperial Crown.—"Frederick William had from early years cherished the hope of seeing some closer union of Germany established under Prussian influence. But he dwelt in a world where there was more of picturesque mirage than of real insight. He was almost superstitiously loyal to the House of Austria; and he failed to perceive, what was palpable to men of far inferior endowments to his own, that by setting Prussia at the head of the constitutional movement of the epoch he might at any time from the commencement of his reign have rallied all Germany round it. Thus the revolution of 1848 burst upon him, and he was not the man to act or to lead in time of revolution. Even in 1848, had he given promptly and with dignity what, after blood had been shed in his streets, he had to give with humiliation, he would probably have been acclaimed Emperor on the opening of the Parliament of Frankfort, and have been accepted by the universal voice of Germany. But the odium cast upon him by the struggle of March 18th was so great that in the election of a temporary Administrator of the Empire in June no single member at Frankfort gave him a vote. Time was needed to repair his credit, and while time passed Austria rose from its ruins. In the spring of 1849 Frederick William could not have assumed the office of Emperor of Germany without risk of a war with Austria, even had he been willing to accept this office on the nomination of the Frankfort Parliament. But to accept the imperial crown from a popular assembly was repugnant to his deepest convictions. Clear as the Frankfort Parliament had been, as a whole, from the taint of Republicanism or of revolutionary violence, it had, nevertheless, had its birth in revolution: the crown which it offered would, in the King's expression, have been picked up from blood and mire. Had the princes of Germany by any arrangement with the Assembly tendered the crown to Frederick William the case would have been different; a new Divine right would have emanated from the old."—Fyffe: *Modern Europe.*

REFERENCES

Alison Phillips: *Modern Europe*, pp. 318–328; Judson: *Europe in the Nineteenth Century*, Chapter VIII.

§ 36. The New Empire

Frederick William IV, who so successfully quenched the fires of German patriotism in 1849, became mentally incompetent in 1857.   His brother William became regent, and on the death of Frederick William, in 1861, succeeded to the crown.   The autocratic spirit of King William was shown at his coronation.   "The kings of Prussia," he said, "receive their crowns from God."   At the outset the king found himself in conflict with the Prussian House of Representatives.   The "Progress" party demanded the completion of the "Constitutional State," and enforced its opposition by refusing to vote appropriations for the increase of the army.

Bismarck and absolutism.

BISMARCK AT THE OPENING OF HIS POLITICAL CAREER.

The King dissolved the House of Representatives, and called to his aid Otto von Bismarck-Schönhausen, a gentleman of Brandenburg, known for his distrust of parliamentary institutions and his devotion to the principle of absolute rule. The policy of Bismarck became the policy of the crown. Together King William and his minister created the Germany of to-day. Their methods were unconstitutional, and their diplomacy was wily, but their plans were well formulated, and their efforts crowned with success. "It is not Prussia's liberality that Germany looks to, but her military power," said Bismarck; and again: "The unity of Germany is to be brought about not by speeches, nor by the votes of majorities, but by blood and iron." In this spirit Bismarck solved the difficulties with the legislature; the protests of the House of Representatives were disregarded, and the crown raised directly the money needed for the army.

The union of Germany under Prussian leadership was accomplished by means of three wars: one with Denmark

The Schleswig-Holstein controversy.

in 1864; the second with Austria in 1866, and the third with France in 1870. The Danish war arose from a dispute over the succession to the duchies of Schleswig and Holstein. King Frederick VII of Denmark was the last of the male line which united under one crown the kingdom of Denmark and the Duchies. The future of the Duchies had been taken up by a convention of the great Powers in London, in 1852, when it had been decided to continue the union under Christian IX, the successor of Frederick VII to the throne of Denmark. The Estates of the Duchies, however, had not ratified the decision of the London Conference. A majority of the inhabitants of the Duchies were German, and desired a separation from Denmark; but on his advent to the throne, King Christian sought to carry out the decision of the Powers.

This led to an explosion of German national feeling.

The Diet of the German Confederation, championing the cause of the Germans in the Duchies, ordered the occupation of Schleswig and Holstein by the troops of Saxony and Hanover. But Bismarck disregarded the action of the Diet. Inducing Austria to act with him, he caused Prussian and Austrian troops to be moved into the Duchies, and swept aside the forces of the Diet. The war with Denmark was brief. By the treaty of Vienna (October 30, 1864) Denmark ceded the Duchies to the King of Prussia and the Emperor of Austria jointly. They were divided, Austria taking Holstein, and Prussia Schleswig.

But Bismarck was not content with this solution. The time had come for a trial of strength with Austria, a contest for the leadership of Germany. The Prussian army had shown its metal, and was ready for the task. The affair of the Duchies furnished the occasion; urging as a pretext that the Austrian government of Holstein was working in a way prejudicial to Prussian interests, Prussia marched her troops into Holstein and drove the Austrians out of the Duchy.

The Seven Weeks' War (June-July, 1866).

Meanwhile Bismarck had been making his preparations for a war with Austria. The neutrality of Russia, the "backbone of the Bismarckian policy," had been assured; to Napoleon III, Bismarck held out vague hopes of a recompense in the lower Rhine country, perhaps the Duchy of Luxemburg; and with Italy an offensive alliance was formed, the price of Italy's aid to be the province of Venetia, an Italian state still held by Austria. Even to the Diet of the Confederation, which both Prussia and Austria had discredited in the scramble for the Danish lands, he made overtures, announcing that Prussia "held to the unity of the German nation," and promising a new federal constitution with an elective parliament.

The war was brief. The minor German states, fearful of Prussia's power, armed against her. Hanover and

CORONATION OF EMPEROR WILLIAM I AT VERSAILLES.

Hesse-Cassel were overrun, and the great battle of the war was fought against the Austrians at Sadowa in Bohemia (July 3, 1866). Austria was beaten at the start, with the Prussians invading from the north and the Italians on her southern borders. The issue of the war established the supremacy of Prussia over the German states. Hanover, Hesse-Cassel and Nassau, Schleswig-Holstein, and the free city of Frankfort were annexed to Prussia ; Venetia went to Italy. The German Confederation was dissolved and a new union formed, the North German Confederation, with the King of Prussia as president. The new Confederation more nearly fulfilled the dreams of German patriots. Its upper house was composed of representatives of the several states ; its lower house elected by universal suffrage. Here was a German national government, with a strong executive and a democratic parliament. It lacked only the final step to convert it into the Empire.

Napoleon III committed a grave error in passively contributing to the rise of Prussia. His true policy would have been to keep open the question of German leadership, and this might have been done, if he had inclined to Austria in the Seven Weeks' War. But he was wheedled into neutrality by Bismarck with the vague promise of Luxemburg. After the Peace of Prague Bismarck had no further need of Napoleon, but by a series of subtle irritations he kept alive the French sense of humiliation, until it burst forth in bitterness, of which the war of 1870 was the result. That magnificent engine of war, the Prussian army, projected by the patriots of the Liberation period, and perfected by the genius of von Moltke, swept over France almost without resistance. By its side marched the armies of the South German states, Bavaria, Würtemberg, and Baden, upon whose hostility to Prussia Napoleon had counted, but who were won for German unity. In the Hall of Mirrors of the palace of Versailles, surrounded by a victorious army, the King of

The Empire.

Prussia was crowned Emperor in the presence of the German sovereigns (January 18, 1871) receiving the crown "from himself and his equals." The Empire included all the German lands, save those of Austria. The conquered territory of Alsace and Lorraine was not annexed to Prussia, but became an imperial province, common to all the Empire.

THE PRINCE OF PRUSSIA,
in 1849.
(Afterwards Emperor William.)

The history of the Empire of Bismarck and William has been one of remarkable prosperity and growth. In commerce and manufacture Germany has become the second power of Europe, rivalling Great Britain. In education, in invention, in the arts and sciences, she has no superior. Her political organization differs from that of the states of western Europe. The Emperor is an autocrat; his will constitutes the policy of the nation; no real parliamentary government exists. Thus far the Emperor's policy has been acceptable to the nation, so great is the gratitude of the German people to the Hohenzollern founders of Germany's greatness.

Germany of to-day.

WILLIAM II.

Prosperity as well has made all things tolerable. The real problem of popular government has yet to receive its solution in Germany.

SOURCE REVIEW

Military Service in Germany.—"In Germany the army is the nation in a literal sense. According to the letter of the law, every male subject is liable to be called on to serve when he has completed his seventeenth year, and the liability continues to the end of his forty-fifth year. The term of service in the standing army is seven years, and it usually begins with the twenty-first year. Two years (instead of three, as formerly) are now passed with the colors, after which the time-expired soldier passes by successive stages into the first reserve, the *Landwehr*, and finally into the *Landsturm*. This last is the army of emergency, comprising all male citizens between the ages of seventeen and forty-five who do not belong to the army or navy, and it is only intended to be called up in the event of the regular forces proving insufficient for home-defense. Though obligation to serve his country under arms applies to every able-bodied German save the members of reigning and mediatized houses—who, nevertheless, are seldom slow to act upon the principle of *noblesse oblige*—the law is applied with all possible leniency. Physical weakness, even of a slight character, exempts, of necessity ; but the sole bread-winners of families, theological students, and even the sons of farmers, tradespeople, and others who cannot be spared from home, are also excused. Further latitude is allowed by the enrollment of what are known as 'One-year volunteers,' who enjoy a curtailed service in consideration of their satisfying certain high educational requirements, and undertake to clothe, maintain, and house themselves during the year with the colors without cost to the state."—Dawson : *German Life in Town and Country*.

REFERENCES

Alison Phillips : *Modern History*, Chapters XVII, XVIII ; Judson : *Europe in the Nineteenth Century*, Chapter XVII.

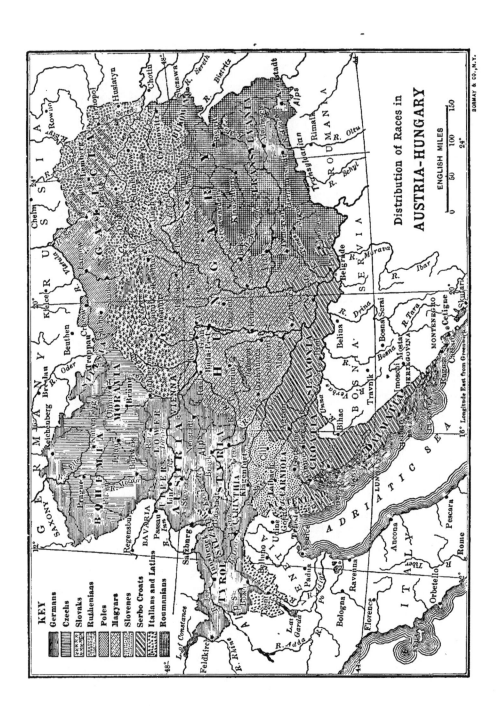

Distribution of Races in
AUSTRIA-HUNGARY

ENGLISH MILES

0   50   100   150

KEY
Germans
Czechs
Slovaks
Ruthenians
Poles
Magyars
Slovenes
Serbo Croats
Italians and Latins
Roumanians

CHAPTER XIII

Austria since 1848

§ 37. The Race Question

No understanding of the problems of Austria in the nineteenth century is possible without taking into account her racial composition. The Empire of Austria is a conglomeration of peoples, living side by side under the same sovereign. It has often been remarked that the name "Austrian," unlike the names "Italian" or "French" or "Spanish," has no racial signification. An "Austrian" may be one of a dozen different nationalities, each speaking a different language and representing a different stage of civilization. In early times this mosaic of peoples was held together with the cement of German culture. The Germans, although a minority of the population, possessed the learning and the ability to govern. They were the ruling classes, and the other races were content to occupy a subordinate position. With the spread of intelligence, however, and the general improvement in the condition of the subject races, these non-German peoples came to possess a sense of national pride ; each race began to cultivate its language, literature, and traditions, and to insist upon a recognition of its nationality in the councils of the Empire. The German nationality has given way before the non-German majority with great reluctance. The struggles of the rising nationalities for power has threatened and still threatens the integrity of the Empire, and is to-day the factor in European politics most likely to bring about a reconstruction of European boundaries.

Its importance in Austria.

For the study of the races of Austria it is convenient to divide them into seven groups :

Races of Austria.

1. *The Germans.*—The central lands of the Austrian crown, lying west of Vienna along the upper Danube, comprising the provinces of Upper and Lower Austria, Styria, Carinthia, Salzburg, and Tyrol, are essentially German. At Vienna and elsewhere throughout this region the German language and culture prevail.

2. *The Czechs.*—In the provinces of the Crown of Bohemia, Bohemia and Moravia, the population is mainly Slavic (Czech), although there are islets of German population scattered here and there, particularly in the northwest portion of Bohemia, adjoining Saxony. The Czechs are proud of their nationality, and for centuries have protested against German supremacy. The fact that they are a small national group, surrounded on three sides with Germans, and intermixed throughout with German population, makes the problem of their political future one of especial difficulty. Their nearest kinsmen are the Poles, also a Slavic people, on the east.

3. *The Poles.*—Galicia, on the northeast, is the part of Poland that fell to the share of Austria. The inhabitants of Galicia are mostly Poles, although in the eastern part the peasantry are Ruthenians, another Slavic people.

4. *The South Slavs.*—Slovenians, Croats, and Serbs. These people, the last to come forward in the path of intellectual and national aspiration, were simple peasants at the beginning of the nineteenth century. They inhabit the southern tier of provinces of Austria and Hungary, the coast lands—Krain, Croatia, and Slavonia. A group of Slavs of less development are the Slovaks, in the northwestern part of Hungary, adjoining Moravia. These are the people who come in large numbers to the United States under the name of Hungarians.

5. *The Magyars or Hungarians.*—They are the ruling element of the Kingdom of Hungary, which lies between

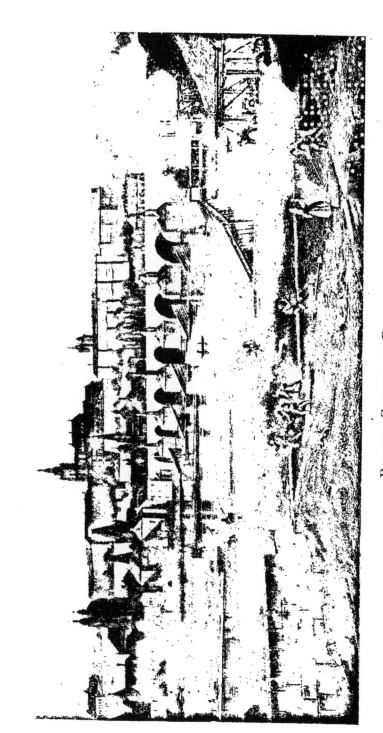

Prague, Capitol of Bohemia.

Austria and the Carpathian Mountains on the east. Of Tartar origin, speaking a language which has no relationship with the other languages of civilized Europe, the Magyars have ever been a proud, independent people, conscious of their racial isolation and jealous of foreign control. By constant protest and armed resistance they have prevented their absorption by the Austrian Germans, and have kept the Crown of St. Stephen, the national emblem of Hungarian independence, distinct from the imperial crown of Austria.

6. *The Roumanians.*—These people, claiming to be descendants of ancient Roman colonists, and speaking a language related to Italian, inhabit the eastern part of Hungary, the province of Transylvania. The greater part of the Roumanian race lies still farther east, in the Kingdom of Roumania. Until recently the Roumanians of Hungary were rude, ignorant people, peasants and shepherds, kept in subjection by the Magyars and the German (Saxon) colonists, who migrated from the west centuries ago and settled on the borders of Hungary. Of late the Roumanians have felt the spur of national pride, and have been developing in sympathy with their kinsmen of the Kingdom of Roumania.

7. *The Italians.*—In 1848 Austria ruled over a large Italian population, all northern Italy, from the Adriatic to the Kingdom of Sardinia. The greater part of these people have since been gathered into the Kingdom of Italy ; but a few Italians still remain under the rule of Austria. They are found in the southern portion of Tyrol, which stretches down through the Alps toward the plains of Lombardy, and in the towns of the eastern coast of the Adriatic, from Triest southward, which were formerly part of the maritime state of Venice.

From this brief review of the distribution of races in Austria and Hungary, it will be evident that her political problem is a complicated one, increasing with the development of the national spirit in the various nations of which she is composed. It is a new separatist tendency, more serious than the old separatism of Germany, which so long prevented German unity, because it is based upon the deep and wide distinctions of race. The internal history of Austria since 1848, when the great impetus was given to racial development, has been an effort to avoid, in so far as possible, the claims of the warring racial units to a proportionate share in the government of the Empire, at the expense of former German supremacy.

SOURCE REVIEW

I. Development of the Czechs.—" Whoever knows what Bohemia was thirty years ago, and compares the racial conditions then with those of to-day, must wonder at the changes that have taken place. The Czech has progressed materially and intellectually in a manner which cannot fail to strike the impartial observer with wonder. Up to the end of the fifties, most of the towns in Bohemia had a decided German character. The better classes almost exclusively spoke German ; the schools, the academies, the theatres, commerce and industry— all these were entirely German. The Czech language was only spoken by the peasant and the villager, or, in the case of the towns, by the working-class and domestics. How all this has altered !

" In the course of thirty years the Czechs have created a powerful political party, a literature and a musical school of their own. We have it on the authority of the *Encyclopædia Britannica*, that at the present day their more prominent names in philosophy, theology, and politics are too numerous to be mentioned in detail. In all Slavic districts a network of savings banks, public credit institutions to advance money to small traders, co-operative societies and manufactories, has been spread out far and wide. Slavic schools are everywhere largely attended, commerce and industry are flourishing. In short, the Czechs have everywhere risen to the level of their German competitors."—Whitman : *The Realm of the Hapsburgs.*

II. Modern Hungary.—" The world has been accustomed to marvel at the growth of trans-oceanic communities. Hungary, however, can show an almost equally remarkable spectacle. Here is a great country of the past, in which national independence had been forfeited 250 years prior to the collapse of Poland, and which continued to exist at one time as a Turkish province, at another as a portion of Austria, but which suddenly becomes endowed with new life, makes peace on equal terms with its conqueror, and rises up again a new nation. In the course of a short space of twenty-five years, this people succeeds in creating commerce and manufacture, a network of railways, a thorough system of public education, a national school of literature, science, drama, painting, and music. These, and many other things besides, have the Hungarians succeeded in bringing into life, mainly by the force of national enthusiasm. Other factors as well have, of course, been at work. In the first place, the bounteous hand of Nature herself has given her in the Danube a river similar to what the Mississippi is to North America. Then, again, she is possessed of a soil, the fertility of which qualifies her to be the granary of Europe ; though against this must be placed the excess of heat, and consequently recurring disastrous droughts and floods."—Whitman.

REFERENCES

Judson : *Europe in the Nineteenth Century*, pp. 167–169; Alison Phillips : *Modern Europe*, pp. 241–249.

§ 38. REVOLUTION OF 1848 IN AUSTRIA

Up to 1848 the iron rule of Metternich held together the nations of Austria; but in spite of all repressive measures the new ideas of liberty found their way into the Hapsburg dominions. In Prague the Czechs established reviews and clubs ; in Hungary Louis Kossuth, a young lawyer, founded the first Magyar political paper ; Galicia was a centre of Polish plots ; and in the south the Croats were dreaming of a

Insurrection of Vienna.

16

Kingdom of Illyria. To make matters still more complicated, the Italian provinces of Lombardy and Venetia,
held by Austria and bitterly hating Austrian rule, were on
the verge of revolution. Even in the German lands a
spirit of liberalism was abroad.

Only a spark was necessary to set Austria aflame ; and
this was furnished by the French Revolution of February.
In Vienna the revolution came with a single riot. A mob,
headed by students, cried " Down with Metternich ! " A
provisional government was established in Vienna by the
insurrectionists. The imperial authorities were terror-
stricken, and, yielding to the demands of the revolutionary
committee, convoked an assembly, elected by universal
suffrage, for the purpose of drafting a constitution. Metternich escaped to England, and the Emperor, a feeble
man, fled with his family to the fastnesses of Tyrol. The
Constitutional Assembly met at Vienna, July 22d ; among
the deputies were ninety-two peasants. It abolished all
feudal rights, as the French Assembly had done fifty years
before, and suppressed all distinctions between nobles and
commoners.

In Hungary the liberal elements were unchained. A
Committee of Safety was chosen, and a demand made
upon the Emperor for a liberal constitution.
Throughout the Empire. Reforms were voted : *liberty of the press,
equalization of taxes*, and the *abolition of
feudal rights*. A constitutional Assembly met at Budapest, and henceforth Hungary was governed separately
and made independent of Vienna ; an army was formed,
the national Hungarian colors adopted, and a separate
currency.

Likewise in the Slavic provinces the separatist tendency prevailed. The Czechs in Prague formed a Slavic
militia and prepared for resistance. A provisional government was formed and a National Assembly promised from
Vienna. The South Slavs rose in revolt under the leader-

BUDAPEST.

ship of Jellačič, a Croatian colonel. Even in Transylvania the Roumanian peasants held a mass-meeting, and demanded equality with other nations of the Empire.

In Italy Lombardy and Venetia strove to break the Austrian bonds. At Milan the Austrian troops were driven from the city. Venice proclaimed the Republic of Saint Mark, and, thinking the time had come to strike for Italian unity, marched to the aid of the Italians of Lombardy and Venetia. The fate of Austria seemed at hand.

Fortunately for the house of Hapsburg, the army was faithful and unconquered. Two able generals turned the fortunes of the Empire, General Radetsky in Lombardy and Count Windischgrätz in Bohemia. The collision between the populace and the garrison in Prague came on the 12th of June. A week later Windischgrätz was in possession of the city, and the Bohemian revolution was at an end. In Italy Radetzky met the Sardinian king, Charles Albert, routed him in a series of battles, and won back Lombardy.

The reaction.

This gave the government at Vienna a breathing spell, and set free troops for the reduction of Vienna and the East. With Hungary a fatal weakness lost her her cause. Much as the Magyar hated the German, he hated the Slav with equal intensity. It was one thing for Hungary to seek her national independence ; but quite another thing to concede the same to the Croats, especially when it meant the separation of Croatia and Slavonia from the Crown of St. Stephen. This jealousy of the South Slavs was made use of by the government at Vienna. Hungary was put under martial law, its liberties revoked, and Jellačič, the Croat, appointed to supreme military and civil command. In this manner the Croats were played off against the Magyars.

But now the trouble shifted to Vienna. The populace of the capital had no sympathy with the Emperor's vacillating policy toward the Hungarians. It rose to prevent troops from going against Hungary ; a mob surrounded the residence of the minister of war, called him out, and

Revolt in Vienna. hanged him. The Emperor fled again in terror, this time into Moravia, and in an imperial manifesto called upon the Austrian people to rise against the revolution. Again the army saved the day. Windischgrätz marched upon Vienna from the north ; Jellačič advanced from the east, while a Hungarian army came up the Danube to the aid of the Viennese insurgents. The Hungarians were repulsed by Jellačič, and Windischgrätz took the city. Vienna was subjected to a reign of terror.

A stronger hand came to the helm ; the weak-minded

The Hungarian war. Emperor Ferdinand was induced to abdicate in favor of his nephew, Francis Joseph. Aided by an able minister, Count Schwartzenberg, the new Emperor set aside the conflicting promises of his predecessor, and pro-

KOSSUTH.

ceeded to crush the liberal-national movement throughout the Empire. In Hungary the radical party, led by Kossuth, secured control and declared the independence of Hungary, proclaimed the Hungarian Republic, and elected Kossuth president. With 50,000 men in the field Hungary was no mean antagonist ; but Austria's resources were not yet at an end. She called on Russia for aid, and Nicholas the Tsar, fearing the establishment of republican institutions on his borders, readily responded and sent an army of 80,000 men into the Magyar country. The Hungarian Republic was lost ; Kossuth and his immediate followers fled to Turkey. (Capitulation of Vilagos, August 13, 1849.)

In Austria the imperial government dissolved the Assembly, "for having placed itself in contradiction with the actual conditions of the monarchy." A con-

The return of absolutism.

stitution was granted by the Emperor, with a legislature and a responsible ministry ; but it was never put into operation and was revoked by imperial decree in 1851. Hungary was declared to have forfeited, by its late revolt, its ancient privileges ; was cut into five administrative districts, and governed by officials from Vienna. An imperial manifesto announced the intention of " uniting into one great state all the countries and races of the monarchy." The dream of Joseph II seemed likely to be realized with force.

Yet the revolution of 1848 was not entirely without results of the better sort. The hasty abolition of feudal rights, accomplished by the revolutionary assemblies in Vienna and at Budapest, could not be undone. If politically the Empire and its dependencies were projected into a deeper gloom of absolutism, yet socially and economically much had been gained.

SOURCE REVIEW

How Kossuth became famous.—"He was a gentleman of noble origin, of course, but his whole fortune lay in his talents, which at that period (1832) were devoted to journalism, a profession which the Hungarians had not yet learned to estimate at its full value. At this time no printed proceedings of the Hungarian parliament had ever yet been published. To supply this defect, Kossuth resolved to devote the time, which would otherwise have been wasted in idle listening, to carefully reporting everything that took place, and circulated it all over the country in a small printed sheet, which was read with extraordinary eagerness. The Cabinet, however, took alarm, and prohibited the printing of the reports. This was a heavy blow, but Kossuth was not baffled. He instantly gathered around him a great number of young men to act as secretaries, who wrote out a great number of copies of the journal, which were circulated in manuscript through Hungary. The government stopped his journal in the post-office. He then established a staff of messengers and carriers, who circulated it from village to village. The enthusiasm of the people was fast rising to a flame. Kossuth was seized and thrown into prison. The charge brought against him was, that he had circulated false and inaccurate reports; but the real ground of the offense was, as everybody knew, that he had circulated any reports at all."—Condensed from E. L. Godkin : *History of Hungary.*

REFERENCES

Judson : *Europe in the Nineteenth Century,* Chapter IX ; Alison Phillips : *Modern Europe,* pp. 275-308 passim.

§ 39. · THE DUAL GOVERNMENT OF AUSTRIA-HUNGARY

The system of absolutism and national repression remained intact so long as Austria continued prosperous.

Fall of absolutism. When, however, she met with the first of a series of reverses, which drove her out of Italy and reduced her to a second place among the states of Germany, she found it necessary to make peace with her subjects.

In 1859 Italy, under the leadership of Sardinia, and with the help of Napoleon III, achieved her unity. In a series of battles fought on the plains of northern Italy the Austrian troops were defeated by the combined forces of Italy and France. Lombardy was lost, and Venetia alone left to Austria south of the Alps. After the defeat of its army, the government of Francis Joseph, wishing to reorganize its military establishment, found its credit gone. A loan offered in 1860 was only partially subscribed. Evidently the people were out of sympathy with the government.

The Emperor appealed directly to his subjects, offering reforms in exchange for their support. A certain liberty of political discussion being permitted, the political elements of the empire soon formed themselves into two parties: the party of unity, which sought a continuance of German administration at Vienna; and the federalist party, which wished to make the various national governments independent of Vienna. These were the Magyars, Czechs, Poles, Croats, and Slovenians.

Effort at centralization, 1860-1861.

The Emperor was at first inclined to give full play to public opinion. The federalist party was in the majority,

FRANCIS JOSEPH, EMPEROR OF AUSTRIA, KING OF HUNGARY.

and in 1860 Francis Joseph restored the national Diets, abolishing the common ministry of the Empire. But with this measure of liberty Hungary rapidly took the lead to complete independence of the Empire. Her Diet declared for the Constitution of 1848, the constitution of the Revolution which had constituted Hungary an independent state. The Emperor, hastening to check the disintegration of his Empire, published the Additional Act of 1861, which, while pretending to amend the Constitution of 1860, introduced quite another system. Its leading feature was an annual parliament for the Empire, consisting of two houses : a House of Lords, appointed by the Emperor, and a House of Representatives of 343 members, chosen by the provincial Diets. The Emperor was to appoint his ministry and retain absolute control of the government. It was altogether a constitution differing not widely from the French Charter of Louis XVIII.

The greater nationalities protested. Hungary, under the leadership of Deák, refused to accept the constitution,

declaring that it would never "sacrifice the constitutional
independence of the nation." The Magyars refused to
Dualism. send delegates to the central parliament, and
refused to pay taxes. The Czechs and Poles
eventually followed, and withdrew their delegates. There
remained in the parliament only the Germans and the delegates of the lesser nationalities. The Vienna authorities
were obliged to govern temporarily as best they could,
abandoning constitutional methods. The deficit contin-

SCHÖNBRUNN, SUMMER PALACE NEAR VIENNA.

ued, debt increased, and prosperity waned. At length,
Francis Joseph, disgusted with the system of unity, despairing of breaking down the resistance of Hungary,
opened negotiations with the Magyars on the basis of the
old relations between Austria and Hungary.

The war of 1866 with Prussia, the defeat of Sadowa,
the humiliation of Austria and the loss of Venetia to the
Italians broke the spirit of the Emperor, and made him
willing to adopt a policy of complete reconciliation with
his subjects. It was a choice between Dualism, which

would reconcile the Hungarians, and win them to the side of the Empire, and thereby stave off for a while the claims of the lesser nationalities ; and Federation, a complete concession of the nationalist principle. The Emperor chose the former. By the Compromise of 1867 the present Austro-Hungarian dualism was established.

By the Compromise of 1867 Hungary remains an independent Kingdom. The Emperor of Austria is recrowned *Austria-Hungary.* at Budapest with the crown of St. Stephen, as " Apostolic King " of Hungary. The Kingdom of Hungary includes Hungary, Croatia, Slavonia, Transylvania, and the Military Frontier. The remaining states are under the imperial crown of Austria.

The two states are joined together not only by the personal union through the sovereign, but by a union government, which has charge of affairs common to both states. Such affairs are: foreign relations, the army and navy, and the finances necessary for carrying on these joint establishments. For the management of these common affairs there exists a union ministry, and a union legislature, known as the Delegations. The Delegations consist of two bodies of delegates, chosen respectively from the Austrian and the Hungarian legislatures, sixty members from each. The Delegations meet alternately at Vienna and at Budapest. They sit separately, each deliberating in its own language, and communicate with each other by written messages. They control the expenditure of the common funds, of which Hungary contributes thirty per cent., and Austria the remainder. All other matters are determined by each of the two states for itself in its own legislature.

At the close of the war waged by Russia in 1877 against Turkey, in behalf of the Christian nations of the lower *Later events.* Danube, the Congress of Berlin detached from Turkey the Slavic provinces of Bosnia and Herzegovina, and placed them under the guardianship of Austria-Hungary. The population of the protected provinces consists mainly of Croats and Serbs, in racial sympathy with the Austrian subjects across the border, and their progress since the union has been rapid.

The present trend of politics in Austria-Hungary is a continuance of the race problem. What the Magyars have achieved is eagerly sought for by the Czechs and other races. To concede their claims would be to split the Empire-Kingdom into a dozen federated fragments; an arrangement which would be greatly complicated by the intermixture of races. The force which at present holds together these warring groups is the personal popularity of the Emperor Francis Joseph. Unfortunately for the future, the death by suicide of his only son and heir, Rudolph, has weakened the dynasty, by throwing the succession into a collateral branch, whose members are less popular. Meanwhile in the Austrian legislature the Slavs have crowded the Germans to the wall, creating a dissatisfaction among the Germans, which, in the event of a reorganization of Austria, would impel them toward a union with the German Empire.

SOURCE REVIEW

Warring Races of Austria-Hungary.—Views of an Austrian.—"The Czechs want the re-establishment of the Kingdom of Bohemia, and finally the union with Russia. The Ruthenians, oppressed by the Poles, and differing in language and religion from them, look forward to an incorporation with the Empire of the Tsar. The Poles proclaim secretly, if not openly, the restoration of the Kingdom of Poland. *Italia irredenta* * is ever alive in the Trentina and Trieste, no matter how hard the Slavs, officials and police, try to suppress it. The southern Slavs of the coastlands, Dalmatia, Croatia, and Slavonia, are clamoring for a unification, and their ultimate

---

* A patriotic society of Italians, who have vowed never to cease their efforts, until all the regions inhabited by Italians, now held by Austria and France, are united with the Kingdom of Italy.

aim is the re-establishment of the old Servian Kingdom, embracing also Servia, Bosnia, Herzegovina and Montenegro. The Roumanians wish their annexation by the young and vigorous Kingdom of Roumania; and lastly, not least, the Germans of Bohemia, Austrian Silesia, Lower Austria, Styria and the most advanced and politically educated inhabitants of the Alpine regions desire a union of the German provinces with Germany. Every visitor to Bohemia must notice in the German districts the ostentatious display of the pan-Germanic banner (black, red, gold) instead of the Austrian colors (black, yellow), and that scarcely a peasant hut is without the pictures of the Emperor William and Bismarck; while, on the other hand, in the Czech districts, he will find likenesses of Huss and the Tsar hanging side by side.

"The cement that holds the centrifugal forces loosely together is Emperor Francis Joseph. Although neither a genius, nor a man of initiative, nor a ruler of will and energy, he is liked by the people at large because he is a fairly good and decent man, has tried his best, to be a constitutional ruler, and does no harm wilfully."

REFERENCES

Judson : *Europe in the Nineteenth Century*, Chapter XV ; Alison Phillips : *Modern Europe*, pp. 444–448.

CHAPTER XIV

The Union of Italy

§ 40. EFFORTS TO ACHIEVE UNITY UNAIDED

THE struggle for Italian unity is as old as modern times. Dante and Petrarch, inspired by the glory of ancient Rome, dreamed of a New Italy, rising from the degradation of medieval anarchy. But a different fate was in store for Italy; the land fell into the hands of foreigners, French and Spaniards, and, on the dissolution of the Spanish empire, came under the influence of Austria. The hopes of unity were never so slight as in the eighteenth century, when the peninsula, parceled out into a dozen petty kingdoms and duchies, was dominated by the Austrians.

Contribution of Napoleon I.

Napoleon I broke the spell, and paved the way for eventual unity. By the erection of the Cisalpine Republic, afterward the Kingdom of Italy; by the incorporation of the Papal State and the Grand Duchy of Tuscany into the territory of France, and by the mild rule of Joseph and of Murat at Naples, he taught the Italians a lesson in democracy and the benefits of good government. More than this, he broke down the prestige of the old governments, which had existed so long that they seemed to be a part of the nature of things. With this he roused a hope of unity, and kindled the fires of Italian patriotism from Milan to Palermo. The Congress of Vienna brought back the old system, but it had lost its sanctity.

Five years after the restoration of Austrian influence and the re-establishment of the "legitimate" sovereigns upon their thrones, Italy burst forth into revolution. The

characteristic of the revolutionary movements of this period is that they were local, independent of one another,
and without common head or direction.
They were largely incited by the *Carbonari*, a secret society, organized in lodges,
after the model of the Freemasons.   At Naples in 1820,
in Sardinia in 1821, insurrections forced the kings to grant
liberal constitutions.   In each instance the revolution was
quelled by Austrian troops at the behest of the Allies.
The Sardinian revolution was accompanied with an event
which was important for the future fortunes of Italy.   On
the side of the conspirators, who were moving for a liberal
constitution, was Charles Albert, nephew of the king,
popularly supposed to be a member of the *Carbonari*.
The king, Victor Emmanuel I, was without direct heirs,
and after the king's brother, Charles Felix, an old man
and childless, the succession would pass in due order of
events to the nephew, Charles Albert of Carignano.   His
participation in the revolution brought down upon the
Prince of Carignano the hatred of the Austrian court.
Metternich sought to have him deprived of the right of
succession, but the other powers resisted, and he was obliged
to expiate his liberalism by joining the French expedition
against the Spanish liberals.   It is also said Charles Albert
promised Metternich that he would never grant a constitution to Sardinia.   King Victor Emmanuel I retired in
1821, and at the death of Charles Felix in 1831 the Prince
of Carignano came to the throne.   The eye of Italy was
upon him as the future champion of Italian unity.

In 1830 the Revolution of July in Paris and the accession of Louis Philippe aroused Italian hopes.   In the
Papal States and in the Duchies of Modena and Parma insurrections took place.   But the Italian liberals soon
found out that Louis Philippe was not disposed to lend
his aid to foreign insurrections, and the insurgents were
put down with Austrian bayonets.   At Rome the ambassa-

Period of Local revolutions, 1820-30.

NAPLES, WITH VESUVIUS IN THE BACKGROUND.

dors of the Powers presented a memorandum to Pope Gregory XVI, recommending certain reforms in the administration of the Papal States ; but nothing came of it, and the pope engaged two Swiss regiments for twenty years for the defense of his throne against the liberals.

Up to 1831 the efforts toward Italian unity had been local and under the direction of secret societies. Now the movement entered the domain of literature and political speculation. Various literary works of the time contain the most diverse suggestions for the achievement of Italian unity. Mazzini, a Genoese, proposed the establishment of the Republic of Italy. In 1831 he founded " Young Italy," a secret society, into which were admitted only men of forty years of age and over. Later he enlarged his project and founded " Young Europe," looking to a republicanization of all Europe. Each country was to form its own republic, and all of Europe was to be bound together with ties of fraternity. Mazzini lived much of his life abroad, published much, earning his livelihood by literary work, and directed his movement from France and England.

The Risorgimento.

In contrast with Mazzini the republican, was Gioberti, a priest, who in 1843 inaugurated a pacific movement looking toward unity. He sought the desired result under the papacy, with the papacy as the center of the new Italian state. His book was called " *Moral and Political Headship of Italy.*" Among others who contributed to the discussion through the medium of the press were Count Balbo and the poet d'Azeglio. Thus began the period called the *Risorgimento* (Resurrection), when the idea of united Italy became a sentiment which pervaded the intellectual classes. It was admitted that Italy must rise and throw off the foreign yoke ; but as to the manner and the means there was much difference of opinion. Who should be the head ? How might it be done ? The latter question was solved for the time being by the remark of Charles Albert.

When asked how Italy might carry out her plan for unity, he replied, "*Italia farà de se* (Italy will do it of herself)."

The impulse of the Revolution of February gave Italy an opportunity to try the suggestion of the King of Sardinia. The weakening of the Austrian power seemed to be Italy's opportunity. With the news of the fall of Metternich, Lombardy revolted, and Charles Albert marched at the head of a Sardinian army to the aid of Milan and Venice. But in vain ; under the command of Radetzky the Austrian troops were everywhere victorious. At Novara (March 23, 1849) Charles Albert, having sought death in vain in the front of battle, recognizing that Austria would never forgive him his breach of faith, resigned his crown to his son, Victor Emmanuel II, and went into exile, dying a few months later at Lisbon, broken-hearted. The revolution was crushed, and the stern military rule of Austria displaced the hopes of national liberty in Lombardy and Venetia.

At Rome the revolution raged most fiercely. Pope Pius IX, elected in 1846, had been greeted by many as the head of New Italy, heralded by Gioberti. He adopted a most liberal policy, and when in 1848 the revolution broke out, granted a constitution. But the republican elements of Rome swept away the liberal régime of Pius IX, drove the pope from Rome, and established the Roman Republic, under the leadership of Mazzini. Four Catholic powers offered aid to the pope—France, Austria, Spain, and Naples. The Neapolitan troops were repulsed by the republican army of Rome ; Spain sent only two ships ; Austria occupied Bologna and the northern part of the Papal States. It was left for a French republic, under the presidency of Louis Bonaparte, to escort the pope back to Rome. After a brief resistance, Rome, defended by Garibaldi and his "red-shirts," was taken by French troops (July, 1849), who guarded the papal throne until 1870. Thus Italy had failed in the attempt to achieve unity for herself.

SOURCE REVIEW

I. Rome, the True Center of Italian Unity : from Mazzini's Address " To the Young Men of Italy."—" Love your country. Your country is the land where your parents sleep, where is spoken that language in which the chosen of your heart, blushing, whispered the first words of love ; it is the home that God has given you, that by striving to perfect yourselves therein you may prepare to ascend to him.   It is your name, your glory, your sign among the people.   Give to it your thoughts, your counsel, your blood.   Raise it up, great and beautiful, as it was foretold by our great men, and see that you leave it uncontaminated by any trace of falsehood or of servitude ; unprofaned by dismemberment.   Let it be one, as the thought of God.   You are twenty-five millions of men, endowed with active, splendid faculties ; possessing a tradition of glory, the envy of the nations of Europe.   An immense future is before you ; you lift your eyes to the loveliest heaven, and around you smiles the loveliest land in Europe ; you are encircled by the Alps and the sea, boundaries traced out by the finger of God for a people of giants—you are bound to be such, or nothing.   Let not a man of that twenty-five millions remain excluded from the fraternal bond destined to join you together ; let not a glance be raised to that heaven which is not the glance of a free man.   Let Rome be the ark of your redemption, the temple of your nation.   Has she not twice been the temple of the destinies of Europe ?   In Rome two extinct worlds, the Pagan and the Papal, are superposed, like the jewels of a diadem ; draw from thence a third world, greater than the two ; from Rome, the holy city, the city of love (*Amor*), the purest and wisest among you, elected by the vote and fortified by the inspiration of a whole people, shall dictate the Pact that shall make us one, and represent us in the future alliance of the peoples.   Until then you will either have no country, or have her contaminated and profaned." —From *World's Best Orations*.

II. Novara.—" All day long the king courted death, pressing forward where the balls fell like hail and the confusion was at its height, with the answer of despair to the devoted

17

officers who sought to hold him back : 'Let me die, this is my last day.' But death shuns the seeker. Men fell close beside him, but no charitable ball struck his breast. In the evening he said to his generals : 'We have still 40,000 men, cannot we fall back on Alessandria, and still make an honorable stand?' They told him that it could not be done. Radetsky was asked on what terms he would grant an armistice ; he replied : 'The occupation of a large district in Piedmont and the heir to the throne as a hostage.' Then Charles Albert knew what he must do. 'For eighteen years,' he said, 'I have made every effort for the good of the people ; I grieve to see that my hopes have failed—not so much for myself as for the country. I have not found death on the field of battle, as I ardently desired ; perhaps my person is the only obstacle to obtaining juster terms. I abdicate the crown in favor of my son, Victor Emmanuel.' And turning to the Duke of Savoy he said : 'There is your king.' "—Countess Cesaresco : *The Liberation of Italy.*

References

Judson : *Europe in the Nineteenth Century*, Chapters X, XI ; Alison Phillips : *Modern Europe*, 237–241 ; 280–311.

§ 41. Unity Achieved Through Foreign Aid

The revolution of 1848 had failed, and Italy found herself once more parceled out and controlled by foreign powers. Something, however, had been learned. It was evident that unity, if achieved, must be won under the leadership of a temporal, and not of a spiritual power. Sardinia, and not Rome, must be the champion of Italian national aspirations.

Leadership of Sardinia.

Fortunately, Sardinia was the one state which preserved her liberties through the storms of 1849. The liberal constitution of 1846, granted by Charles Albert, and preserved by Victor Emmanuel II, secured for Sardinia a parliamentary government, a senate, appointed by the king, a Chamber of Deputies, elected by the people, and a ministry responsible to the chambers. Sardinia became the only liberally governed state in Italy.

Victor Emmanuel was passionately fond of hunting, and was by taste a military man. Left to himself, it is not likely he could have solved the problem of Italy ; but, like William of Prussia, he found a servant greater than himself, who made his reign illustrious. Cavour was educated for the army, discharged for liberalism in 1830, and spent some years traveling in France and Germany. In 1847 he founded a liberal monarchical paper, *Il Risorgimento,* at Turin. During the Revolution of 1848 he was a moderate, and in 1850 was called to the king's ministry. There he evolved the policy that was to lead to the Kingdom of Italy.

Camillo di Cavour.

VICTOR EMMANUEL II., KING OF SARDINIA, 1849–1861; KING OF ITALY, 1861–1878.

Ten years were devoted to the preparation. The resources of Sardinia were strengthened. Cavour sought to revive agriculture and commerce, and added to the royal revenue by secularizing the estates of the regular clergy. At the same time the army, in which the king took great pride, was reorganized after the Prussian model by General La Marmora. Cavour put himself in touch with Italian patriots thoughout Italy. These local leaders, defeated in their efforts to achieve independence through their personal efforts, turned to Sardinia and Cavour as the sole remaining means for the redemption of Italy. A secret organization, the " National Union," served to bind together the scattered elements of resistance to Austrian control.

The foreign policy of Cavour was masterful, and marks

him as one of the great diplomats of the nineteenth century. Convinced that Italy could never hope to win her liberty without foreign aid, he sought the friendship of the great liberal powers, England and France. Napoleon III was especially well disposed toward Italian unity, because as a boy, while visiting his father, the ex-King of Holland, in Italy, he had taken, it is said, the oath of the *Carbonari*, and thus allied himself for life with the cause of liberal Italy. In the Crimean War Cavour offered troops to France and England ; and although Sardinia drew no territorial advantage from the war, yet she won the fellowship of two great powers, and raised the reputation of Italian troops in the eyes of Europe ; and at the Congress of Paris, which established the conditions of peace at the close of the war, Cavour succeeded in bringing the Italian question before the attention of the world.

England refused to intervene, and the fate of Italy depended on the will of Napoleon. Cavour's influence over the Emperor was great, but Napoleon hesitated to involve his Empire in a costly war, from which no great advantage could accrue to France. The attempt of the Italian, Orsini, against the Emperor's life (January 16, 1858), and a letter, in which Orsini told Napoleon that his life was forfeit as a recreant *Carbonaro*, may have turned the scale. Cavour was summoned to an interview at Plombières (July, 1858), and there the conditions of French aid were arranged. Napoleon was to deliver Lombardy and Venetia, and to receive for his reward Savoy and Nice. The warlike preparations of France and Sardinia alarmed Austria ; she sent to demand explanations ; they were refused, and war was declared.

The War of 1859-60.

It was a war of absolutism against the liberal elements of Europe. Against Austria were arrayed, not only France and Sardinia, but all Italian patriots, Freemasons and Republicans. Garibaldi and his volunteers fought beside the regular army of Sardinia. The Austrians were defeated at Montebello and Magenta, and driven out of Lombardy ; coming back to the attack they were checked at Solferino (June 24th). All at once Napoleon stopped and began to negotiate for peace ; he dared go no farther. The battles of Magenta and Solferino had set France to counting the cost, and dangerously strengthened the clerical opposition to his Italian policy. Prussia was mobilizing her troops on the French frontier. The Peace of Zürich November 10, 1859, freed Lombardy, which was annexed to the Kingdom of Sardinia, but left Venetia in Austrian hands. Cavour, in despair, resigned. Napoleon, although he had not "freed Italy as far as the Adriatic," insisted on his pay, Savoy and Nice. He could not do otherwise ; France was at his back, demanding the price of Magenta and Solferino, the immense loss of men and treasure. But Italy never forgave her liberators for their hard bargain.

GARIBALDI.

The central states came of their own accord to Sardinia ; Tuscany, Modena, Parma, and the papal province of Romagna rose against their rulers and annexed themselves to the kingdom of Victor Emmanuel. The south of Italy was smoldering with revolution, and needed only a spark to set it into flames. Sardinia dared not interfere, lest Europe should interpose a hand ; but Garibaldi, secretly aided by Cavour (who had resumed his post in January, 1860), organized his "Marsala Thousand," and invaded Sicily. Garibaldi defeated the Neapolitan troops at Milazzo, freed Sicily, crossed to the mainland and entered Naples, while King Francis II fled to Gaëta (September 6,

The Kingdom of Italy..

1860). Garibaldi now prepared to march on Rome, and Cavour, seeking to forestall French or Austrian intervention, moved Sardinian troops into the northern provinces of the pope, under pretext of checking the advance of Garibaldi. The pope was reduced to the possession of Rome itself; Garibaldi yielded to Victor Emmanuel and the union of Sicily and Naples with Sardinia was accomplished. The first Italian parliament, meeting at Turin in February, 1861, proclaimed Victor Emmanuel King of Italy by the grace of God and the will of the people. The Sardinian liberal Constitution of 1848 was adopted for Italy, and Florence chosen as the capital.

VICTOR EMMANUEL III.

In this manner Italy, under the dynasty of Savoy, by republicans and monarchists, working together, and with the aid of France, was welded into a united state. But Italy was not yet complete. Venetia was still in the hands of Austria, and Rome, the traditional center of Italy, was still lacking to the kingdom. Garibaldi sought to make his work complete by adding Rome; but he was checked by the troops of the king at Aspromonte and wounded (August, 1862). It seems pathetic, after his great work for unity, that this should happen; but his judgment was at fault; Rome was the one spot that Italy dare not touch. France and the Catholic powers were pledged to the preservation of the pope's temporal power. In 1866 the Austro-Prussian War gave Venetia to Italy; and finally, in 1870, when the Second Empire fell, France recalled her troops from Rome, and the Italian forces, through a breach in the wall, to signify that Rome was

Completion of Italy.

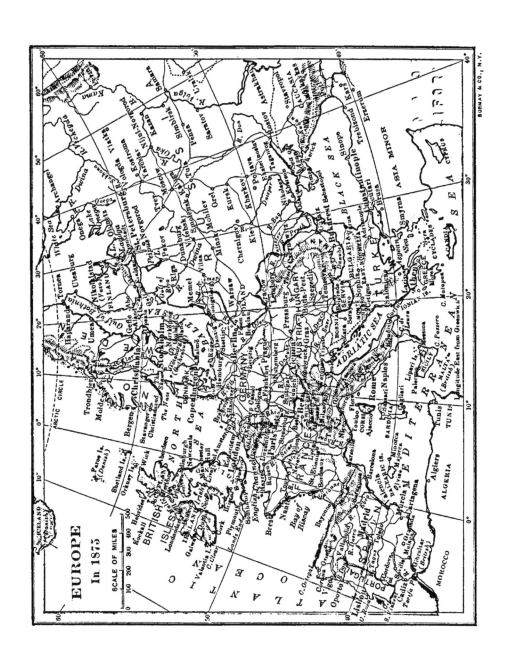

EUROPE
In 1875

SCALE OF MILES
0   100   200   300   400   500

taken by force, entered the city. The Romans voted for annexation, 130,000 against 1,500. The papacy was deprived of temporal power, and to this day has never recognized the government of Italy. The capital of Italy was established at Rome.

Thus was created the new kingdom of Italy, by Cavour and Garibaldi, aided by Napoleon III. The history of Italy since 1870 has been uneventful. Drifting away from France, she joined the Triple Alliance with Germany and Austria. This has involved a heavy burden of expense for the army and navy, which has been a serious drain upon Italy's slender finances. Aspiring to a part in the world's work, Italy sought to establish colonies in East Africa (Erythræa); but her efforts were unsuccessful.

SOURCE REVIEW

I. Count Cavour: His Devotion to Italy.—"Many generals have passed terrible hours on the field of battle; but he passed more terrible ones in his cabinet, when his enormous work might suffer destruction at any moment, like a fragile edifice at the tremor of an earthquake. Hours, nights of struggle and anguish did he pass, sufficient to make him issue from it with reason distorted and death in his heart. And it was this gigantic and stormy work which shortened his life by twenty years. Nevertheless, devoured by the fever which was to cast him into his grave, he yet contended desperately with the malady in order to accomplish something for his country. 'It is strange,' he said sadly on his death-bed, 'I no longer know how to read; I can no longer read.'

"While they were bleeding him, and the fever was increasing, he was thinking of his country, and he said, imperiously: 'Cure me; my mind is clouding over; I have need of all my faculties to manage important affairs.' When he was already reduced to extremities, and the whole city was in a tumult, and the king stood at his bedside, he said, anxiously, 'I have many things to say to you, Sire, many things to show you ; but I am ill ; I cannot, I cannot ; ' and he was in despair.

"And his feverish thoughts hovered ever round the State, round the new Italian provinces which had been united with us, round the many things which still remained to be done. When delirium seized him, 'Educate the children!' he exclaimed, between his gasps for breath, '—educate the children and the young people—govern with liberty!'"—Edmondo de Amicis : *Cuore.*

II. Garibaldi, the Patriot. —"Garibaldi died last night (June 2, 1881). Do you know who he is? He is the man who liberated ten millions of Italians from the tyranny of the Bourbons. He died at the age of seventy-five. He was born at Nice, the son of a ship captain. At eight years of age he saved a woman's life; at thirteen, he dragged into safety a boatload of his companions who were shipwrecked; at twenty-seven he rescued from the water at Marseilles a drowning youth; at forty-one, he saved a ship from burning on the ocean. He fought for ten years in America for the liberties of a strange people; he fought in three wars against the Austrians, for the liberation of Lombardy and Trentino; he defended Rome from the French in 1849; he delivered Naples and Palermo in 1860; he fought again for Rome in 1867 ; he combated with the Germans in defense of France in 1870. He was possessed of the flame of heroism and the genius of war. He was engaged in forty battles, and won thirty-seven of them.

"When he was not fighting, he was laboring for his living, or he shut himself up in a solitary island, and tilled the soil. He was teacher, sailor, workman, trader, soldier, general, dictator. He was simple, great, and good. He hated all oppressors, he loved all peoples, he protected all the weak; he had no other aspiration than good, he refused honors, he scorned death, he adored Italy. When he uttered his war-cry, legions of valorous men hastened to him from all quarters; gentlemen left their palaces, workmen their ships, youths their schools, to go and fight in the sunshine of his glory. In time of war he wore a red shirt. He was strong, blond, and handsome. On the field of battle he was a thunderbolt, in his affections he was a child, in affliction a saint.

Thousands of Italians have died for their country, happy, if, when dying, they saw him pass victorious in the distance; thousands would have allowed themselves to be killed for him; millions have blessed him and will bless him."—*Cuore*.

REFERENCES

Judson: *Europe in the Nineteenth Century*, Chapter XIV; Alison Phillips: *Modern Europe*, pp. 356–484 passim.

CHAPTER XV

Russia and the Eastern Question

§ 42. THE RUSSIAN EMPIRE FROM 1814

THE Russian Empire in Europe was already in its present form in 1814, and was by far the largest of the European states. It had come to be a factor in the political life of Europe at this time, although its internal history scarcely reflects the great political and social changes that were going on in Europe. It is the policy of Russia toward the other powers with which it has come in contact that constitutes the important part of Russian history in the nineteenth century.

The foreign policy of Russia.

Russia is also a conglomeration of peoples; but, unlike Austria, Russia controls her subject nations, and is not controlled by them. This is due to the fact that Russia contains so large a nucleus of Muscovite Slavs, who are the dominant race, and their supremacy has been sustained by the absolutism of their Tsars. Instead of yielding to racial decentralization, as Austria has been obliged to do, Russia has pursued a rigid policy of Russianization, against the Germans of the Baltic provinces, the Lithuanians and Poles of the West, the Cossacks and Asiatic tribes of the South, and, last of all, the Finns of the North. Each one of these non-Muscovite elements is too small to offer serious resistance, and too isolated from other subject nationalities to effect a union for defense.

Russia, like Austria, has its race questions.

Alexander I was the most liberal of the Tsars. This he owed to his education, which was superintended by

250

THE KREMLIN, MOSCOW.

Laharpe, a liberal of the French school. When Napoleon I had been defeated, and the allies assembled at Paris

Alexander I.

to divide the spoils, it was the influence of Alexander that saved France from the fury of the English and Germans, and secured for her the liberal Charter of 1814. Later, at the Congress of Vienna, Alexander disclosed his cherished hope, to solve with general satisfaction the Polish problem. He wished to acquire the whole of ancient Poland ; then grant to the Poles a separate constitution, making the crown of Poland distinct and separate from the imperial Russian crown. His effort to acquire Prussian Poland was thwarted by Talleyrand ; but Alexander carried out his Polish policy in the Polish provinces of Russia, and the Kingdom of Poland was re-established in 1815, with a constitution, securing to the Poles a native administration, with a partially elective legislature ; a greater degree of political liberty than was possessed at that time by any other people in central Europe.

The system, however, did not become popular in Poland. Secret societies, copied from the *Carbonari*, even plotted against the Tsar's life. Alexander became discouraged with his experiments in liberalism, and after 1818 became converted to the views of Metternich. A religious mysticism veiled the closing years of his life, and he died in 1825 on the coast of the Black Sea, conscious of the failure of his early hopes. His younger brother, Nicholas, who succeeded to the throne, put down the Poles with an iron hand, abolished the Charter of 1815, and gave Poland a Russian governor. "Poland shall henceforth be a part of the Empire," he said, "and form one nation with Russia."

Nicholas had none of the sympathy with liberalism which formed so large a part of his brother's character. He abhorred constitutions and hated western ideas. His policy was to shut out Russia from the west, which was, perhaps, the better policy for Russia. Up to this time Russian life had been an Asiatic travesty of western European ideas and customs ; the policy of Nicholas called forth a Russian literature and national sentiment, and promised Russia an indigenous development. Although Nicholas withdrew Russia from the leadership of Metternich, yet he had no sympathy with revolutions. When the Hungarians were struggling against Austria in 1849, it was with willingness that Nicholas sent a Russian army to crush them.

Nicholas I.

In 1848 Nicholas, confident of the strength of his army, thought the time had arrived for the conquest of the Ottoman Empire. He looked upon Turkey as already in the throes of dissolution. To the English ambassador he suggested in 1852 that, as the "Sick Man" at Constantinople was about to die, England and Russia "ought to agree about the funeral." Finding an opportunity for intervention in the quarrels of Roman and Greek monks about the Holy Sepulchre, Nicholas advanced his army into Turkey, coming as the protector of the Orthodox (Greek) Church. To his surprise he had to meet the combined armies of England, France, and Sardinia, which were prepared to defend the integrity of the Ottoman Empire. The war was carried into the Crimea (1854), and Nicholas, defeated by the western powers he affected to despise, died broken-hearted.

The Crimean War.

Alexander, son of Nicholas, reversed his father's restrictive policy, and entered upon a career of reform. The great act of his reign was the abolition of serfdom. The peasants, bound by law to the soil, paid dues to the proprietor of the land, labored in his fields, and obeyed him as their master. There were forty-six millions of the unfree, half of them on crown lands. By the Emancipation act of 1861 all serfs were freed. They were given parcels of land, on payment of an annual rental, and at any time they might become proprietors of the land

Alexander II.

by the payment of a fixed sum. The government stood ready to advance the purchase money, to be repaid in installments. In addition to the emancipation of serfs, Alexander introduced other reforms : local assemblies (*Zemstvos*), public schools after the western model, and a reorganization of the army on the Prussian plan.

ALEXANDER II, LIBERATOR OF THE SERFS.

But a constitution Alexander would not grant; and with the growth of political discussion which his reign permitted, there rose up against him a great secret association of terrorists, recruited largely from the student class, whose object was the destruction of the absolutist system. Persecuted by the secret police, the " Nihilists " resolved upon the death of the Tsar, and, after three unsuccessful attempts, succeeded in March, 1881. His son, Alexander III, turned by this event from the reform policy of his father, restored the despotism of Nicholas I. The press was muzzled, the land filled with spies, and Siberia became the fate of suspected persons. The policy of Russianization was continued by Alexander III, and the aim of the Empire to-day is to make the Russian language and the Russian church sole and supreme throughout the land. For this

NICHOLAS II.

reason the Jews have been persecuted, and the condition of their residence in Russia made intolerable. The Grand

Duchy of Finland was the last country to be Russianized. Unmindful of his coronation oath, the Tsar, who had sworn to preserve the constitutional liberty of the Grand Duchy, began there also the policy of Russianization. Nicholas II, who succeeded Alexander III in 1894, continues the policy of the first Nicholas. Russia stands in much the same position as France in 1789, in respect to her political and economic problems ; with a population, however, much less enlightened and advanced. Her modern period is yet to come, and her rulers hope, by excluding western influences, and keeping Russia close in the fold of the Orthodox Church, to direct her development along a path which shall avoid those pitfalls into which, in their estimation, western Europe has stumbled.

SOURCE REVIEW

Russian Students as Revolutionists.—Of late years Russian university students have been prominent in the reports of political and socialistic agitation. The government has been obliged at times to close the universities on this account. The following extract attempts to account for this phenomenon : " For some time past the disturbed condition of the student world, especially in the universities and theological seminaries, has caused the government no little anxiety. For several reasons the Russian students of both sexes are far more inclined to revolutionary ideas than those of almost any other European nation. Conscious of the backwardness of their own country, the susceptible nature of the Slav leads the younger generation to seek a remedy for this reproach by adopting what they believe to be the very latest and most advanced theories of modern civilization. Besides this, a large proportion of the students are in a state of poverty, almost of destitution, which renders them yet more disposed to give free play to their imaginations, and build up society anew upon a system in which hunger and cold and suffering shall be abolished forever.

" When the universities were thrown open to all classes of

society a vast number of scholarships were founded for the support of indigent students.   The Emperor Alexander II gave half a million rubles to the university of St. Petersburg for this purpose, and his example was at once followed by an immense number of private persons.   As a result of this well-meant munificence nearly two-thirds of the students in the universities are now dependent upon Government or private subsidies, but these are generally so small in amount as hardly to suffice for even the barest necessaries of life.   Quite recently, in several of the universities, many of the students were unable to leave their lodgings to attend the classes for weeks at a time, as in their ill-clad and shoeless condition they dared not face the cold of a Russian winter.   Male and female students crowd together in the cheapest lodgings that they can find, while their families, generally living far away in some remote corner of rural Russia, are unable to exercise any wholesome influence to counteract the atmosphere of discontent and suffering and wild dreams of a 'Social Reformation' that their condition almost necessarily creates around them.   It is hardly surprising that in the days of Nihilism nearly all the revolutionists condemned for political offenses had received 'superior instruction' and only one per cent were illiterate."
—Palmer : *Russian Life in Town and Country.*

REFERENCES

Alison Phillips : *Modern Europe*, pp. 339–360 (for Crimean War) ; Judson: *Europe in the Nineteenth Century*, Chapter XXII.

§ 43.   THE EASTERN QUESTION

The Ottoman Empire, founded at the close of the Middle Ages by a Turkish dynasty, retained in 1814 an immense territory.   In Asia there was Asia Minor, Syria, the Euphrates country up to Persia,   and the suzerainty of Arabia; in Africa, Egypt and the northern coast of Africa to Morocco ; in Europe, the whole of the Balkan peninsula, and north of the Danube the principalities of Moldavia and

The Ottoman Empire.

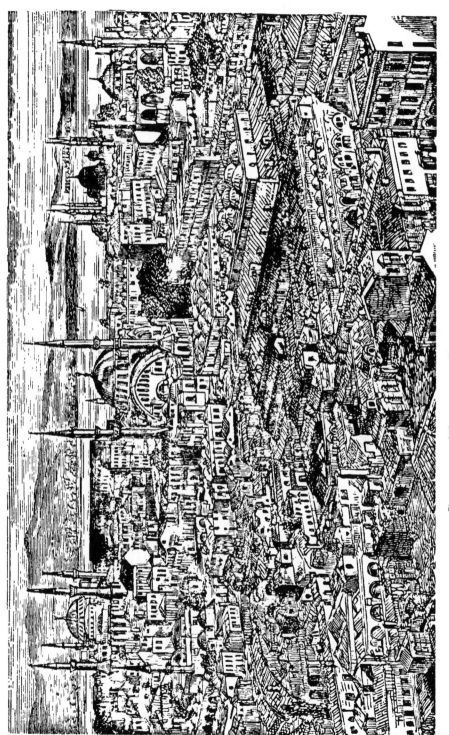

GENERAL VIEW OF CONSTANTINOPLE.

Wallachia. The empire, however, although vast, verged on ruin. The task of the Turk in Europe was impossible. An arbitrary government, without method in administration, seeking its law, religious, civil, and political, in the Koran, its existence was based upon the ignorance of its subject peoples. Intelligence and the knowledge of liberty, as it progressed across Central Europe, was certain to bring about the dismemberment of Turkey.

Whoever became a Mussulman, no matter what his origin—Greek, Croat, or Albanian—became a Turk, and *The Turkish nation included only Mussulmans.* was entitled to all the privileges of the original founders of the empire. The Koran permitted no inequality amongst believers. Society in the Ottoman Empire was divided, therefore, into two great classes, Mussulmans and *raias*, as the subject Christian peoples were called. All offices of whatever class, civil or military, were held by Mussulmans; the *raias* retained their languages, their customs, their clergy, and their village administration; they paid a special head-tax, due from infidels, and were at the mercy of the unsalaried, rapacious officials of the Sultan.

In Asia the *raias* were relatively few and scattered—Greeks, Jews, and Armenians; but in Europe the Turks were in the minority, holding by force great groups of conquered peoples. North of the Danube were the Roumanians, occupying the principalities of Moldavia and Wallachia, governed by Greek governors appointed by the Sultan. South of the great river were the Serbs, a race of peasants with Turkish lords; farther to the south and west the Bosniaks and Albanians, partly Christian, partly of the Moslem faith; and on the east, occupying both slopes of the Balkan Mountains, the Bulgarians, in the three provinces, Bulgaria, Roumelia, and part of Macedonia. South of the Bulgarians were the Greeks, inhabiting the extremity of the peninsula and the adjacent islands.

The position of the Sultan was that of a stranger in Europe—a conqueror encamped on the shores of the Bosphorus. When the Christian sovereigns of Europe came together to discuss and arrange matters of importance to all Europe, the Sultan did not form one of the council. At the Congress of Vienna, Turkey first came into the field of general European politics. Austria, extending the policy of Metternich to all Europe, asked the Congress to guarantee to the Sultan the integrity of his possessions. This Russia refused to do; but since all the Powers were more or less interested in the fate of Turkey, it was agreed that all must be consulted in the disposition of her affairs. Thus the Eastern Question was born, in 1815. The "Question" was this: Should the Turkish Empire be preserved intact; or, if dismembered, what disposition should be made of its territories? But the rivalry of the states kept the Turkish power erect in Europe. The policy of Russia was to push southward, and seek an outlet in the Mediterranean; the policy of the other Powers was to prevent her, and to preserve the "balance of power" in Europe. England in particular feared the extension of Russia to the southward, as threatening her possessions in India.

The Eastern Question.

But while the European concert tended to protect the Turk in Europe, his power was threatened from another source. Up to 1821 the danger was from without; later it came from within. The awakening of a sense of national consciousness in Greece led to revolt, and the Greek insurgents appealed to the Christian states for aid against the Turk. Metternich sought to restrain the Russian Tsar, while Turkish soldiers massacred the inhabitants of the Greek Isles, and the Sultan hanged the Greek Patriarch, with three archbishops, in the doorway of their church. But liberal Europe was particularly attracted to the cause of the descendants of the ancient Greeks; Philhellenic socie-

Beginning of dismemberment.

ties were formed, and step by step statesmen were brought around by the force of public opinion. England joined with Russia in negotiations with the Porte for the independence of the Greeks. This the Sultan refused, and the two powers, allying with them France, proceeded to intervene; a Russian army forced the Porte to terms, and Greece

THE TURKISH EMPIRE IN EUROPE.

was made free. Thus through the force of public sentiment the concert of the powers was overthrown and the integrity of Turkey violated.

In 1852 the question rose again, when Nicholas sought to settle the affairs of the "Sick Man of Europe." The Congress of Paris, which followed the defeat of Russia in the Crimea, defended the Turkish Empire against the further spoliation, closed the Black Sea to ships of war, declared the Danube a neutral river, and guaranteed again the integrity of Turkey. In return, the Sultan promised reforms and a mild government for his Christian subjects. But it was in vain ; it was impossible for the Turks to look upon the Christians as their equals before the law. " The doctrine of the Koran draws an indelible line between Turks and Christians ; equality before the law will remain a dream in Turkey." This project of the Powers, however sincerely entertained, was no solution of the problem ; that was to come in the dismemberment of the empire, and the political separation of the Christians from the Mussulmans.

Twenty years later events occurred which made the policy of the Powers untenable. In 1876, while the insur-

The break-up of the empire.

gent mountaineers of Herzogovina were holding the attention of the Turkish army, the Bulgarians rose in arms and declared themselves independent. The Sultan sent against them the *Bashi-bazouks*, irregular volunteers, serving for the opportunity of plunder, who destroyed a hundred villages, massacred 30,000 inhabitants, and carried off 12,000 women into slavery. The " Bulgarian Atrocities " aroused the indignation of Europe ; the Powers dared no longer attempt the defense of the Turkish Empire. Servia entered the war in July and Russia followed with the invasion of Turkey in the name of the persecuted Christians. The Turks fought with valor, but were overcome, and Constantinople lay in the grasp of Russia (Peace of San Stefano, March 3, 1878). Here the Powers intervened, however, and the Congress of Berlin (June 13–July 13, 1878) arranged the final conditions of peace. The Sultan recognized the complete independence of the Christian states of Roumania, Servia, and Montenegro. Bulgaria, between the Danube and the Balkans, was erected into a

Christian principality, subject to Turkish suzerainty.   Of
the other Bulgarian states Roumelia was to be allowed a
certain amount of self-government, enough to make the
condition of her Christian population tolerable, with a
Christian governor appointed by the Sultan.   Greece was
given Thessaly, and Austria was invited to occupy the
provinces of Bosnia and Herzegovina.   The introduction
of Austria into the Balkan Peninsula was intended as a
check to Russian influence.   Russia, as the material reward of her victory, received an addition to her Asiatic

territory on the south shore of the
Black Sea ; while England, as protector of Turkey, received the gift
of Cyprus.

Thus Turkey in Europe was almost wholly torn from the Sultan's
grasp.   There remained to him the
Mussulman lands of Albania and
the province of Constantinople ; of
Christian subjects, the Bulgarian
and other Christian nationalities of
Macedonia, and the Greeks of the
province of Salonika.   The Christian
countries of the Turkish Empire in

ABDUL HAMID, SULTAN
OF TURKEY.

Europe have become independent states, as before the
Ottoman conquest ; and the Eastern Question is in a fair
way to solve itself, in spite of the diplomats of Europe.

SOURCE REVIEW

Synopsis of the Treaty of Berlin.—"(1) Bosnia, including
Herzegovina, was assigned to Austria for permanent occupation.   Thus Turkey lost a great province of nearly 1,250,000
inhabitants.   Of these about 500,000 were Christians of the
Greek Church, 450,000 were Mohammedans, mainly in the
towns, who offered a stout resistance to the Austrian troops,
and 250,000 Roman Catholics.   By the occupation of the Novi

General View of the Acropolis at the Present Day.

(From a recent photograph.)

Bazar district Austria wedged in her forces between Montenegro and Servia, and was also able to keep watch over the turbulent province of Macedonia. (2) Montenegro received less than the San Stephano terms had promised her, but received the seaports of Antivari and Dulcigno. It needed a demonstration of the European fleets off the latter port to make the Turks yield Dulcigno to the Montenegrins (who alone of all the Christian races of the peninsula had never been conquered by the Turks). (3) Servia was proclaimed an independent principality (became a kingdom in 1881). (4) Roumania also gained her independence and ceased to pay any tribute to the Porte, but had to give to her Russian benefactors the slice acquired from Russia in 1856 between the Pruth and the northern mouth of the Danube. In return for this sacrifice she gained the large but marshy Dorbrudscha district from Bulgaria, and so acquired the port of Kustendje on the Black Sea. (5) Bulgaria, which according to the San Stephano terms, would have been an independent state as large as Roumania, was by the Berlin Treaty subjected to the suzerainty of the Sultan, divided into two parts, and confined within much narrower limits. Turkey was allowed to occupy the passes of the Balkans in time of war." J. H. Rose : *A Century of Continental History.*

REFERENCES

Judson : *Europe in the Nineteenth Century*, Chapters XXIV, XXV; Alison Phillips : *Modern Europe*, Chapter XIX (for Treaty of Berlin).

§ 44. GREECE

The ancient Greek nation, overrun by Slavs and Albanians during the Middle Ages, fell into the hands of the Turks and shared the general fate of the Balkan Christians. Under the dominion of the Turks the Slavs and Albanians dwelling in Greece were Hellenized, and little by little there was formed a hybrid nation, speaking the Greek tongue and occupying the territories of ancient Greece. Outside of Greece men of Greek extraction were scattered through the Turkish

Under Turkish rule.

Empire; in Constantinople they occupied a quarter of the city, called the Phanar, whence they received the name of "Phanariots." A sharp, shrewd race, equal to the Jews as traders, they largely controlled the commerce of the Danube, and were found in the ports of the Adriatic and even as far west as Leghorn and Marseilles.

During the French Revolution and the Napoleonic wars Greek sailors, under the neutral Turkish flag, drove a thriving trade in the Mediterranean, carrying Russian grain from Odessa to the ports of western Europe. In 1816 they possessed a fleet of 600 vessels with 17,000 sailors. These Greek sailors inhabited three barren rocks, called the Nautical Isles—Hydra, Spezzia, and Psara—facing the Gulf of Argolis. There they lived in three little republics, tributary to the Sultan. Their vessels were armed with cannon, for defense against the Barbary pirates. The general peace of 1814 put an end to their trade and made them ready for adventure of any sort. On the mainland bands of mountaineers, half brigands, lived in defiance of the Turkish authorities.

The contact with western nations roused the national spirit of the Greeks. Merchants, grown rich in trade, established schools at Bucharest, Corfu, and Constantinople. The Greek language, debased with foreign elements, began to be studied in its classical form, and a consciousness of the ancient grandeur of their race spurred the educated Greeks toward a resurrection of their national life. The revolt against Turkish rule took place at the same time in the Morea, in Epirus, and among the Danubian Greeks of Roumania. In the north the insurgents were soon suppressed, but in the Morea they were more successful, and drove out the Turks. A brutal war ensued, which lasted for four years. To make matters worse, the Greek revolutionists quarreled among themselves, and civil war was added to the horrors of Turkish invasion. At length, in 1825, the Sultan called

Struggle for independence, 1821-1829.

upon his vassal, Ibrahim Pasha, Viceroy of Egypt, for aid. Two armies invaded Greece : a Turkish army from the north, while troops from the Egyptian fleet landed in the south and devastated the Morea with fire and sword, until Greece was again in Turkish hands.

But the Powers came to the rescue. England and France, driven by the force of public opinion, joined with Russia, whose motive was to rescue her brethren of the Greek Church from the hands of the infidels. The Powers projected a naval demonstration to compel Ibrahim Pasha to withdraw. A mixed fleet under the command of an English admiral took possession of the harbor of Navarino, where the Egyptian fleet was at anchor. The bitter feeling between Christian and Mohammedan sailors led to hostilities which were not intended ; a shot from an Egyptian gunboat brought about the battle of Navarino (October 20, 1827), in which the Egyptian fleet was destroyed. The Sultan demanded an indemnity, which was refused ; and after fruitless negotiations an English fleet, threatening Constantinople, secured the recall of Ibrahim Pasha, while France sent an army into the Morea. Russia moved southward across the Danube, and, defeating the Turks in Bulgaria, approached Constantinople. The peace of Adrianople (1829) granted the independence of Greece within narrow limits, stripped of Thessaly and Crete, a poverty-stricken state of 750,000 souls.

Capodistrias, a Greek, who had been in the Russian service, was chosen President in 1827. He fell a victim to local jealousies and was murdered four years later.
Kingdom of Greece. Meanwhile the Powers had been seeking a foreign king for Greece. Leopold of Saxe-Coburg, who subsequently became King of Belgium, refused the honor. In 1832 Prince Otto, of Bavaria, was chosen king. He brought with him Bavarian advisers, and put the army into German uniform. As a Catholic and a German he failed to make himself popular with his new subjects, but succeeded fairly

well in organizing the government and introducing institutions of western Europe, such as the University of Athens in 1836, and a national bank in 1841.   In 1843 the Greek soldiers rose against the king, a National Assembly was called, and the king was compelled to accept a constitution, with a ministry responsible to a Chamber of Deputies chosen by universal suffrage.   But Otto continued unpopular, and a revolution in 1862 drove him from the throne. Prince George of Denmark, the English candidate, was chosen king in the following year, and England turned over to Greece the Ionian Islands, held by England since the Congress of Vienna.

The Constitution of 1864 abolished the Senate established by the Constitution of 1843, and gave

Modern Greece.

the whole parliamentary power to the *Boulé* or National Assembly, elected by universal suffrage. Since then the history of Greece has largely consisted of repeated attempts to add to the Greek kingdom those parts of Turkey which are Greek in population. Through the good offices

GEORGE I. OF GREECE.

of France and England, Thessaly and a part of Epirus were added in 1881, a delayed result of the rearrangement of the Turkish Empire by the Treaty of Berlin.   The Greeks were yet unsatisfied.   The island of Crete revolted against Turkish dominion in 1896, but its union with Greece was prevented by the Powers.   In 1897 Greece declared war against Turkey, and was defeated by the Turkish army, which had been reorganized under the direction of military experts loaned by the Emperor of Germany.

Greece has been made possible by the sympathy of Europe, and the ancient traditions of her name.   The enthusiasm which accompanied her resurrection has been only partially justified by her progress as a nation. Her extension northward is checked by the growth of the Slavic states, Servia and Bulgaria, and by the entrance of Austria into the Balkan peninsula. But Greece is growing in wealth, and her population includes 2,200,000 out of a total eight millions of Greek-speaking people.

SOURCE REVIEW

Execution of the Patriarch: An Episode of the Greek Revolution (see § 43).—"While the new patriarch was assuming the insignia of his official rank the deposed patriarch was led to execution. He was hung from the lintel of the gate of the patriarchate, with a *fetva*, or sentence of condemnation, pinned to his breast.[1] The old man met death with dignified courage and pious resignation. His conscience was at ease, for he believed that he had fulfilled his duty as a Christian priest by concealing from an infidel sovereign the existence of an orthodox conspiracy, of which he may have obtained detailed information only in the confessional. In the evening the grand-vizier, Benderli Ali, walked through the streets of the Phanar, attended by a single *tchaous*. On reaching the gate of the patriarchate, he called for a stool, and sat down for a few moments, looking calmly at the body hanging before him. He then rose and walked away without uttering a word. Ottoman justice is deeply imbued with the principle that men in high office are hostages to the Sultan for order in his dominions and that they ought to expiate crimes of the people which are attributable to their neglect.

"The body of Gregorios remained publicly exposed for three days. It was then delivered to the Jews to be dragged through the streets and cast into the sea. This odious task is rendered a source of horrid gratification to the Jew-

---

[1] The patriarch (head of the Greek Church) was accused of concealing knowledge of the plots of Greek revolutionists. It was held that as official of the Sultan (by whom he was appointed) he was in duty bound to disclose such knowledge to the Turkish authorities.

VIEW IN FRANKFORT-ON-THE-MAIN.

ish rabble at Constantinople, by the intense hatred which prevails between the Greeks and the Jews throughout the East. The orthodox, who regarded Gregorios as a martyr, watched the body, and at night it was taken out of the water and conveyed in an Ionian vessel to Odessa, where the Russian authorities welcomed it as a holy relic, which the waters had miraculously cast up to strengthen the faith, perhaps to animate the bigotry, of the Sultan's enemies. The body was interred with magnificent ecclesiastical ceremonies and much military pomp."—Finlay : *History of Greece*.

REFERENCES

Alison Phillips: *Modern Europe*, pp. 114–168; Judson: *Europe in the Nineteenth Century*, pp. 260–263 ; 278–281.

§ 45.   THE DANUBIAN STATES

Of the Danubian states which formed at one time a part of the Turkish Empire, Roumania was least affected

Roumania.

by Ottoman dominion, on account of her remoteness from the center of Turkish power. Modern Roumania is made up of two states which formerly existed as the principalities of Wallachia and Moldavia, tributary to the Porte. Wallachia lay between the Danube and the Carpathians ; Moldavia between the Carpathians and the Black Sea. At the beginning of the nineteenth century they were governed by *Hospodars*, governors selected by the Sultan from the *Phanariots* of Constantinople. In 1834, through the intervention of Russia, they were permitted to choose their own *Hospodars*.

The Roumanians, as their name implies, are traditionally of Roman origin. They claim to be descended from the colonists settled by the Roman Emperor Trajan upon the Danube. Their speech is a Romance tongue, related to French, Spanish, and Italian ; in religion they are adherents of the Orthodox church. The population in 1834 consisted of peasants, who tilled the plains, and land-owning nobles, who lived in the cities, Bucharest and Jassy. The peasants were abject serfs ; the nobles, influenced by their supposed common origin with the French, imitated in a rude way the customs of Paris.

The Treaty of Paris (1856), which terminated the Crimean War, placed the principalities under the protection of the Powers. . Their union, which was

Formation of Roumania.

forbidden by the Sultan, was effected in 1859, when a Moldavian noble, Couza, elected *Hospodar* in both principalities, took the title of Alexander I, "Prince of Roumania," and called a National Assembly at Bucharest, the capital. The servile peasantry were made proprietors in 1864, buying the interest of the nobles in their holdings by means of fifteen annual instalments.

CHARLES I, KING OF ROUMANIA.

Alexander was the victim of local jealousies, and was forced to resign in 1866. Convinced that the nobles would never endure the rule

A foreign king.

of a native prince, the Roumanians chose a Catholic German prince, Charles of Hohenzollern, who came to the throne as Charles I, and still reigns. Under his able constitutional rule the kingdom has prospered. The army was reorganized after the German model, and co-operated with the Russians against the Turks in the war of 1877–78. The war made Roumania a sovereign state, obtaining from the Sultan a formal recognition of her independence. Charles took the title of king in 1881.

The problem of Roumania, apart from her industrial development, is to extend her borders to include the whole of the Roumanian nation. Apart from the subjects of

King Charles, there are over three millions of Roumanians in adjacent states, of whom two millions and a half are in the Kingdom of Hungary.

Servia is called the "Peasant Nation." Its ancient native aristocracy was lost in the conquest by the Turks, and replaced with Mussulmans, who settled as conquerors in the country. The industry of Servia was swine-raising, and such prominent individuals as there were among the native Serbs at the beginning of the nineteenth century had arrived at distinction through success in this industry. The two families about which the history of Servia revolves were of this character: the Karageorgewitches, taking their origin from Kara Georges (Black George), a heroic leader of the Serbs against the Turks in the early years of the century; and the Obrenowitches, who furnished the first modern prince of Servia.

Servia.

Kara Georges, worsted by the Turks, fled to Austria. His rival, Milosh Obrenowitch, pursued a different policy, bowing to Turkish authority, and received from Constantinople the title of "Prince of the Serbs of the Pashalik of Belgrade." In 1830 he was made hereditary prince, and the Turkish garrisons removed from Servia. Thus Servia was formed, as yet a dependency of Turkey, but self-governing. Meanwhile Milosh had murdered his rival, Kara Georges, who returned from Austria in 1818. In 1837 Russia and the Sultan, listening to complaints of Milosh's absolutism, imposed upon him a ministry, who asked him for an accounting of the national funds, whereupon he abdicated in favor of his son, angry at such questioning of his authority. Three years later a revolt drove the Obrenowitches from the throne, and seated there a son of Kara Georges, Alexander. He in turn was driven out in 1859, and the Obrenowitches returned to power. These rapid changes of dynasty reflect the intrigues of the two great powers, Russia and Austria, each seeking to make good its

The two dynasties.

influence in Servia.   In 1868 Milan Obrenowitch, educated
at Paris, came to the throne, and in the following year a
constitution was adopted, and an attempt made to introduce a western form of government.   The *Skouptchina*,
an ancient assembly of heads of families, was made into
an elective parliament.

In 1876, excited by the revolt of Christians in Herzegovina, Servia declared war against Turkey.   Conquered
Kingdom of Servia. and overrun, she was saved by European intervention ; but during the Russian inva-
sion of Turkey in 1877 Servia reopened the war.   The

ALEXANDER I, KING OF
SERVIA.

Peace of Berlin gave her greater
territory and complete independence ; but the establishment of
Austria in Herzegovina was a severe blow to the national aspiration, since it cut her off from the
hope of a larger Serbian union.
She saw a chance for Serbian expansion on the south.   There
Greeks, Serbs, and Bulgarians,
each looking to the establishment
of a great Balkan state, were in-
triguing to secure a paramount influence in the mixed provinces of
Roumelia and Macedonia, still sub-
ject to Constantinople.   When Roumelia chose for its governor the Prince of Bulgaria, thereby effecting a union with
Bulgaria, Servia rushed into war.   She was completely
beaten, and was happy when Europe intervened to stop
the victorious Bulgarians.   Thus for a time her schemes
for a greater Servia were checked.   Milan abdicated in
1889, and his son Alexander I, the reigning king, pre-
serves his throne with difficulty, leaning upon Austrian
influence, while Russia holds a Karageorgewitch in reserve.

The Montenegrins are the Swiss of the Balkans.   A

democracy of warriors, of Serbian blood, although nominally subject to Turkey, they were governed by a family,
succeeding from uncle to nephew, under the title of Prince-Bishop (*Vladika*). In

Montenegro (Italian for Tchernagora).

1851 Danilo dropped the episcopal title, married, and founded a dynasty. He was succeeded by his nephew, Nikita. Montenegro has been in continual struggle with the Turks, looking to Russia as her protector. In 1878 her territory was made independent, and a seaport added on the Adriatic (Dulcigno). The sovereign is absolute, with a Council of State, half appointed by himself, half elective. A daughter of the Prince is now Queen of Italy.

The principality of Bulgaria was created by Russia, and accepted by the Congress of Berlin. As contemplated
by Russia, it comprised Bulgaria and Roumelia, almost wholly peopled by Bulgarians,

Bulgaria.

and Macedonia, a mixture of Bulgarians, Serbs, Greeks, and Wallachians (Roumanians). The Congress of Berlin cut it down to Bulgaria, which remained tributary to the Porte, with a prince, elected by the people and approved by the Sultan. Alexander of Battenberg, a German prince, was chosen. The constitution established a ministry and a single assembly, the *Sobranje*, elected by universal suffrage.

In 1885 Roumelia, desiring union with Bulgaria, revolted against its Turkish governor, and called for aid upon Prince Alexander. The Prince could not resist the desire of his subjects, took the title of " Prince of the Two Bulgarias," and occupied the province. The Powers protested, and Servia went to war. The Turkish Government finally accepted a compromise, and Alexander was appointed governor of Roumelia. In 1887 Alexander, refusing to submit his policy to Russian control, was surprised by conspirators, forced to resign, and hurried out of the country. In the absence of a prince, Stambouloff, president of the *Sobranje* (Bulgarian legislature), governed

19

the country. It was not an easy matter to find a prince ; but finally Ferdinand of Coburg, an officer in the Hungarian army, accepted the title, and was recognized by the Sultan. The agitation for the union of Macedonia is now the sensitive point of Bulgarian politics.

SOURCE REVIEW

" Carmen Sylva," **Queen of Roumania.**—"Prince Charles had occupied the Hospodarial throne of the United Principalities for a little more than three years and a half before he sought and obtained the hand of one of the most highly gifted and accomplished young ladies in Europe, the Princess Elizabeth of Wied. From the date of her arrival in the country of her adoption, Princess Elizabeth addressed herself to the difficult task of winning the hearts of her subjects, instinctively averse to and suspicious of foreign-born persons. She devoted several months of unremitting labor to the study of the Roumanian language, literature, legendary lore, and music. She and all the ladies of her court (at her instance) wore the national costume, setting an example of reaction against Paris fashions and extravagance which the great Boyarins could not but follow. She founded charitable institutions in the principal towns of both Principalities, reorganized the public hospitals, and was an unwearied visitor of the poor. She translated ballads, fables, and love-songs, and published them under the pseudonym of ' Carmen Sylva,' thus spreading the fame of Roumania's cherished bards far and wide throughout civilized Europe. Her gentle manners, engaging appearance, sweet disposition, and, above all, inexhaustible interest in the history, traditions, and customs of Roumania, rapidly effected the conquest of Trajan's rugged but warm-hearted descendants, and before she had been a year on the throne, ' *Marea Sa* ' (her Highness) had attained the summit of her ambition, an unexampled popularity in her brave and sagacious husband's realm."—Condensed from W. Beatty-Kingston : *Monarchs I Have Met.*

REFERENCES

Judson : *Europe in the Nineteenth Century,* Chapters XXIII, XXIV,

CHAPTER XVI

The Smaller States

§ 46. SPAIN AND PORTUGAL

WHILE the Spaniards were waging their war of liberation against Napoleon I, and their king, Ferdinand VII, was a prisoner in France, a liberal movement, stimulated by contact with French and English, took place in the peninsula. A Cortes, or National Assembly, chosen by universal suffrage, came together in 1811, and proclaiming the doctrine of the French Revolution that "Sovereignty is vested essentially in the nation," drew up the Constitution of 1812, a charter not unlike the French constitution of 1791. It vested the executive power in the king, and provided for a Cortes of a single chamber, elected by universal suffrage. Thus the Spaniards, although jealously repulsing French control, had ended by accepting the principles of the French Revolution.

The Restoration in Spain.

The English army brought back the king. Once seated on the throne, he gave free rein to his Bourbon instincts, abolished the Constitution of 1812, condemned to prison or to exile the liberal leaders, and restored the old system, with its absolutism, privilege of nobles, Inquisition and all. But the government was embarrassed on all sides; the country was impoverished with war, its debt increased, and armies were necessary to subdue the American colonies, which had risen in revolt. A military expedition was prepared against Buenos Ayres and lay for three years at Cadiz, awaiting ships to carry it to America.

The general dissatisfaction found expression in 1820.

THE ROYAL PALACE AT MADRID.

The army at Cadiz, idle and unpaid, led the revolt, and was followed by the liberal sympathizers in the cities. A

Revolution of 1820.

Junta, or insurrectionary committee was formed, which proclaimed the Constitution of 1812. The king, alarmed and stripped of military support, yielded, and expressed his readiness to accept the charter. A Cortes was elected, and for three years Spain lived under a constitutional monarchy.

But the Powers of the Congress of Vienna were not disposed to permit so grave a disturbance of their labors. In 1823 a French army, commissioned by the Powers, crossed the Pyrenees and restored the absolute monarchy. Persecutions followed, liberals and Freemasons were executed, liberal and foreign books were forbidden; students of the universities were obliged to swear not to recognize the sovereignty of the people, nor to join secret societies.

Ferdinand had two children, both of them girls. The Salic law, introduced with the Bourbons from France

The Carlist trouble,

(1713), forbade succession through the female line, and by law the crown would pass to the king's brother, Carlos. Ferdinand, however, wishing to preserve the crown for his daughter, Isabella, published an edict restoring the old Spanish order of female succession. Carlos protested, and on the death of the king in 1833, Spain was divided into two parties, devoted respectively to the claims of Carlos and of Isabella. England and France supported Isabella; the absolute governments, the claims of the pretender, Carlos.

The government of the Queen Regent, Christina (for Isabella was an infant), sought liberal support, and granted a constitution similar to the charter of Louis XVIII. But the country was disturbed with Carlist plots. For five years (1834–39) the issue was in doubt; but the incompetence of Carlos turned the scale against him; his partisans, weary of the struggle, withdrew, and Carlos fled abroad. His claim still lives with his descendants, and a Carlist party still stands ready to profit by the weakness of the Spanish Government.

The regency of Christina and the reign of her daughter, Isabella, were vacillating, unprogressive, and filled with scandal. In 1868 the army and navy rose with pronunciamentos against the crown, Madrid joined the insurgents, and Isabella fled to France. A provisional government offered the crown in vain to one prince after another. The offer to the Prince of Hohenzollern-Sigmaringen was the immediate cause of the Franco-Prussian War. Finally, Amadeo, son

Revolution and republic.

ALPHONSO XIII, KING OF SPAIN.

of Victor Emanuel of Italy, accepted the honor, but finding it impossible to reconcile the Spanish political factions, resigned in 1873. The Cortes proclaimed a Republic. The Republic was, however, no solution. A struggle of embittered partisans, it degenerated into a military dictatorship under Marshal Serrano. In 1874 Martinez Campos, a military leader, proclaimed in favor of Alphonso XII, son of Isabella, and he was accepted. His rule was liberal, politically; but in order to reconcile the pope, who had declared in favor of the Carlist claimant, Alphonso closed Protestant chapels and schools, and abolished civil marriage. The army was reorganized on the German model; civil affairs were left to a ministry responsible to the Cortes. Alphonso died in 1886, and was succeeded by his posthumous son, Alphonso XIII.

In colonial matters Spain has been unsuccessful. This is due in part, no doubt, to her methods; but it remains to be shown that any other power can deal successfully with the same material. In the West Indies and in the Philippines her colonial subjects have been for years in constant revolt. The Cuban War of 1895 resulted in the intervention of the United States, and in the brief war which followed Spain betrayed her poverty and lack of military resources. The treaty of Paris stripped her of her chief possessions, Cuba, Porto Rico, and the Philippines.

Spanish colonies.

John VI, King of Portugal, of the house of Braganza, fled before Napoleon to the greater Portugal, Brazil. There he remained after the restoration, and governed Portugal from Rio de Janeiro. In 1820 John VI died, and left two sons. Pedro, the elder, chose to remain in Brazil, and proclaimed himself emperor; Miguel, the younger, came to Portugal, but was driven out in 1824. Pedro, not wishing to come to Europe, yielded his rights to his daughter, Maria da Gloria, who granted a constitution in 1826, similar to the French charter of 1814.

Portugal.

A struggle for the throne ensued between Maria and Miguel, which lasted until 1834. The powers intervened and drove Miguel out of the kingdom; he promised, in return for a yearly allowance, to renounce the crown, and live in exile. Maria married a German prince of the house of Coburg.

Portugal has reflected, in her political development, the movements of Spain. The constitution has been modified and made more liberal; the suffrage made more general. Portugal remains, however, the most backward country of western Europe.

SOURCE REVIEW

I. Decline of Spain's Colonial Empire.— "The people standing at the threshold of the twentieth century have viewed the collapse of the last important edifices in the Spanish colonial domain. Spain, after a reign of just about four hundred years over an empire on which the sun never set, retained, at the termination of the war with the United States, but a remnant of its vast realms. In the Oceanica, the Caroline Islands and Palos, as well as the Ladrones (except Guam), with a total area of 610 square miles and a population of 37,000 souls, were yet Spanish; but since then they have been sold to Germany. In Africa, Spain still owns territory amounting to 243,877 square miles, and having 136,000 inhabitants. A further district on the Campo and Muni rivers, measuring 69,000 square miles and counting 500,000 residents, is in dispute with France.

"A detailed discussion of the reasons for the misfortunes suffered by the Spaniards in colonization is not necessary. In every epoch and region the seeds were sown to reap the whirlwind. Too centralized an administration, utter lack of self-government, corrupt officials, avaricious greed for quick returns at the sacrifice of future prospects, a restrictive commercial system, trade monopoly, erroneous economic doctrines, the admission of the Church to an exaggerated share in public affairs, and general wastefulness of resources, accompanied with enormous taxation, are the elemental defects to which disaster was due. The Crown always clung to the maxim that it was the right of the parent state to draw all possible benefit and advantage for itself from the colonies, irrespective of the interests of the latter. Conquest would more aptly designate its motive of action in taking possession of foreign territory. Whatever may have been the temporary objects, the results are clear; the record must inevitably be closed with the verdict of failure due to false policy and deplorable methods."— Morris : *History of Colonization.*

II.—In spite of the disasters which have fallen to the lot of Spain in the nineteenth century, she has not escaped the liberalizing and progressive influences of the times. Emilio Castelar, the great democratic leader, has written as follows : "When we turn the eyes of our memory to the sad realities of the past and compare them with the realities of the present, we see what may be accomplished without the fulfilment of Utopian dreams and unrealizable ideals. Those who have seen an almost absolute monarchy may to-day see a democratic monarchy. Those who once scarcely dared to express their thoughts, to-day can write whatever they think proper. Those who were once excluded from the universities for proclaiming free thought and the proper standards of science, to-day have a right to teach what they think and believe. Those who once felt their hearts stirred with indignation against slavery and the markets where human beings were bought and sold, as in Nineveh and Babylon, now know that to-day there is not one slave under the Spanish flag. We may well feel content with the work of the past forty years."

III.—The Spanish Succession

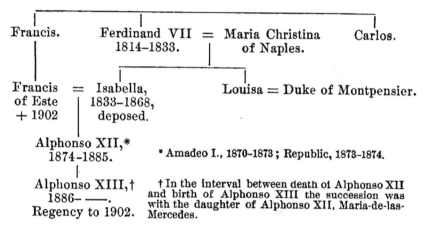

Francis.

Ferdinand VII = Maria Christina
1814–1833.   of Naples.

Carlos.

Francis = Isabella,
of Este | 1833–1868,
+ 1902 | deposed.

Louisa = Duke of Montpensier.

Alphonso XII,*
1874–1885.

* Amadeo I., 1870–1873 ; Republic, 1873–1874.

Alphonso XIII,†
1886– ——.
Regency to 1902.

† In the interval between death of Alphonso XII and birth of Alphonso XIII the succession was with the daughter of Alphonso XII, Maria-de-las-Mercedes.

REFERENCES

Judson: *Europe in the Nineteenth Century*, pp. 299–304; Alison Phillips : *Modern Europe*, pp. 122–129.

§ 47. SWITZERLAND

In the eighteenth century Switzerland was a league of thirteen sovereign states, loosely bound together for purposes of defense. The Peace of Westphalia had recognized their independence in 1648, but two centuries had failed to knit the states together into a common government. Differences in religion, which each canton had settled for itself, was one of the obstacles to closer union. In mountain cantons, where the population was pastoral or agricultural, and poverty was the rule, democratic institutions prevailed ;

Switzerland in the eighteenth century.

the people met together in open-air assemblies, and regulated their common affairs; but in the cities, an aristocracy, enriched with trade and manufacture, governed with despotic powers.   Indeed the bond of union between the states was as slight as could be imagined, and civil liberty, as understood in later times, was not a feature of Swiss life in the more populous cantons.

THE LION OF LUCERNE.

The French Revolution broke rudely in upon these self-satisfied communities, and forced upon them unity and liberty against their will.   In 1798 Switzerland was invaded by the armies of the French Directory, and a Helvetic Republic established after the pattern of the French Republic then existing, with a central government and civil equality.   The conservative Swiss resented vigorously the reformation from without, and a period of civil war ensued.   In 1803 Napoleon restored the sovereignty of the cantons, and restricted the central government to the conduct of foreign and military affairs; but he added six new cantons, and

The Revolution and Napoleon.

forced each canton to adopt a constitution, based on civil and religious liberty.

The fall of Napoleon and the spirit of reaction which prevailed in Europe gave to the Swiss conservatives an

Restoration.

opportunity to show their dislike of French institutions. The older cantons withdrew their representatives from the Diet and demanded back their eighteenth-century institutions. The new cantons held to the Napoleonic constitution, and Switzerland found herself divided into two hostile camps. At length moderate counsels prevailed, and the " Federal Pact of 1815 " was adopted, a loose federation, leaving to each canton the right of regulating its internal affairs, and giving to the central government, the Diet, the organization of the postal service, the regulation of the coinage, and the control of foreign affairs. The reaction did not carry Switzerland completely back to its pre-Revolutionary status, but it emphasized the principle of state rights and gave evidence of the determination of the Swiss not to be hurried by outside influences along the line of political reform. The Federal Pact of 1815 was not unlike the Confederation of the United States before the adoption of the Constitution of 1787. The individual cantons, left to organize their own governments, restored for the most part their aristocratic forms. The Congress of Vienna added three cantons, taken from French territory, making the number twenty-two, as at present.

But the political and civil reforms which Switzerland would not receive from strangers came gradually about

Growth of democracy.

through internal progress. Situated in the midst of Europe, the Swiss were not insensible to the growth of liberty about them. A democratic party, consisting of the people crowded out of public affairs in the aristocracies, demanded in 1830 a revision of the cantonal constitutions. The governments were alarmed and yielded. One by one the cantons amended their constitutions in a liberal sense. In some cases this was accomplished peacefully, in some by revolution; but in the end civil and political rights were generally established.

Religious differences were the causes which eventually brought union out of disunion. The Pact of 1815 guaranteed the rights and privileges of religious institutions; but the wave of democratic reform broke down this guaranty, demanding the abolition of monasteries and the expulsion of the Jesuit order. In 1843 the seven Catholic cantons formed a league for mutual defence, the "*Sonderbund*," and withdrew their deputies from the Diet. For four years this league within a league existed, but in 1847 war broke out. The great powers, Austria, Russia, Prussia and France, agreed to intervene and reinforce the Pact of 1815; but before they could act the army of the Diet struck a quick, sharp blow, and in eighteen days the *Sonderbund* was defeated. (Lucerne, November 24, 1847.)

Constitutional revision followed at once; a strong progressive government had become a necessity. A committee of the Diet was appointed to draft a new constitution, and under liberal influences the Constitution of 1848 was produced. By it a Federal state was established in place of the old, loose Federation of 1815. Switzerland became, like the United States, a Federal Republic. Each canton preserved its state government, and exercised all rights not specially conferred upon the federal power. The federal legislature is composed of two houses: a Senate, with two members for each canton; and a National Council, elective, representing the people, like our House of Representatives. The executive is a board of seven men, sitting in joint session; the President merely chairman of the board. In 1874 a Federal Supreme Court was added.

A peculiar Swiss institution is the *Referendum*, much admired in other countries. Any bill which has passed the

QUEEN VICTORIA,

two houses must be submitted, on demand of thirty thousand qualified Swiss citizens, or of eight cantons, to the vote of the people, before it can become law.

Switzerland to-day is one of the most progressive of European nations. In education, in legislation governing the hours and conditions of labor, in industry, Switzerland of and in general well-being Switzerland stands to-day. in the van of modern progress. Her constitution, with its large allowance of local self-government, suits admirably a country whose population is composed of three race elements. The Germans, who make up two of the three millions of the Swiss people, live harmoniously with the French of the five western cantons, and the 150,000 Italians of the Canton of Ticino on the South.

SOURCE REVIEW

Switzerland a Voluntary Union.—"Look at Switzerland, as she is even now. Does she not stand for a representation—on a small scale and imperfectly, it may be—of what poets and philosophers have pictured to themselves the world might some day become? Is she not already, in her way, a miniature Parliament of Man? For she is not a national unit, like France and Spain, existing as such in spite of herself. The nucleus of the Swiss Confederation was perhaps formed by nature to be free and independent, but the outlying districts joined the Union of their own accord ; in other words, it is the will of the Swiss people and their fixed determination which keep them united. Consider the mixture of races and religions which they represent. Of the twenty-two Cantons, thirteen are German speaking, four are French ; in three German and French both are spoken, in one Italian, and in another Romansch. The population of German Switzerland is almost purely Teutonic ; that of French Switzerland about half-and-half Teutonic and Celto-Roman ; while Italian and Romansch Switzerland can boast of Celto-Roman, Ostro-Gothic, and even Etruscan elements. Some of these Cantons are Protestant, others Roman Catholic, and others, again, have a mixed population of both faiths.   If these incongruous, often antagonistic Cantons can meet upon some common plane and conform to some common standard, can live side by side in peace and prosperity, surely the task of some day uniting the nations of the world upon a similar basis is not altogether hopeless and chimerical."—McCrackan : " *The Rise of the Swiss Republic.*"

REFERENCES

Judson : *Europe in the Nineteenth Century*, pp. 284-287 ; Alison Phillipps: *Modern Europe*, pp. 262-265.

§ 48. THE SCANDINAVIAN STATES

Norway, Sweden, and Denmark are ranked in the nineteenth century among the minor states.   Their great importance in the Middle Ages, when they sent forth hordes of conquering Northmen to rule the destinies of western Europe, has found no counterpart in modern times.   The meteoric appearance of Charles XII of Sweden was the last gleam of Scandinavian greatness.

The three states of the north.

In Napoleon's time the northern states were much disturbed by the ambitions of the Emperor and the Tsar. Sweden lost the Grand Duchy of Finland to Russia.   One of Napoleon's generals, Bernadotte, was chosen by the childless Swedish king as his heir.   After the fall of Napoleon, Denmark, which had remained faithful to the Emperor's fortunes, was punished by the loss of Norway, detached by the Allies in 1814, and added to the crown of Sweden, a reward for Bernadotte, who prudently deserted his old commander in his failing fortunes.   The Danish king retained only Denmark and the Duchies of Schleswig and Holstein.   Bernadotte offered the Norwegians a viceroy and a constitution ; but they refused and war began.   Finally an agreement was made between the two countries : the king should be King of Sweden and of

Norway ; but each people should retain its separate government.

Sweden preserved her aristocratic form of government well into the nineteenth century. The king governed
Sweden. with a Council of State; a Diet, consisting of four orders, nobles, clergy, citizens, and peasants, registered the will of the king. The Lutheran church was secured and all other religions were prohibited. Religious freedom was not secured until 1858 ; a reform movement resulted in the Constitution of 1866, which transformed the old Diet into a modern parliament.

In Sweden, as elsewhere in Scandinavia, the composition of political parties was peculiar. In France, Italy, and Germany, as we have seen, the cities were the centers of the liberal movement. In France, for example, the revolutions have ever proceeded from Paris, and were echoed in the lesser towns, such as Lyons and Marseilles. This is due to the fact that the cities contained a large population of laborers

OSCAR II, KING OF SWEDEN.

and of the unprivileged classes, who were always seeking to improve their condition. But in the Scandinavian states the cities, where the courts and their officials predominated, were the centers of conservatism, and the liberals were the country people, intelligent, accustomed to independence, and jealous of their liberties.

After the separation from Denmark Norwegian society was reduced to peasant proprietors, merchants, sailors, and pastors ; a democratic nation, with no idle nobility to support. The scattered population, orderly and accustomed to the regulation of local affairs, demanded little government, and the national legislature met but once in three years.   It was in conflict with Bernadotte (Charles XIV) during the whole of his reign (1818–1844).

Norway.

Oscar I (1844–59) yielded to the Norwegians, recognized their national flag, and lived in peace. Religious liberty was established, and in 1869 the sessions of the legislature, the *Storthing*, were made annual.

Norway soon became prosperous.   The population increased rapidly; the debt was paid off, and Norway came to be one of the leading maritime nations, owning

one-fourth of the merchant shipping of Europe.   With Oscar II, who succeeded Charles XV in 1872, the struggle with Sweden was renewed.   The constitution of Norway (1814) forbade the king's ministers sitting in the *Storthing*, lest their presence should influence the deputies.   Now, however, wishing to establish the English system of a responsible ministry, the Norwegians sought to amend their constitution, making the ministers responsible to the *Storthing*, and compelling their appearance before that body.   The king refused to concede .this, and claimed that the constitution could not be amended, except with his consent.   The *Storthing* passed the measure three times over the king's veto, and declared the constitution amended, against the protest of the king.   War seemed inevitable ; but in 1884 King Oscar yielded, and Norway passed over to the parliamentary system, which means the government of the country by the people.

BJÖRNSON, LEADER OF THE SEPARATIST PARTY IN NORWAY.

But Norway was not satisfied with this.   Jealous of any restriction upon her national independence, she now demands the right to regulate her own foreign affairs and establish consuls abroad. In 1895 the *Storthing* voted for a Norwegian flag without the symbol of union. There is a mutual lack of confidence in the united kingdoms, and the union seems strained almost to breaking. One party in Norway demands the establishment of a republic.

In 1814 Denmark was much lessened in importance by the loss of Norway. In 1864 Denmark was still further reduced by the loss of Schleswig and Hol-

Denmark.

stein, forcibly torn away by Prussia and Austria. One article of the treaty in which Denmark surrendered the duchies provided " that the people of northern Schleswig, if by a free vote they signify their desire to be reunited to Denmark, shall be ceded to that country ; " but this provision was never carried out, and was canceled by Germany in 1878. The Schleswig Danes have never been reconciled to the separation.

The adversities of Denmark, as so often happens in the histories of nations, modified the absolutist form of her government, and brought about the Constitution of 1866, under which the country has been governed since that time. This constitution, like the French Charter of Louis XVIII, left in doubt the control of the ministry—whether by king or by parliament. Since 1873 a parliamentary conflict has raged about this question, and it is still unsolved.

Iceland, the frigid dependency of Denmark, has had her political experiences. She demanded financial independence, freedom from control at Copenhagen, and received a new constitution in 1893, establishing home rule. Iceland has a legislature, the *Althing*, of two chambers : an Upper Chamber of twelve members, half of which are appointed by the king; and an elective Lower House.

SOURCE REVIEW

Norwegian Dissatisfaction.—Many things tend to make the union with Sweden unpopular in Norway. Sweden, directed by the aristocratic tendencies of her court, leans toward an intimacy with Germany; but democratic Norway turns for sympathy toward the liberal nations of the West, France and England.   The same tendencies bring together Norway and Denmark, the latter state still smarting under the losses of the Schleswig-Holstein wars.   An eminent French historian, Charles V. Langlois, has given the following estimate of Norway : " Norway has in recent years excited much interest in the outside world.   Her writers, such as Ibsen ; explorers, such as Nansen, and artists like Thaulow and Grieg enjoy an international reputation.   The Norway of to-day, which is in many respects, as, for example, in her school system, and in her efforts to restrict the excessive use of alcohol, notably in advance of the larger countries of Europe, is at the height of her material and intellectual development.   She is now passing through a phase of national existence somewhat similar to that which Portugal passed through in the sixteenth, and Sweden and Holland in the eighteenth century.   The Norwegian nation is to-day that people of all Europe which most nearly resembles the peoples of the new world, of North America, of Australia, and of South Africa."

REFERENCES

Judson : *Europe in the Nineteenth Century*, pp. 293–298. (For constitution of Norway-Sweden) Woodrow Wilson : *The State*, Chapter IX.

§ 49.   BELGIUM AND HOLLAND

The Kingdom of the Netherlands, created by the Congress of Vienna out of the United Provinces (Holland) and the Austrian Netherlands, was an ill-assorted

Kingdom of the Netherlands. union.   The Belgian provinces of the south had little in common with the Dutch provinces of the north.   The former had received their language and ideas from France ; the latter, inhabited by people speaking a language closely allied to German, had ever been open to German influences.   Besides this the Dutch were Protestant ; the Belgians, Catholic.

French occupation, during the Revolution and the Napoleonic period, swept away the old political and social institutions, which had existed in the Netherlands since the Middle Ages, and made the foundations ready for the erection of a modern state. It did for the Netherlands what Joseph II wished to do for his Belgian provinces in the eighteenth century, and more. Although the Netherlands had suffered from the trade restrictions imposed by Napoleon in his attempt to incorporate them into his Continental System, yet the people were shrewd enough to recognize the advantages of the French methods of administration. The Fundamental Law of 1814, which organized the Kingdom of the Netherlands, established a constitutional monarchy after the pattern of the French charter of Louis XVIII.

LEOPOLD II, KING OF BELGIUM.

Belgium is a product of the Revolution of July. The Kingdom of the Netherlands fell to pieces at the first shock to the system of the Congress of Vienna. The Belgians made good

Creation of Belgium.

their revolt, secured recognition from the Powers, and chose for king Leopold of Coburg. The Dutch king refused to recognize the decision of the Powers, and a French army drove the Dutch troops from Belgian soil. It was not until 1839 that King William accepted the inevitable division of his kingdom.

At the time of their revolt the Belgians declared in favor of a hereditary monarchy with representative institutions. A liberal constitution was adopted, which declares that "all powers emanate from the nation." The king governs through a ministry responsible to the Chambers, the ministers resigning when they have no longer a majority in the Chamber of Deputies; an arrangement which makes the Chamber the ruling power in national affairs. Complete liberty of the press and of worship was established. Thus in 1830 Belgium was far ahead of all the nations of the Continent in the possession of constitutional privileges and parliamentary government.

Since 1830 political struggles in Belgium have turned upon two questions : education and suffrage. The Liberal and the Catholic party have had about equal chances at the helm of government. The liberals have labored to make the school system independent of the church ; but this the Catholic party has vigorously opposed.

Belgium of to-day.

The Constitution of 1830 limited the suffrage to men paying taxes to the amount of twenty florins ($8.00). In 1891 it had come to be recognized quite generally that the requirements for voting needed to be changed ; because, in a population of 6,000,000, there were only 135,000 voters. After two years of debate a system of plural voting was adopted. Each man over twenty-five years has one vote. If he is the head of a family, he has an additional vote ; if possessor of real estate or of 2,000 francs in the savings-bank, a vote ; if graduate of a high school, a vote ; provided that he may not have more than three votes in all. This system of voting produced 1,350,000 voters with 2,066,000 votes. Voting is obligatory.

The political struggles of Belgium have never endangered the constitution nor prevented a rapid increase in the population and wealth. The population has nearly doubled since 1830, and Belgium has become one of the foremost industrial countries in the world. King Leopold II has sought to furnish a colonial outlet for Belgian enterprise in the creation of the Congo Free State in Africa.

After the loss of Belgium, affairs were quiet in the Netherlands for several years. In 1844 a Liberal party began the

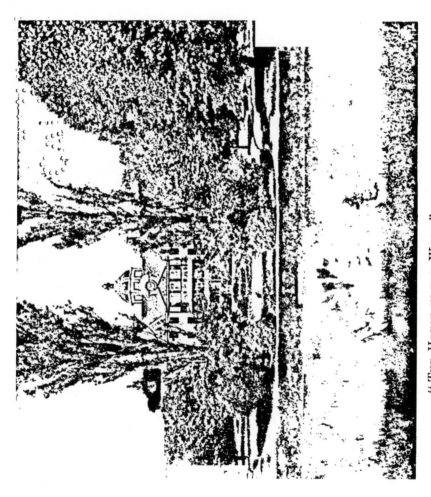

"THE HOUSE IN THE WOOD."
Royal Palace, The Hague, Netherlands

agitation for a modern constitution, and this was drafted by the States-General and promulgated in 1848. A leg-

Holland; officially the Netherlands.

islature of two chambers was established, the members of the Upper Chamber appointed by the local governments of the provinces ; the members of the Lower Chamber elected by voters paying a certain amount of direct taxes. Universal suffrage, although demanded by the Liberals, has never been adopted in the Netherlands. The ministry is responsible to the legislature, which still retains the ancient name of States-General.

As might be supposed in a country formed by the union of independent provinces, the individual provinces retain large powers of local self-government. Each province has its estates, which are largely concerned with the important task of keeping up its canals. The communes (towns and villages) are responsible for the repair and maintenance of the dykes. The

WILHELMINA, QUEEN OF THE NETHERLANDS.

nineteenth century has been a period of prosperity for the Netherlands ; her population has doubled since 1830.

The Grand Duchy of Luxemburg was given to King William in 1814 as an indemnity for the loss of certain

Dependencies.

Rhenish lands belonging to his family, which were ceded to Prussia. It was attached to the Dutch crown through a personal union, and was not made a part of the Netherlands. Since succession in the Grand Duchy is through the male line only, on the death of William III in 1890, and the succession of his daughter Wilhelmina, the Grand Duchy was lost to Holland, passing to the Duke of Nassau, next in succession in the male line.

The Netherlands looks small on the map, but it possesses a huge colonial empire, which forms an outlet for ambitious young men, and brings vast wealth to the home country. From 1850 to 1873 the colonies produced a surplus of revenue, which went toward defraying home expenses and the retirement of the national debt. In 1873 the war against the Atchinese in Sumatra necessitated heavy military expenditures, and turned the account.

SOURCE REVIEW

Peace Conference at The Hague.—On the 24th of August, 1898, Count Mouravieff, Russian Minister of Foreign Affairs, on behalf of his imperial master, the Tsar Nicholas II, placed in the hands of all foreign representatives at St. Petersburg a proposal for an international conference, looking toward the maintenance of universal peace and a possible reduction of the excessive armaments with which the Powers are burdened. "The ever-increasing financial burdens," the proposal reads, "strike at the root of public prosperity. The physical and intellectual forces of the people, labor and capital, are diverted for the great part from their natural application and wasted unproductively. Hundreds of millions are spent in acquiring terrible engines of destruction, which are regarded to-day as the latest inventions of science, but are destined to-morrow to be rendered obsolete by some new discovery. It is the supreme duty, therefore, at the present moment, to put some limit to these increasing armaments, and to find means of averting the calamities which threaten the whole world."

In response to this invitation representatives of nearly all independent governments (the exceptions were the South American republics, the Emperor of Morocco, the King of Abyssinia, and the Grand Lama of Thibet) met at The Hague on the 18th of May, 1899, and there organized a system of courts for international arbitration. Nothing was accomplished in the way of reducing the standing armies of the European states.

REFERENCES

Alison Phillips: *Modern Europe*, pp. 186–199 ; Judson : *Europe in the Nineteenth Century*, pp. 287–292.

CHAPTER XVII

England

§ 50. Political Reforms in England

ENGLAND is the only one of the European states which has gone through the nineteenth century without revolution. She has preserved in the main the form of government which was established at the end of the seventeenth century, after the expulsion of the Stuart kings. Such changes as have taken place have not involved the writing of new constitutions; for England has no written constitution, and the introduction of new forms and usages gradually accommodates the form of government to the needs of the times. Such forms and usages, once adopted, become precedents, with the force of law; and in this manner the unwritten constitution of England keeps pace with the demands of progress.

England at the beginning of the nineteenth century.

At the beginning of the nineteenth century the government of England consisted of a king, a ministry, and a Parliament of two houses, Lords and Commons. The king governed through his ministry, and the ministry was in theory responsible to Parliament. This parliamentary system, which set the mark toward which all liberal Europe was tending during the first half of the century, would, if carried out to its logical conclusion, have resulted in England in the rule of Parliament. But certain of the English kings were not disposed to surrender the supreme power without a struggle. George III was the last of the kings who sought to impose his personal will upon the nation, and the failure of his policy in the American Revolution gave a final blow to personal government in England. The desperate struggle in which England was engaged against revolutionary and Napoleonic France checked for a time her internal development, and the fear of liberal ideas, which was the outcome of this struggle, postponed the reform movement in England for a generation.

WESTMINSTER ABBEY.

But England's political liberties at the beginning of the nineteenth century were more apparent than real. It is true that Parliament governed the coun-

Need of reform.

try ; but Parliament did not represent the people. It represented a relatively small group of persons, the land-owners and wealthy manufacturers, an aristocracy of blood and money. Owing to the traditional aversion of the English for change, the system of parliamentary representation remained practically the same as in the seventeenth century, although during that period the population of England had undergone a complete change of distribution. In the seventeenth century the South of England, a rich agricultural country, with Channel ports controlling the foreign trade, was most populous; but toward the end of the eighteenth century a new era of steam manufacture built up great cities in the north, such as Manchester and Birmingham, near to the mines of coal and iron. Yet these cities of 100,000 population were given no representation in Parliament, while the old decayed towns, often dwindled to a hundred souls, still preserved their two members each in the House of Commons. Places of this kind were called "pocket boroughs," because they were controlled by a single man or family. Sometimes the memberships, to which the borough was entitled, were sold, and the proceeds divided among the few inhabitants. The borough of Sudbury advertised itself for sale to the highest bidder.

Apart from the towns the conditions were no better. In the English counties no one but landowners had the right of voting. In Scotland matters were still worse; out of a population of 2,000,000, there were less than 3,000 voters. "The county of Bute, with a population of 14,000, had only twenty-one voters, and of those only one was resident. He took the chair, moved and seconded his own nomination, put the vote, and elected himself unanimously as county member." The result was that the seats in Parliament were almost wholly acquired by inheritance, by purchase, or by family influence. The House of Commons was not representative of the people; it was an assembly of landlords and plutocrats, and their nominees, who represented their interests. It was impossible to secure such legislation as would meet the needs of the growing industrial centers.

In 1815 public opinion was aroused upon this question. An association was formed at Birmingham for the purpose of bringing the subject to the attention of the people, by means of the press and public meetings. The government was obliged at length to meet the issue. The Duke of

Wellington, chief of the Tory (conservative) ministry then in power, refused to yield; he declared that "the representative system, just as it stood," was "a masterpiece of human wisdom." In 1830 Wellington was overthrown, and a Whig (liberal) ministry under Earl Grey presented a Reform Bill. Twice it passed the House of Commons, but went no farther; it was shattered against the aristocratic tradi-

Movement toward reform.

GLADSTONE.

tions of the House of Lords. Riots broke out, and revolution seemed at hand; but the cool common sense of the English prevailed; a way was found to circumvent the House of Lords. The ministry announced that the crown would create enough Liberal peers to overcome the Tory majority. Upon this the Lords weakened; enough stayed away to permit the passage of the bill, and in this manner the Reform Bill became law, in 1832.

The Reform Bill broke down the aristocratic majority in Parliament, and let the Newer England into the government. This was accomplished by redistricting the country. From the old "rotten boroughs" were taken away members, who were distributed among the new, vigorous towns. The suffrage was enlarged, and political power was transferred from the upper to the middle classes. The same reforms were extended by Disraeli in 1867. The secret ballot was introduced in 1872. In 1884 Gladstone extended the ballot to 3,000,000 rural votes, mostly agricultural laborers. In 1885 electoral districts were constituted on the American

English democracy.

plan, and the last vestige of the old apportionment disappeared. London, which before the Reform Bill of 1832 had six members, now received sixty-two. Gradually and without disturbance the tendency is toward the inclusion of the whole people in the task of self-government.

SOURCE REVIEW

Abolition of Slavery in the West Indies, 1833.—The period which succeeded the passing of the Reform Bill was characterized by an immense activity and earnestness in legislation. One of the greatest of its products was the complete abolition of the system of slavery in the British colonies. The slave trade had itself been greatly limited through the efforts of Great Britain, but now the whole system of West Indian slavery was brought to an end. A long agitation on the part of a small but energetic anti-slavery party brought about this result in 1833. The name of William Wilberforce (1759–1833) is most intimately connected with this reform. The bill which passed Parliament, and which took effect from the first of August, 1834, gave immediate freedom to all children subsequently born, and to all those who were then under six years of age, while it prescribed for all other slaves a period of apprenticeship lasting five years (and in the case of agricultural slaves, seven years), after which they obtained absolute freedom. The bill also appropriated £20,000,000 for the compensation of the slave-owners. Two colonies, Antigua and the Bermudas, dispensed with the apprentice system altogether, and in no case did it last beyond 1838. The number of slaves at the time of the emancipation was estimated at 674,000.— Adapted from McCarthy : *The Epoch of Reform.*

REFERENCES

Gardiner : *A Student's History of England,* Chapter LVI ; Judson : *Europe in the Nineteenth Century,* Chapters XVIII, XIX, XX.

§ 51. The Corn Laws and Other Problems

Before the reorganization of Parliament by the Reform Bill the landowners were in power, and saw to it that their interests were protected. Laws were passed early in the century for the purpose of keeping up the price of grain. When grain fell to eight shillings a quarter, importation was forbidden. The benefit of this artificial price of grain went, not to the tenant, who cultivated the soil, but to the landlord, who confiscated the additional profit by advancing the rent. On the other hand the Corn Laws kept the price of food high for the laborer, and so increased the cost of manufacture. England was then hanging in the balance between her agricultural and her industrial interests; and as Parliament was controlled by the class whose interests were agricultural, little attention was paid to the demands of the industrial class for cheap food.

The change in the composition of Parliament brought about by the Reform Bill solved the problem. The old landowning aristocracy was unseated in the Commons, and the new element stood for trade and industry. The results were soon apparent. In 1838 an Anti-Corn Law League was formed. The leading spirits were Richard Cobden and John Bright. Through the press they carried on a "Campaign of Education," which ended in convincing the majority of Englishmen. The fact was that the industrial element had by this time grown so strong that it would no longer permit dear food to stand in the way of England's commercial supremacy. About this time the great famine in Ireland, by which Ireland lost about 2,000,000 of her population, strengthened the demand for cheap food. The Corn Laws were repealed in 1846 in the ministry of Sir Robert Peel, and by 1852 the protective duties were all gone. England had passed over to the doctrine of free trade, under which she grew to be, in the nineteenth century, the greatest trading and manufacturing nation in the world.

Since 1673 Roman Catholics were debarred from holding public office and sitting in either house of Parliament by the requirement of a declaration against some of the main points of Catholic doctrine. In 1793 the Irish Parliament, seven years before its abolition, admitted Catholics to the right of voting, but after the union in 1801 none but Protestant members could be sent from Ireland into Parliament in England. Both George III and George IV, when there was talk of removing the disability, declared that they were bound by their coronation oaths to uphold the Anglican Church against Catholicism.

Catholic emancipation.

In 1828 O'Connell, a powerful orator and a Roman Catholic, was sent to Parliament from Ireland. He was refused a seat. The ministry desired to yield, but George IV refused his consent. The ministry resigned, and the king, unable to form another ministry to uphold his policy, was obliged to concede the general demand for toleration. In 1829 the Catholic disabilities were removed ; Catholics were admitted to sit in both houses of Parliament, and to hold all offices, civil and military, with one or two exceptions.

Sir Robert Peel, England's Free Trade Minister.

England has solved most of her vexatious questions ; but the Irish question seems incapable of solution. It is her race question, but a race question embittered with religious differences. The Irish are pure Celts ; the English are of mixed origin, but

The Irish question.

largely of German blood, with an admixture of Norman French. The Irish have remained attached to the Catholic Church ; the English are for the most part Protestants.

Ireland has been governed as a conquered country ; ever since the conquest in the seventeenth century the Irish have been ruled by the English. In 1815 the Anglican Church was the State church in Ireland, supported by tithes and the income from church estates. Although its adherents were only 620,000 out of a total population of 5,000,000, yet the whole of Ireland was taxed to support it. In some parts there was a church and a rector, but no congregation at all ; nevertheless the tithes were collected and the rector paid, and the peasantry were obliged, in addition to the tithes, to support Catholic services out of their voluntary contributions. The land belonged to English landlords, who for the most part were "absentee," living out of Ireland. The Irish peasant occupied for generations a small farm, on which he built his cabin, and for which he paid rent. Likely to be evicted at the pleasure of the landlord, he was not disposed to make improvements, which would only induce the landlord to seek a new tenant at a higher rental. The shiftlessness and wretchedness of the Irish peasant became proverbial.

In 1782 Ireland was a dependency of Great Britain, with a Parliament of its own at Dublin. This Parliament was not representative of the Irish people, for it was wholly Protestant, no Catholic being allowed to hold office in the island. In 1793 the disabilities of Catholics as to voting were removed ; but in 1801, at a time when the Irish were looking to Napoleon to free them from the hated bondage to England, Ireland was united to England by the Act of Union, its Parliament suppressed, and representation given to Irish Protestants in the English Parliament, both in Lords and Commons. Locally Ireland was governed by a Lord-Lieutenant, appointed by the English crown.

During the nineteenth century the condition of the Irish has been improved. In 1869 Gladstone brought about the disestablishment of the Irish church. Ireland was no longer obliged to support with tithes a church in which she had no interest. The tenure of land by Irish peasants has been much improved. In a series of acts, from 1870 to 1885, Mr. Gladstone brought to the peasantry fair rents and fixed tenure, and now the government advances to the tenant, upon easy terms of payment, the cash for the purchase of his holding. In time the Irish, with any showing of thrift, will become free proprietors, and Irish rents will become a thing of the past.

The Irish struggle.

But Ireland is not satisfied with this. She wants at least self-government. Whether, with self-government in Ireland, England would find a friend or an enemy on the west is an important question. Mr. Gladstone undoubtedly believed in Ireland's friendship, for he set to work to crown his benefits to Ireland with the gift of Home Rule, which the Irish party in Parliament, under the leadership of Parnell, had advocated since 1870. In 1886 the Liberal (Mr. Gladstone's party) introduced a bill into Parliament providing for an Irish legislature. The Conservatives opposed it as a step toward Irish independence, and they were joined by a considerable body from the Liberals (the Liberal-Unionists, led by Joseph Chamberlain). The bill, defeated at the time, was reintroduced in 1893. It passed the Commons, but was rejected by the Lords. In 1894 Mr. Gladstone, on account of age, was obliged to retire from the leadership of his party, his projects for Ireland unaccomplished. Since then the Liberal party has never been strong enough to urge the Irish question, even if it were disposed to do so.

HOUSES OF PARLIAMENT, LONDON. OPENED 1852.

SOURCE REVIEW

The Irish Famine of 1845-47.—" In 1841 the population of Ireland was 8,175,124 souls. In 1845 it had probably reached to nearly nine millions. To anyone looking beneath the surface the condition of the country was painfully precarious. Nine millions of a population living at best in a light-hearted and hopeful hand-to-mouth contentment, totally dependent on the hazards of one crop, destitute of manufacturing industries, and utterly without reserve or resource to fall back upon in time of reverse. Yet no one seemed conscious of danger. The potato crop had been abundant for four or five years, and respite from dearth and distress was comparative happiness and prosperity. Moreover, the temperance movement (of Father Mathew) had come to make the 'good times' still better. Everything looked bright; yet signs of the coming storm had been given; quite recently warnings that ought not to have been mistaken or neglected had given notice that the esculent which formed the sole dependence of the peasant millions was subject to some mysterious blight. In 1844 it was stricken in America, but in Ireland the yield was healthy and plentiful as ever. The harvest of 1845 proved to be the richest gathered in many years. Suddenly, in one short month, in one week, it might be said, the withering breath of a simoom seemed to sweep the land, blasting all in its path. I myself saw whole tracts of potato growth changed in one night from smiling luxuriance to a shriveled and blackened waste. A shout of alarm arose." [Nearly two million of people died, and as a result of the hard times one million emigrated from Ireland to America between 1847 and 1851.]—Sullivan : *New Ireland*.

REFERENCES

Gardiner : *A Student's History of England*, Chapter LVIII ; Judson : *Europe in the Nineteenth Century*, Chapter XXI.

§ 52.   England's Possessions

England may be regarded as the most successful in colonization of all nations.   This is due to three facts :

Colonial Policy.

1. She has had a surplus of population, energetic enough to seek to improve their condition in the colonies.

2. Her colonists have not mingled with the natives with whom they came in contact.   In this way the colonists have kept intact their European institutions, ideals, and culture.

3. England developed a liberal policy toward her colonies, giving them full measure of self-government.   The result has proved the wisdom of the policy.   Free to go, they have preferred to stay.   The bond of blood grew stronger as the political bond was relaxed.

But this liberal policy was not adopted by England until the loss of the United States and the threat of further loss brought her to a closer study of the colonial problem.   In 1837 Canada, after having for a generation protested against the aristocratic government thrust upon her from London, rebelled against the crown.   The rebellion was put down with some severity, and in the following year a commissioner was sent from England to examine carefully and report upon the situation.   As a result of his report, the home government decided to reverse its policy of repression and concede the Canadian demands. In 1840 Upper and Lower Canada were united and given a representative government, afterwards enlarged unto the Dominion of Canada, 1867.   A Governor-General, appointed by the crown, is the only tie of political connection with the mother country.   Although England has a right of veto over Canadian legislation, it is never used.

The English first became interested in Australia through the explorations of Captain Cook, who took possession of the eastern coast in the name of England in 1770.   No immediate settlement was made. In 1788 an expedition was sent out and a penal colony founded at Botany Bay.

Australasia. Early in the nineteenth century sheep-raising was begun and other parts of the continent occupied. Tasmania was settled in 1803 ; New Zealand in 1838. The settlements flourished, and before 1840 they numbered 80,000 souls. In 1851 the discovery of gold aroused additional interest in Australia. The self-government granted to Canada in 1840 was extended to Australia. New Zealand received representative institutions in 1852, New South Wales in 1855, and other colonies as soon as they were prepared for self-government. The use of the colonies as penal settlements was objected to by the new element that came to make homes, and the system was abandoned in 1860.

On January 1, 1901, the commonwealth of Australia came into being, a federation of the five continental colonies of Australia and Tasmania. New Zealand, on account of its distance from

CAPTAIN COOK.

the continent, remains apart. The constitution of the new Commonwealth is similar to that of the Dominion of Canada, with a Governor-General, appointed by the crown, and two Houses of Parliament.

The defeat of Napoleon left England in possession of the Cape of Good Hope, which had been taken from the Dutch

The Cape Colony. allies of France. England's actual possession dates from 1806. The Cape Colony acquired self-government in 1853, with the same parliamentary system as Canada and the Australasian colonies. The Dutch colonists were never reconciled to British rule. In

1834, dissatisfied with the proximity of the English, a large body of them migrated ("trekked," as they called it) northward into the African wilderness. There, in Natal, supposing themselves to be beyond the reach of English ambitions, they set up a republican government of their own. In 1843 Natal was declared a British colony, and a great part of the Dutch "trekked" again up into what was afterward known as the Orange Free State. Again civilization pursued them, and the more unreconciled of the "Boers" moved away in 1848 into the wilderness across the river Vaal. Here in the Transvaal they were

for many years undisturbed, and those who remained in the Orange Free State were acknowledged independent in 1854.

The Boers had fierce struggles with the native blacks, and looked to England for aid;

The Boer War.

but the aid came at too high a price, when the government of Disraeli, England's "Jingo" prime minister, planted the English flag in the Transvaal. In 1880 the Boers took up arms,

A BOER GENERAL.

and defeated the British in the battle of Majuba Hill; but the government changed in England, and Gladstone reversed the policy of his predecessor and acknowledged the independence of the Boers, reserving to England the control of the foreign relations of the Transvaal.

Unfortunately for the Boers, the discovery of gold brought into their land an invasion of foreigners, who soon outnumbered the Boers and built up, at Johannesburg, the largest of the South African cities. The Boers resented the intrusion, and refused political rights to the newcomers; and, when England attempted to bring pressure upon them, sprang to arms, the Transvaal and the Free State together (1899). The vastness of the country and the valor of the Boers made the war a difficult and costly one for England. Canada, Australia, and New Zealand came to the aid of the mother country, showing their willingness to share the imperial burden ; but the sympathy of the rest of the world was with the Boers.

Besides the Anglo-Saxon lands the British Empire includes the great and populous countries of southern

India. Asia, known as India. The Sepoy mutiny of 1857, due partly to religious scruples, and partly to a dislike of British rule, put an end to the government of the East India Company, and India was transferred to the crown. In 1876 Queen Victoria took the title of Empress of India. India is governed by a Viceroy and Council appointed by the crown.

Edward VII.

The tendency of English occupation has been toward expansion, to reach northward for a natural boundary against the aggressions of Russia. These two states, England and Russia, have absorbed between them western and central Asia ; Persia, Afghanistan, and China alone remain independent, and they are threatened.

English rule in India has in later years been wise and just ; but the problem of India remains for the future to solve, if, indeed, it is capable of solution. The English have put a stop to the constant warfare between the petty states which made up India in earlier times ; she has given to this mass of oriental peoples the " *Pax Britannica;* " life is safe as it has never been before ; but the mass of the population remains at the same low level of poverty and degradation.   Of 200,000,000 in British India, only six per cent. can read and write ; famines increase in intensity, and it is doubtful whether the more intelligent Indians are grateful for British efforts in their behalf or are in sympathy with British rule.

SOURCE REVIEW

I. The English in India.—" The truth is, the English are by nature unfitted to win the affections of a fanciful and dreamy oriental people.   For the English temper is arrogant, hard, stubborn, practical, and unimaginative.   Endowed with a genius for government, the Englishman has scant respect for races which have no capacity for politics and no aptitude for progress.

" What, then, is to be said of the contact of these two incongruous races ?   Is India really benefiting by a rule which arouses her antipathy?   That she is well governed cannot be denied.   Law and order reign throughout her wide domains as they never have reigned through the efforts of her native people, and from such an efficient and well-ordered rule the Hindoos must inevitably acquire new standards of political conduct.   But chafing under the haughty and unbending dominion of a people whom they hate, they can hardly put on more than a veneer of civilization, and their longing to live their own life seems wholly natural and justifiable."—Sears : *Political Growth in the Nineteenth Century.*

II. The Lesson of Honesty.—"Of chief importance, perhaps, is the fact that, from the natives as well as from the administrators themselves, one learns that the Europeans have established among the natives, who, generally in most countries of the Orient, are themselves disposed to be corrupt and untruthful, a reputation for rigid honesty as regards all financial matters, and for truthfulness and justness in their dealings with others.   Justice is done by the Europeans even against the personal interests of their own fellow-countrymen if need be, or against themselves in the settlement of disputes between Europeans and natives or among the natives.   It is practically universally true throughout the English and Dutch colonies alike that if a native has a good case in which he wishes justice done, whether the case be civil or criminal, he will prefer the European judge.

" When one realizes that the chief obstacle among oriental peoples to the establishment of self-government is not a lack of intelligence, but rather a lack of trustworthiness and truthfulness, qualities upon which all successful organization in both business and politics must rest, the deep significance of such facts must not be overlooked."—J. W. Jenks : *Report to War Department*, 1902.

CHAPTER XVIII

Africa

§ 53. EGYPT

THE nineteenth century witnessed an extension of European influence into Africa. Previous to 1800 the interior of the "Dark Continent" was unknown

Ottoman states in Africa.

and uncared for. A few stations on the West Coast had been established, centers of the traffic in ivory, gold, and slaves. The states along the northern coast, bordering the Mediterranean, were remnants of the once great Mohammedan empire, still loosely attached to the center of the faith at Constantinople. The conquests of Napoleon in Egypt had been abandoned when

MEHEMET ALI.

the emperor gave up his oriental schemes for the greater project of the control of Europe, and Egypt had returned into the hands of her Turkish governors.

In the troublous times which followed the French invasion of

Mehemet Ali.

Egypt a new and strong dynasty arose. Mehemet Ali, Pasha of Egypt, while nominally governing as viceroy of the Sultan, set to work to reorganize the country. The estates of the great landholders were converted into national do-

312

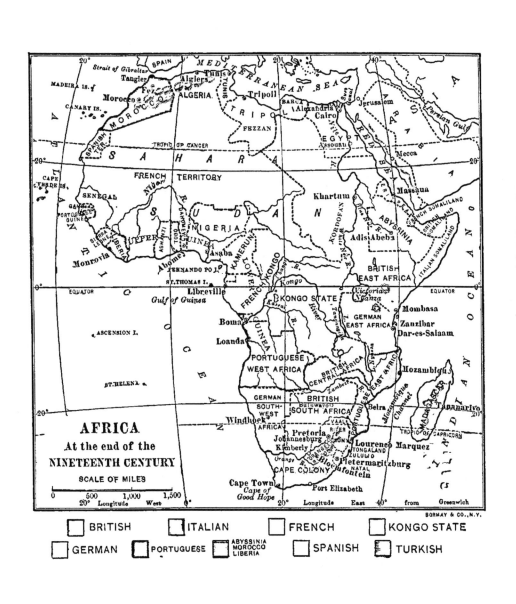

AFRICA.
At the end of the
NINETEENTH CENTURY

SCALE OF MILES

BRITISH	ITALIAN	FRENCH	KONGO STATE
GERMAN	PORTUGUESE	ABYSSINIA MOROCCO LIBERIA	SPANISH	TURKISH

BORMAY & CO., N.Y.

main, and from the income of these lands and from taxes
Mehemet Ali built up an able army after the European
pattern, officered with French military experts. His fleet
was greater than the Turkish fleet and better manned.

The Greek revolt gave Mehemet Ali an opportunity to
try his forces. The Sultan, unable with his own resources
to put down the Greeks, called his Egyptian vassal to his
aid, and the invasion of Crete and the Morea followed.
That the Greeks were not wholly crushed was owing to the
sympathy aroused in Europe and the intervention of the
Western Powers. Mehemet Ali was forced to retire, but
he claimed his reward, the government of Syria, which the
Sultan had promised him in return for his assistance.
Waiting three years in vain, he advanced into Syria, took
the province by force, and made his way northward toward
Constantinople. The powers intervened and Mehemet Ali
was checked, but retained, through the good offices of
France, the government of Syria. In 1839 Turkey sought
to drive him out, but the Egyptian army was again successful, and marched once more upon Constantinople.
Nothing but the intervention of the Powers prevented the
Egyptian Viceroy from seizing the throne of Turkey.
England and France sent their fleets to the Bosphorus and
co-operated with the Turkish troops in the defence of the
city. Again Mehemet Ali was driven back, and forced to
terms of peace, by which he gave up Syria and contented
himself with the hereditary government of Egypt, conferred upon him and his descendants by a decree of the
Sultan. Thus the Powers again saved Turkey from conquest, and established a hereditary dynasty on the throne
of Egypt.

Egypt, regenerated and strongly governed by the family of Mehemet Ali, extended its influence, in the reign of
Ismaïl Pasha (1863-1879), into the heart of Africa. The
region of the Upper Nile was conquered by the Egyptian
army, commanded by European officers, and the empire of

Ismaïl extended to the great lakes at the Nile sources
and to the Indian Ocean on the Somali coast.   During

Ismaïl Pasha.

his reign the Suez Canal was constructed,
through the indomitable energy of Ferdinand
de Lesseps. It was formally opened with great celebration in
the presence of the Empress Eugénie, on November 19, 1869,
"the last great day of the Second Empire," as it has been
called.   England was doubtful of the success of the undertaking, but, when once it had been accomplished, she saw
that the safety of the route to India lay in her control of
the canal.   With commercial shrewdness she took advan-

FERDINAND DE LESSEPS

tage of the financial needs of the
Khedive, Ismaïl, and purchased
his 177,000 shares in the Suez
Company, thereby obtaining a
majority interest. Ismaïl, carried
away with the sudden importance
and prosperity of his rule, plunged
into extravagances and borrowed
freely in Europe.   Bankruptcy
was threatened, and French and
English creditors urged their respective governments to intervene.   Thus a new motive was introduced into the international

politics of the world, a financial motive, likely to be as important for the future as the earlier motives of legitimacy
and balance of power.   The orientals are good borrowers,
and their chronic inability to pay leads in the end to foreign intervention.

Under this pressure England and France intervened to
force Ismaïl to entrust the administration of

The
Condominium.

his finances to English and French agents.
He refused and was deposed and replaced
with his son Tewfik, who accepted the joint control, and
made a place in his ministry for two financial agents, one

French and one English. This was the end of Egyptian independence.

This intervention was not cheerfully accepted, however, by the national Egyptian party. A military agitator, Arabi Pasha, organized a movement against the foreign control. At the same time, in the Upper Nile country, a pretended prophet or *Mahdi*, Mohammed Ahmed, preached a crusade against the hated Christians. This double insurrection came to a head in 1882 : Arabi Pasha, with the Egyptians of the Lower Nile, pillaged the houses of Europeans and seized Alexandria. The English invited the French to intervene, but, in an evil hour for her, France refused. An English fleet bombarded Alexandria; General Wolseley disembarked 20,000 men, defeated Arabi Pasha at Tel-el-Kebir and entered Cairo. In this manner England broke the *Condominium*, and has since remained in possession of Egypt, to the exclusion of French influence.

It remained to conquer the Mahdi, who showed great powers of resistance. His troops, under the command of Osman Digma, swept the valley of the Nile, and took Khartoum, where the Anglo-Egyptian general, Gordon, was murdered (January, 1885). A national hero, his fate aroused great indignation in England, and hastened the reconquest of the Soudan. General Kitchener, with admirable organization and well-planned advances, overthrew the Mahdi, and re-established Egyptian rule in the Upper Nile country.

The Soudan.

Meanwhile, English rule has greatly benefited the Egyptians. Extensive works for regulating the overflow of the Nile, upon which the fertility of Egypt depends, are now in progress, and their completion will largely increase the area of Egyptian tillage.

§ 54.   THE CONGO FREE STATE

The explorations of Livingstone opened up the heart of the Dark Continent.   Before his death in 1873 he had

Central Africa.

carried the British name and influence into regions up to that time unknown.   In 1871 Stanley began his travels, destined to draw the attention of Europe to the valley of the Congo, and to set in motion that scramble for land which in a few years caused the whole of this great continent, hitherto despised, to be

divided up among the Powers of Europe.   An important discovery was that the Lualaba River, found by Livingstone in Central Africa, was the upper stretches of the Congo.   This gave a great waterway from the West Coast to the interior, and promised to make Central Africa accessible as it had never been before.

In 1876 Leopold II, King of the Belgians, gathered together at Brussels a con-

HENRY M. STANLEY.

African International Association.

vention of geographers and other persons interested in African explorations from all parts of Europe.   The African International Association was formed, the main object of which was to extinguish the slave-trade in Central Africa, where thousands of poor negroes were captured by bands of slave-hunting Arabs, and carried off for sale in the slave-markets of the Mohammedan world.   The International Association did little of itself, but French, Belgian, and German explorers were sent out in national expeditions to explore East Central Africa.

In January, 1878, Stanley landed at Marseilles, coming

directly from his Congo explorations. King Leopold proposed to him to attack Africa from the west, by way of the Congo. Stanley accepted and entered the service of the Belgian king. In the following year his expedition arrived at the mouth of the Congo, and carried around the cataracts, which interrupt the navigation of the river not far from the coast, several steam-launches, which were put together in the upper river, at Stanley Pool. With these the expedition proceeded along the upper river, establishing posts and laying the foundations of a new African state.

The activity of King Leopold hastened the scramble for African possessions. France sent de Brazza into the new Congo country, and even Portugal was awakened to the fact that her old African claims, long neglected, were becoming valuable. Out of this jumble of conflicting claims Prince Bismarck summoned order by suggesting an International Conference at Berlin, for the purpose of discussing African questions and arranging boundaries.

The Berlin Conference (1884).

In the meantime the Congo Association, formed under the auspices of the Belgian king, had arranged its difficulties with the separate powers. It conceded to Portugal the south bank of the Congo at its mouth, but secured by the north bank the access to the ocean which it desired. The powers of the Berlin Conference recognized the existence of an Independent Congo State, under the control of the Congo International Association. There was to be absolute freedom of trade and navigation of the Congo basin, and all nations were to enjoy equal privileges.

. In 1885 the Belgian parliament authorized King Leopold to accept the headship of the state founded by the Congo International Association. "The union between Belgium and the new state was to be exclusively personal." Soon afterward King Leopold announced to the Powers that the Association had been changed to the Congo Free State, and he

The Congo Free State.

declared the perpetual neutrality of the new state.   Yet it was evident that King Leopold looked forward to the eventual union of the Congo State with Belgium.   By his will, in 1889, he made Belgium heir to the Congo State. In the following year the Belgian Government advanced twenty-five million francs for African improvements (mainly the railroad to Stanley Pool), with the condition that after ten years Belgium might annex the Free State ; in 1894 the constitution of Belgium was amended to permit such annexation.   The government has never yet foreclosed its mortgage, very likely because it is more convenient to have the Congo governed as a separate state, without bringing it into the parliamentary struggles of the home country.

The exploration of the Congo and the establishment of the authority of the Free State along the great river and its tributaries brought the Belgian officials into hostile contact with the Arab slave-hunters.   The methods of these hunters of men were particularly atrocious.   Surrounding African villages, they burn and kill and devastate the settlements, leading the survivors off to the slave markets of Khartoum or Zanzibar.   Whole tribes have been exterminated and great districts laid waste.   In 1885, when the Belgians arrived at Stanley Pool, they found the chief of the slave-hunters, Tippo Tib, already established there.   War was inevitable.

The war against the Arabs.

It broke out in 1891, and lasted three years.   In this time the power of the Arabs was broken ; the slave-hunters were killed off, forced to flee or be taken prisoners.   In this campaign the Congo troops, pressing eastward, established the authority of the Free State to the limits imposed by the Berlin Congress.   Thus through the creation of the Congo State the original purpose of the African International Association has been accomplished, and the slave-trade, attacked in its hunting-grounds, has been practically abolished.

VIEW ON THE CONGO RIVER.

The International State, opened to all nations alike, as contemplated by the Berlin Conference, has been trans-

The Administra-
tion.

formed, in the course of events, into a Belgian colony. But it is not likely that the Berlin project could have succeeded. Immense expenditures were necessary to open the Congo basin, and it is improbable that King Leopold would have invested his fortune in a project of general interest. The 15,000 miles of navigable river in the Congo basin were of no avail until transportation could be secured from the coast to the cataracts; and for this a railroad must be constructed at a cost of many millions. Into this Leopold and the Belgians have turned their resources. It seems likely to be a good investment, both for king and people. By a decree of 1885 all vacant lands are the domain of the king. The royal revenue from rubber and ivory, amounting to many millions a year, are reinvested by the king in agriculture, in the creation of great plantations, which in later times will be immensely valuable. The same is being done by many chartered Belgian companies.

§ 55.　Europe in Africa

English influence in Africa has two lines of extension : from the Cape northward ; and from Egypt southward toward the sources of the Nile. This has sug-

English
Possessions.

gested the project of the " Cape to Cairo " railway, which, with one exception, the crossing of German East Africa, would traverse territory possessed by or controlled by England. From the Cape the English have passed northward, beyond the Dutch Republics, now, by the issue of the Boer War, included within the sphere of British control, annexing the lands of various native tribes, and incorporating them into British Central Africa, reaching to Lake Tanganyika on the north. British East Africa, with the Island of Zanzibar, assigned to England by the Congress of 1885, extends to Lake Victoria on the west, and reaches on the north to the Soudanese protectorate. On the West Coast Gambia, Sierra Leone, and the Gold Coast are possessions dating back to slave-trading times, while Nigeria is a recently acquired protectorate.

France began to interest herself in Africa in 1830. Algiers was then a dependency of Turkey, and the Algerian pirates had been for centuries the bane **French possessions.** of Mediterranean commerce. In 1827 a quarrel between France and Algiers, arising from an interference with the rights of merchants of Marseilles to engage in the coral fishery off the African coast, resulted in hostilities. Charles X sent an army across the Mediterranean and compelled the capitulation of the city of Algiers. Three weeks later came the Revolution of February, and Louis Philippe became King of the French. The military operations in Algiers continued; in 1837 the city of Constantine was taken and the Turkish garrisons driven from Algiers. The Arabs had next to be reckoned with, the military lords of the country, who had in earlier times conquered the Berbers, or natives of Algiers, but were forced to yield in turn to Turkish rule. Abd-el-Kader, emir of Mascara, roused the Arabs to a holy war against the Christians. Defeated, he retired into Morocco, where he induced the Sultan of Morocco, Abd-er-Rhaman, to declare war against France. Hostilities continued until 1847, when Abd-el-Kader was captured and taken to France, where he was held prisoner until 1853, when he was set at liberty. Turks and Arabs having been subdued, there still remained the original population, the Berbers. Their subjugation was a long and tedious affair; it was not until 1880 that the more distant tribes of the Sahara were finally brought under French rule.

The possession of Algeria led to the occupation of the

22

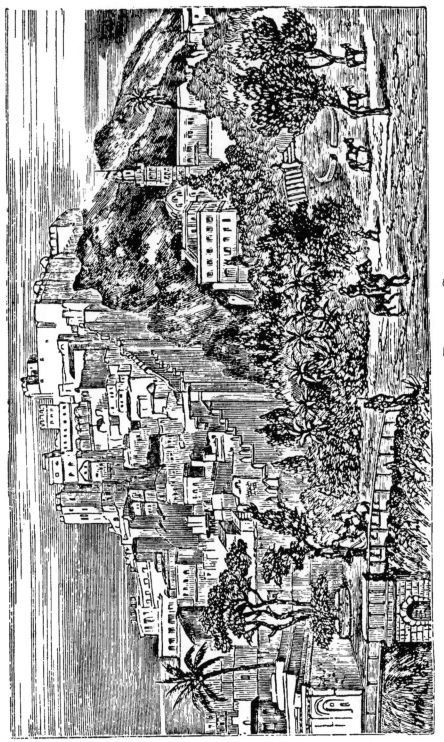

ALGIERS, FROM THE PARADE GROUND.

neighboring state of Tunis. The depredations of the
Tunisian tribesmen in Algeria was the pretext for French
interference; the real motive was the fear of Italian occu-
pation. In 1881, taking advantage of some trifling misun-
derstanding with the Bey of Tunis, French troops entered
the country and imposed upon the Bey the Treaty of
Bardo, whereby the French protectorate was recognized.
This great French state of North Africa, with Algeria and
Tunis on the north, stretches southward across the desert,
including Senegal on the West Coast. Reaching to the
River Niger on the south, it extends eastward to Lake
Tchad, including a rich and populous country, the last of
Africa to be contended for by the Powers. At Lake
Tchad the spheres of French and English influence meet.
During the troubles in the Soudan the French explorer,
Marchand, penetrated eastward into the valley of the upper
Nile, then lost to Egypt, and defeated a band of Dervishes
at Fashoda. Here Marchand met the English column
advancing southward, and, yielding to orders from France,
gave way. An Anglo-French convention in the following
year defined the boundary between English and French
protectorates. The Marchand incident may be regarded
as a French protest against the English occupation of
Egypt (ever a sore point with France), but the French
Government was not prepared to carry the protest to a
point of hostilities.

France also possesses settlements on the West Coast,
French Congo and Dahomey; but next to French North
Africa her most important African colony is
Madagascar. the island of Madagascar. In 1638, in the
reign of Louis XIII, Fort Dauphin was founded at the
south end of the island; but French interests developed
slowly. In 1868 the queen of the Hovas, a tribe of Malay
origin, inhabiting the table-lands of Central Madagascar,
was converted by English missionaries, whose influence
was hostile to the French. In 1878 war broke out with

the Hovas, and continued with some interruptions until
1895, when an expedition was sent from France, which
occupied Tananarive, the Hovas capital, and Queen Rana-
valo was exiled to the island of Réunion. Slavery has
been abolished in Madagascar and efforts made to encour-
age education and industry.

The Germans were also desirous of African possessions.
Coming late into the field, they have found little opportunity for colonial expansion; the Indies were
occupied; American colonization prohibited
by the Monroe Doctrine; only Africa remained. The Congress of Berlin gave to Germany: German East Africa, between Zanzibar and Lake Tanganyika;
Southwest Africa, or the regions of Damara and Nama-
quas, north of the Orange River; the Cameroons, at the
foot of the Gulf of Guinea; and Togo, between the English
Gold Coast and French Dahomey. The Germans have not
shown as yet a marked ability for colonial enterprises. Of
the thousands of Germans who migrate every year from the
Fatherland, the greater part are still seeking their homes
under foreign flags.

*German posses-
sions.*

Italy, arriving late, but wishing to take a hand in the
partition of Africa, seized the territory about Massoura on
the Red Sea, and sought to create the colony
of Erythræa, with a protectorate over the
Kingdom of Abyssinia. The task proved difficult beyond her expectations. In 1896 her troops were
annihilated by the army of the Abyssinian king, Menelik,
and Italy's colonial ardor was quenched for the time. She
has established a protectorate on the Indian Ocean over
the land of the Somalis, and still holds Massowa and the
neighboring territory.

*Italian and Portu-
guese possessions.*

Portugal, once mistress of Africa, still possesses important colonies, unprogressive and badly governed. On
the West Coast she has Portuguese Guinea, and Angola,
south of the mouth of the Congo; on the East Coast,

Mozambique, stretching southward from German East Africa along the coast opposite Madagascar, including the port of Lorenzo Marques, important as the entrance to the Transvaal from the sea. The Portuguese had hopes of uniting Angola and Mozambique, and thus forming a belt across Africa ; but the English have extended their holdings northward from the Cape, cutting away the " Hinterland " of Portugal and confining her to the coast.

Spain's possessions in Africa are few. Opposite the Canaries she has a strip, whose back country extends indefinitely into the Desert of Sahara. In the Gulf of Guinea she has the island of Fernando Po and some small settlements on the main. She looks, however, upon Morocco as her eventual share of Africa, if France ever should allow her to take it, and the Powers permit its appropriation.

CHAPTER XIX

The Far East

§ 56. CHINA AND JAPAN

BEFORE the middle of the nineteenth century the great oriental nations of China and Japan were outside the range of European politics. China had been for centuries, it is true, a field for missionaries and traders. The Chinese are essentially a commercial people, and their teas and silks have long been known in western markets. For purposes of trade Europeans were permitted to establish settlements along the coast, and many ports upon the sea and on the great navigable rivers have been opened for trade, often with force, and always against the desire of the exclusive Celestials. China, however, with her ancient and highly developed civilization, has resisted the introduction of western ideas and has clung tenaciously to her established customs. Her people have migrated into all the lands bordering upon the Pacific Ocean, and given evidence of their ability to compete successfully with other nations in commerce and industry, everywhere preserving their racial characteristics.

Japanese history has been very different. Satisfied with her institutions, and fearful of the intrusion of foreigners, she remained until the middle of the nineteenth century a sealed empire. This policy she was able to carry out successfully, on account of her compact political organization, whereas China is little more than a group of eighteen semi-independent provinces, feebly held together by the imperial power at Pekin.

China.

Japan.

FUSIYAMA, SACRED MOUNTAIN OF JAPAN.

Japan's early experience with the Spanish and Portuguese strengthened her policy of exclusion, and led her to cut herself off utterly from intercourse with the western world. A law of 1637 prohibited all natives of Japan from leaving their country, and visited with the penalty of death any attempt to open communication with foreigners. For over two centuries the only connection of Japan with the outside world was through a little settlement of Dutch merchants, permitted to occupy, under conditions which practically made them prisoners, an island in the harbor of Nagasaki.

In 1852 the government of the United States resolved to establish, by force, if necessary, diplomatic and trade relations with Japan. In the following year Commodore Perry entered the harbor of Yedo with four war vessels, and presented a letter to the regent (or *Tai-kun*), whom he took to be the emperor. Returning in 1854 for his answer, he overawed the Yedo authorities with his show of force and extracted a treaty, which permitted the establishment of trade, and resulted in the opening of the ports of Yokohama, Nagasaki, and Hakodate. The European powers quickly followed, and treaties were signed with England, Russia, and France.

Perry and Japan.

The foreign policy of the *Tai-kun* was resented by the conservative elements of the Japanese people, who viewed with fear the prospect of a foreign invasion. Outrages upon foreign representatives and merchants followed, and these were promptly punished with the bombardment of Japanese ports by American and European fleets, and by the exaction of indemnities. A change of feeling toward foreigners gradually came about, largely through the influence of young Japanese, who visited Europe and America and discovered that the western nations had no other than pacific intentions toward Japan. Upon their return they communicated this to their people and eventually dispelled their fears.

Meanwhile the intercourse with foreigners and the education of young men abroad were working great changes in the national spirit. The sacred emperor, the "Child of Heaven," had for centuries been a recluse, and all powers vested in the

Constitutional changes.

regent. In 1868 the progressive party brought the emperor from retirement, and after severe fighting established his personal power. Mutsohito inclined toward western

JAPANESE INFAN-
TRYMAN.

ideas. He began the new régime by transferring his residence from Kyoto to Yedo, changing the name of the latter city to Tokyo, the "Eastern Capital." Foreigners were welcomed; many young men were sent abroad to be educated; a new military system was introduced, with railroads, telegraphs, and schools; society was revolutionized with the abolition of feudalism. In 1882 an imperial decree established a constitution with representative government. The manner in which Japan has taken on a western civilization and made it in all respects effective is the wonder of the century.

Corea, the "Hermit Kingdom," lies near to Japan, and is a market for Japanese products. Traditionally Corea is a dependency of China, although independent in her internal affairs, and governed, in a wretched manner, by a king. Russia, on the north, looks with envious eyes upon the Corean peninsula, as rounding out the Asiatic Empire of the Tsar on the Pacific. Russia and China were combined to oppose the Japanese influence in Corea.

In 1894 a rebellion broke out in Corea, and the king called upon China for aid. Japan resented the interference of China, and sent troops to offset the Chinese intervention. War was the result; the Chinese troops were rapidly driven

The Chinese-Japanese War.

from Corea, and the war carried into China. The Japanese troops, finely disciplined and equipped, met little resistance from the ill-formed Chinese levies. Pekin was threatened; China sued for peace, and Li-Hung-Chang, a noted Chinese statesman, was sent to Japan to arrange the conditions. China acknowledged the independence of Corea, ceded to Japan the island of Formosa, the Liao-tung peninsula on the coast of China, and agreed to pay a great indemnity. But Russia, France, and Germany intervened and prevented the cession of any portion of the mainland of China to Japan. Under one pretext or another the western powers took for themselves the strategic points on the Gulf of Pechili, which they had denied to Japan. Russia took Port Arthur, gaining a southern terminus for her Trans-Siberian railroad; England, seeking

A TYPICAL
BOXER.

always to check Russian advance in the Orient, took the port of Wei-hai-wei, across the Gulf from Port Arthur; and Germany, seeking reparation for the murder of some missionaries by the Chinese, seized upon the harbor and neighborhood of Kiao-tcheou. Thus, on the Chinese coast, spheres of European influence have been established, and the way opened for an eventual dismemberment of the Celestial Empire.

EMPEROR OF CHINA.
(Alleged portrait.)

In 1900 a wave of anti-foreign feeling swept over China, the result in part of the seizure of Chinese territory by the western Powers. A patriotic society, called the "Boxers," sought to exterminate the Occidentals and

put an end to the invasion of western influences, which
have always been unwelcome, and which seem to threaten,
with railroads and new religions, the ancient
civilization of the "Middle Kingdom." Missionaries were massacred and the foreign embassies at
Pekin besieged. A joint army of the Powers (of which the
United States was one) was sent to the relief of the embassies, and after much effort Pekin was reached and
sacked, and the ambassadors and their families rescued.
The Chinese Government sued for peace, and consented to
make apologies and pay a huge indemnity. In 1902 England and Japan formed an alliance for the preservation of
the territories of China and Corea, an act which is likely
to check for a time the dismemberment of the "Middle
Kingdom."

The Boxers.

§ 57. Russia in Asia

In the reign of Ivan the Terrible the Cossack leader,
Irmak, at the head of 850 men crossed into Asia, and,
traversing the immense forests of Tobol, defeated the Tartar Khan and took Sibir, his
capital. Thus a new crown, that of Siberia,
was added to the crown of Russia. In the seventeenth
century the progress of annexation carried the Russians to
the Pacific Ocean and to Lake Baikal in the south. The
peninsula of Kamtchatka was annexed in 1707. Up to
this time the Asiatic possessions were of small importance
to Russia; the northern portion of Siberia is too cold for
habitation, except by Arctic tribes.

Formation of the Russian Empire.

The eighteenth century added little to Asiatic Russia.
The Kirgis Tartars acknowledged the sovereignty of the
Tsar, and Russia was rid of a race of fierce robbers, who
lived by the plunder of caravans, and barred the way to
the East; but their territory is a desert waste.

The nineteenth century saw a wide extension of the
Asiatic Empire. In 1801 the Tsar Paul, an enthusiastic

admirer of Napoleon, planned a campaign against the English in India, and crossed the Caucasus and annexed Georgia. This was the beginning of the Russian province of Caucasia, where subsequent annexations (Mingrelia, 1803, to Kars, 1877), have built up the most populous and flourishing section of Asiatic Russia. The soil is productive; there are mines of copper, lead, and coal, a district of oil-wells at Baku on the Caspian, and the people are civilized and industrious.

THE MOSQUE OF THE PALACE OF KHIVA.

The second half of the nineteenth century was marked by the extension of Russian power into the southwest of Asia, in the direction of Afghanistan and India. Turkestan was made a Russian province in 1865, a sterile land, except in the valleys of the rivers. The conquest of one Tartar tribe led to further warfare, until the whole country had been absorbed down to the independent state of Afghanistan. Here lay some of the most fertile tracts of Western Asia. The Khanate of Bokhara, taken in 1868, is the richest of the Asiatic lands of Russia, with a population of two and a half millions.

The Khanates.

The Khanate of Khiva, taken in 1873, is smaller, with a population of 700,000. The people are Mohammedan. It has been the policy of Russia to hold these great Khanates as vassal states. This saves the friction and expense of military occupation, and yet insures to Russia the advantages of trade. Surrounded on all sides by Russian garrisons, the Khanates are thoroughly subdued.

In 1880 a new expedition under General Skobeloff subdued the Turkomans south and east of the Caspian, took Merv in 1881 and completed the subjugation of Turkestan.

MONGOLS.

A railway, started from Krasnovodsk on the east shore of the Caspian, runs southeast by way of Merv to Bokhara, Sarmakand, and Tashkend, passing along the northern border of Afghanistan and reaching at one point, Kuskh, to within eighty miles of Herat, the "Gate of India." Between Russian Turkestan and India lies the "buffer state" of Afghanistan, which Russia threatens with her railroad and her chain of fortresses on the northern border. Here, and in Persia on the west, Russian and English influences struggle for control. There are frequent rumors of a Russian railway extension across Persia to the Persian Gulf. This would give Russia access to the Indian Ocean, where a Russian fleet would prove an additional menace to the English power in India. Apart from this, Russia has no doubt given peace and the prospect of advancement to southwestern Asia.

Having reached the limits of her present extension on the borders of Afghanistan and Persia, the later activity of Russia in Asia has been directed toward the extreme East, at the expense of the northern provinces of the Chi-

EASTERN ASIA
AND EAST INDIES
At the end of the
NINETEENTH CENTURY.
SCALE OF MILES

FRENCH   BRITISH   RUSSIAN   CHINESE   GERMAN

DUTCH   NATIVE STATES   AFGHANISTAN   TURKISH

UNITED STATES   OMAN   BHUTAN   JAPANESE

nese Empire. The Treaty of Pekin, 1860, secured to Russia all that former Chinese territory north of the Amur River, together with the maritime province of Ussuri. Here Russia looks across the sea to Japan and joins Corea on the south.

The Chinese Border.

This was a better outlet to the Pacific than the frozen waters of Okhotsh ; but the southernmost harbor of Ussuri, Vladivostok, is still too icebound for a perfect har-

VIEW OF TRANS-SIBERIAN RAILWAY.

bor, and Russia continued to scheme for an outlet into warmer seas.

Meanwhile the great Trans-Siberian Railway was projected and begun by Alexander III. This vast system of railway, connecting St. Petersburg with Vladivostok, has been pushed forward with great energy, until it is now nearing completion. The threatened break-up of China, the result of the war with Japan, gave an opportunity for a more southerly terminus. In the scramble of Russia, Germany, and England for Chinese ports Russia secured Port Arthur, on the Gulf of Pechili. An agreement between the courts of Pekin and St. Petersburg has given

Russia a free hand in Manchuria, and permission to construct a southern branch of the Trans-Siberian Railway through Manchuria, under the name of the "Eastern Chinese Railway." This concession, with a rendezvous for the Russian fleet at the terminus, Port Arthur (or Dalny), gives Russia a fine naval and commercial base on the Pacific. Strategically, its advantages are limited somewhat, perhaps, by the English occupation of the port of Wei-hai-wei, directly across the mouth of the Gulf of Pechili.

These two great powers, England and Russia, have marched across Asia side by side, Russia on the north, England on the south, a zone of high mountains and deserts between them. On the west of Asia their interests clash in Persia and Afghanistan ; on the east, in China. France, with her colonies of Tonking and Annam on the south, bars the way to English advance along the southern line into China. The newly risen power of Japan will have something to say, before she sees her Chinese cousins become the vassals of distant western powers. Already we have the whisperings of an Asiatic "Monroe Doctrine" of " Asia for the Asiatics." But China is to-day the checkerboard of European diplomacy. She is being pushed unwillingly along the path of progress. It will be interesting to see under what guidance and with whose aid she will accommodate herself to western ideas and methods.

England and Russia in Asia.

CHAPTER XX

Material Progress

§ 58. The Art of War

In the Middle Ages the mounted knight, clad in armor, with lance and sword, decided the issue of battle. But little was thought of the foot soldier ; war was the business of nobles, and the task of the peasant and the artisan was to labor for the support of the gentleman-at-arms. The medieval battle had no element of strategy ; no effort to take advantage of the character of the country, its hills and valleys, for superior position. Indeed, the principles of chivalry rather indicated that the opposing armies should meet in a " fair field," without advantage to either host. The battle was a judgment of God, and, when each commander was assured of the justice of his cause, there was no need of seeking a superior position. The opposing armies rode furiously at each other, and the clash of lances and the ensuing play of swords determined victory.

Modern times have revolutionized the art of war with the introduction of foot soldiers. They came from two sources : the English archer, with his long-bow and cloth-yard shaft emptied the saddles of the French knights in the battles of the Hundred Years' War ; but a more important factor was the phalanx of Swiss pikemen, against whom the armed knights dashed themselves in vain. The success of the Swiss made them sought for by all princes, and their presence decided many battles of the fifteenth and sixteenth centuries. Meanwhile their methods were adopted, with some improvements, by the Germans and the

Spaniards.   Behind the rows of defensive pikes were placed men with swords and other weapons of offense. When the horsemen had been routed with the pikes, the front rows parted and let through the swordsmen, who finished with the defenseless cavalry.   The day of the knight was over, and infantry became the important branch in warfare.

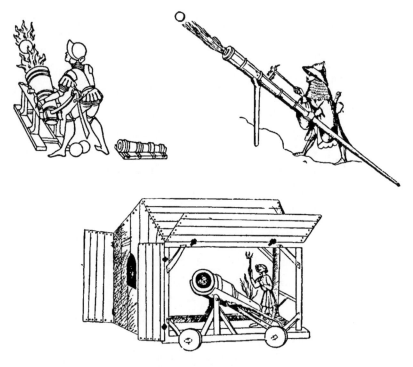

EARLY CANNON.

The use of gunpowder gradually supplanted the bow and cross-bow.   Siege-guns were earlier adopted than explosive hand-arms.   The great weight of the **Firearms.** ancient arquebus, which made it necessary to carry a forked iron for a rest, limited its use.   The complicated mechanism of the later wheel-lock and the firelock retarded their introduction.   In the sixteenth century might be seen, side by side, the bow, the arquebus, and the mechanical cross-bow, the arbalest.

The musket was the arquebus, somewhat shortened and reduced in weight, without the fork. They were made with both wheel and match-locks. In the seventeenth century bands of musketeers were reinforced with pikemen; having fired their shot, the musketeers retired behind the pikemen who guarded them from attack during the tedious process of reloading. In 1664 the French borrowed the paper cartridge from the Spaniards, who seem to have be the military inventors of the time. About 1630, the flint-lock was known in Italy; but it did not supplant the musket until the beginning of the eighteenth century. The bayonet came about the same time. For over a hundred

ARBALEST.

dred years the flint-lock held its place in the armies of Europe. In the eighteenth century, although much progress was made in the science of war, in the organization of battles and the direction of sieges, little was accomplished in the improvement of weapons. The great wars of the French Revolution and of Napoleon were fought with the flint-lock. At a time when the mind of all

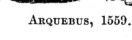

ARQUEBUS, 1559.

Europe was centered upon war, science and invention made no contribution. The battles of Napoleon were won

23

by the superior mobility of his troops, "with the legs of his soldiers." To this must be added the immense enthusiasm which animated a democratic army, in which any man, with bravery and ability, might win a marshal's *baton*.

SEVENTEENTH CENTURY MATCHLOCK.

During the first half of the century progress was not rapid. To be sure, the invention of the percussion cap made possible a lighter and more reliable weapon ; but in military science the period was relatively barren. The Crimean War was a lamentable failure to feed, clothe, and otherwise provide for large bodies of men at a distance from the base of supplies. The Italian campaign of Napoleon III, with its battles of Magenta and Solferino, was a contest of brute force, the hurling of great bodies of men against each other, without ability to foresee the outcome. The carnage was so terrible that Napoleon dared not proceed to the conquest of Venetia.

But military science was growing ; the Prussian school of von Moltke placed war upon a scientific basis. With a perfectly drilled and equipped army, and a knowledge of the enemies' country, war became a great game of strategy. Invention came to the aid of the Prussians. In 1847 the needle-gun, a breech-loading weapon, using a metallic cartridge, was adopted. After the Prussian victory over Austria this weapon became, under various

Nineteenth century.

forms—Chassepot, Mauser, Martini—the weapon of Europe. The breech-loading principle applied to cannon worked a similar revolution. Since 1880 the great makers of ordnance, Armstrong, Krupp, Creusot, have vied with each other in the production of rapid, long-range cannon. The discovery of new and powerful explosives has added much to the efficacy of these new weapons. Nitro-glycerine, dynamite, and other similar compounds have a destructive force much greater than gunpowder.

SHIP OF WAR, SEVENTEENTH CENTURY.

Smokeless powder has made possible a lighter gun, a smaller ball, and longer range. New explosives—melanite, roburite, and the like—have replaced gunpowder for use in high-power artillery.

Since the invention of the high explosives, and since the states of Europe have become, with the introduction of the Prussian system of compulsory military service, great armed camps, no war between powerful nations has taken place. The idea of such a war is frightful ; and in the minds of many, this universal armament and invention, by making war so hideous, paves the way for peace ; and this is at least to be hoped.

In naval warfare, as well, the nineteenth century has brought about great changes. The American War of the Rebellion produced a new type of armored vessel, which rapidly took the place of the old wooden war-ship. Instead of great wooden forts, modern navies are made up of complicated steel mechanisms, filled with wonderful devices, set in motion by steam and electricity. England leads the world in the number and variety of these formidable engines of marine warfare, and she is closely followed by the other great nations. Of late the effort of invention has been toward the perfection of submarine, torpedo-bearing craft. Of all these the real efficacy is unknown. No trial of strength has yet taken place between two modern navies. The events of the Chinese War and of the Spanish-American War were but naval skirmishes, viewed with intense interest by naval experts of all nations. The modern naval battle has yet to be fought.

Naval warfare.

§ 59. INVENTION

The nineteenth century was especially prolific in invention. The sciences, which up to that time were largely the playthings of philosophers, became in the nineteenth century the sources whence came innumerable inventions, tending to increase the wealth and comfort of mankind. The practical arts have been so revolutionized that "the distance is much greater between the industrial processes of the eighteenth century and those of the present day than between those of the eighteenth century and the ancient arts, even those of Egypt."

Steam.

Between 1790 and 1815 the English used water-power for driving their spinning and weaving machinery. The use of steam as a motive-power, the invention of Watt, improved by the American, Oliver Evans, and by others, came into use soon after. The steam engine has been put to three great uses : the stationary engine, first used in mines, now replaces animal, wind, and water power in the manufacture of goods of all kinds, and in agricultural operations, such as threshing ; secondly, it is used for propelling steamboats ; and, thirdly, it furnishes the motive power for land transportation (railways).

The idea of applying steam to transportation seems to have haunted the minds of many men at the close of the eighteenth century. The practical solution, however, is attributed to the American, Fulton, whose steamboat successfully navigated

Steam transportation.

the Hudson River in 1807. In 1814 the Savannah, an American steamship, crossed from Savannah to Liverpool in twenty-five days, six more than was required by fast sailing vessels ; in 1821 the "Enterprise," an English steamship, made the voyage to India in forty-five days. In 1838 the first screw-propeller boat was built in England, and from this time on the propeller began to take the place of side-wheels for deep-water navigation. England has led the nations of the world in the manufacture and use of steam vessels, although of late the German builders have produced some of the swiftest ocean "liners." Iron and steel have replaced wood in the construction of steamships.

The railway, like other great inventions, came gradually. In 1800 Evans propelled a car with steam in the streets of Philadelphia ; but his experiment aroused little interest. In England the idea was taken up, and in 1812 Stephenson constructed a machine somewhat resembling the locomotive of to-day. For several years the locomotive was used for hauling coal-cars from the mines. In 1839 the first steam passenger train ran from Liverpool to Manchester. Railroad lines were rapidly constructed in Europe and America, and now they have become a necessary ele-

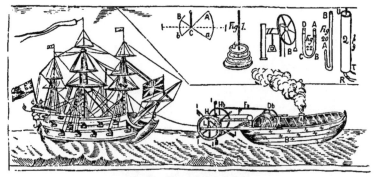

Hull's Steamboat, 1736.

Fitch's First Boat, 1787.

The Clermont, 1807.

EARLY PROJECTS OF STEAM NAVIGATION.

ment in our lives. Great lines of railway traverse both hemispheres from Atlantic to Pacific, and a Trans-Saharan line is the dream of French engineers.

The employment of electricity is a triumph of the second half of the nineteenth century. It has been adapted

Electricity.

to the electric telegraph, to the telephone, to electric lighting, and to the propulsion of vehicles. Before 1850 the aërial telegraph, a method of signaling with semaphores, from hilltop to hilltop, was

STEPHENSON'S NO. 1 ENGINE, 1825.

the most rapid means of transferring intelligence. Between 1833 and 1838 the principle of electric telegraphy occupied the attention of physicists in France, Germany, and England, when Morse discovered a method by which messages could be transmitted along one wire. After 1850 the electric telegraph came into general use. In 1851 the first submarine telegraph cable was laid between Dover and Calais: and a transatlantic cable in 1857. Now all parts of the world, the Indies and Australia, are connected with Europe and America. The telephone is an invention of the end of the century, competing with the telegraph for long-distance land lines, but of greater utility for local communication.

The discovery of the electric light goes back to the beginning of the century, but it was not until the end of the century that a satisfactory electric lamp was produced. Edison and Swann perfected this apparatus about 1881, and since that time electric lighting has been one of the features of town life. The use of electricity for the pro-

The " Rocket," 1829.

pulsion of street-cars has resulted in the general substitution of this power in the place of draft animals, to the great convenience of the public. Electricity has also been adapted to the automobile, or horseless carriage, where it competes with steam and gas as a motive force.

Among the agents of enlightenment which have benefited from invention is the newspaper. The introduction of the steam press (London *Times*, 1814), together with the cheapening of the cost of paper, has brought the newspaper within the reach of all.   In the early years of the nineteenth century the daily newspaper was a luxury re-

The Newspaper. served for subscribers of the middle class; but now the use of the newspaper has become so general that the formality of subscription has in most instances given way to a daily or semi-daily purchase by all classes of the urban population.

The wide circulation of the newspaper among all classes has made it an important political agent.   It brings the government into contact with the people, making unnecessary the formal posting of proclamations and laws, as was formerly done ; it also brings the people into contact with the government, enabling the dissatisfaction of the people with the acts of government to find expression, and making unnecessary the old right of petition, so strongly insisted upon in earlier times as an important element of popular liberty.

The growing importance of industry, as compared with agriculture, has had its effect upon the distribution of

Effects of industry. population.   At the beginning of the nineteenth century the bulk of the population was rural ; few cities had a population of more than 50,000. New industries, which centered in the cities, in order to secure the advantages of transportation and exchange, brought together there workmen and commercial employees in thousands.   In England, where industry has made the greatest encroachment upon agriculture, more than three-fourths of the population is urban.

The contribution of chemistry to modern progress has been very great.   It has revolutionized agriculture in the

Chemistry. use of chemical fertilizers ; it has given us matches, beet-sugar, preserved foods, and photography, together with a thousand other benefits. From a new natural product it has separated a great number of valuable substances.   In Germany the manufacture of coal-tar products adds $60,000,000 yearly to the national wealth. With the biological sciences, it has given us anesthetics, which render surgery painless; antiseptics, which facilitate the cure of diseases; and the two seem likely to ameliorate and prolong the duration of human life.

§ 60. PROBLEMS OF TO-DAY

At the beginning of modern times society was organized on a basis of birth; a man was and remained noble, burgher, or peasant, according to the condition of his parents. A few men of the superior classes, who were called "well-born," monopolized the good things of earth, and possessed themselves of the offices of wealth and·distinction, by virtue of their birth. They controlled public affairs and gave to society its form. Such a society is called an aristocracy.

Democracy.

Little by little the aristocratic form of society became subject to criticism. We find it attacked with vigor by the "philosophers" of the eighteenth century. A numerous and able class of men were coming forward, the "middle class," enriched with trade, and more closely in touch with the changing needs of society than the aristocrats, who were too well satisfied with themselves and with their conditions to wish for, or even tolerate, change. The resistance of the aristocracy to the spirit of democracy in France resulted in their overwhelming defeat. In other countries, where the revolution was more gradual, they have little by little ceased to be a factor of importance. In England, in Hungary, and in some German states they still retain slight privileges of birth, but even here their pretensions provoke amusement rather than alarm.

The word "democracy" is no longer restricted to its original meaning of a direct government by the people. It has come to be used to designate a society free from the distinctions of birth. It is not necessarily associated with a republic ; the French empires were democratic monarchies.

In the political field the democratic spirit demands that all men shall be equal before the law ; that in matters of justice and taxation or of military duty no distinction based on rank or position shall be known ; that all offices of the state shall be open to all persons alike, who are able to give evidence of their fitness ; that there shall be no bar to the entrance of all persons into the various occupations, professional, commercial, and industrial. This freedom of opportunity, declared by the French Revolution and largely realized in the Empire of Napoleon the Great, has now become general in Europe and America. Universal military service is an application of this principle to one side of modern life, and it is further safeguarded in the reformed civil-service establishments of all progressive nations.

Political democracy.

The democratic spirit is not satisfied, however, with its victories in the political field. No sooner had a reasonable degree of political liberty been won than the struggle was begun for economic liberty and well-being. The system of manufacture on a large scale, as it developed during the nineteenth century, aided by steam and by improved means of transportation, divided the persons interested into two classes : the capitalists and the laborers. These two classes began to array themselves against each other about the middle of the century. The feeling of the laborer, who earned so little that he lived from hand to mouth, and was ruined, if he lost his employment, was that he received too small a portion of the product for his share ; and that the capitalist-employer, who lived in much more agreeable circumstances, and accumulated wealth, received too much ; and no amount of explanation on the part of economic philosophers could convince him that he ought to bear his lot with patience and humility.

Economic democracy.

Out of this dissatisfaction of the laborers grew several parties, who sought to establish a juster division of the Labor unions. product of toil. In England, where progress has ever been conservative, the effort toward solution took the form of an organization of labor into unions. These unions, by strikes and other means of coercion, have achieved much for the laborer in the way of bettering his condition. Capital, opposed by organized labor, has been obliged to yield much. Labor legislation, by reducing the hours of labor, and forbidding in many instances the competition of women and children, is an expression of the democratic spirit.

In France, where men have ever been most daring in experimenting with the structure of society, the movement Socialism. took at first the form of socialism. Impatient of winning their way inch by inch with the organization of labor, certain theorists of the labor party advised a short cut to the desired end, by means of a thorough reconstruction of industry. The state was to become the sole capitalist and employer of labor, dividing among the producers the whole product of their labor. The experience of the Revolution of February discouraged this idea in France ; but a similar scheme, more carefully prepared, was advanced by Lasalle and Marx in Germany twenty years later. Out of their writings has grown the Social-Democratic party in Germany. The deputies of this party in the imperial Reichstag have increased in number from two in 1871 to fifty-six in 1898. The Social-Democratic party demands that the ''instruments of labor —factories, mines, railroads, etc.—shall cease to be the property of individuals and shall become the general property of the nation.''

Here we have outlined the two chief methods that have been devised for arriving at economic democracy. Which of them, if either, shall bring about the desired condition is a problem the solution of which lies in the future.

The desire for a democratic society has been a strong stimulus toward universal education, as likely to break

Education.

down one of the obstacles in the way of a more democratic organization of society. Formerly a private or family affair, education is now regarded as one of the most important functions of the state.

Formerly education was under the supervision of the church ; but, like many of the functions of society (poor relief, for example), it has now been transferred to the state, in order that it may have a more general enforcement. In many of the German states instruction is obligatory ; so also in Switzerland, Scandinavia, France (since 1882), and in many of the States of the American Union.

A noticeable feature of the nineteenth century is the increase in wealth. All classes now dispose of an amount

Increase in wealth.

of money per capita that would have seemed fabulous to the men of a century ago. Many things which then were luxuries, to be obtained only by the more fortunate, such as sugar, chocolate, books, silks, and musical instruments, are now in general use, together with a hundred other things of later invention. The manual laborer of to-day has more luxuries, more opportunities for enjoyment and for mental culture than the middle classes in the year 1800. More than all this, he has in many ways, political and social, his own and his children's future in his hands.

LEADING EVENTS OF THE FOURTEENTH AND FIFTEENTH CENTURIES

France.	Spain (and Portugal).	Italy.	Germany.
Bull *Unam Sanctam*, 1302.		Dante, 1265–1321.	Lewis of Bavaria declares Empire independent of Papacy, 1338.
Hundred Years War, 1346–1453.		Petrarch, 1304–1374.	Golden Bull, 1356.
		Residence of Popes at Avignon, 1309–1377.	
		Great Schism of the West, 1378–1417.	Execution of John Huss, 1415.
		Council of Pisa, 1409.	Hussite wars, 1419–1436.
		Council of Constance, 1414–1418.	Albert of Austria, Emperor, 1438.
		Election of Pope Martin V, 1417.	Frederick III, Emp., 1440–1493.
Death of Joan of Arc, 1431.		Council of Basel, 1431.	Maximilian marries Mary, heiress of Burgundy, 1477.
English driven out of France (Calais), 1453.	Marriage of Ferdinand of Aragon and Isabella of Castile, 1469.	Cosimo de Medici, 1434–1464.	
	Diaz rounds Cape of Good Hope, 1486.		
	Grenada taken, 1492.		
	Jews exiled, 1492.		
	Discovery of America, 1492.		
Charles VIII invades Italy, 1494.	Vasco da Gama opens route to Indies, 1497.	Death of Lorenzo de Medici (Lorenzo the Magnificent), 1492.	Erasmus, 1467–1536.
Louis XII invades Italy, 1500.			Maximilian I, Emp., 1493–1519.

LEADING EVENTS OF THE SIXTEENTH CENTURY

Spain.	France.	Germany.	England.
Charles, grandson of Maximilian, King of Spain as Charles I, 1516.	John Calvin, born 1509; died (in Geneva), 1564.	Martin Luther, 1483–1546.	Henry VIII, 1509–1547.
	Francis I, 1515–1547.	The Ninety-five Theses, 1517. Election of Charles V, 1519. Diet of Worms, 1521. Diet of Augsburg; Schmalkaldic League, 1530.	
Voyage of Magellan, 1519–1522.			
Organization of Society of Jesus by Loyola, 1534.			Act of Royal Supremacy, 1534.
Philip II, 1556–1598.	Henry II, 1547–1559. Francis II, 1559–1560 = Mary Stewart.	Death of Luther, 1546. Schmalkaldic War, 1546–1547. Council of Trent (intermittent), 1545–1563.	Edward VI, 1547–1553. Mary, 1553–1558.
Seven United Provinces war against Philip, 1579. Declare independence; birth of Dutch Republic, 1581.	Charles IX, 1560–1574. St. Bartholomew, Aug. 24, 1572. Henry III, 1574–1589.	Peace of Augsburg, 1555. Abdication of Charles V, 1556 Death of Charles V, 1558. Ferdinand I, Emperor, 1556–1564.	Elizabeth, 1558–1603.
Defeat of Armada; decline of Spain, 1588.	Henry IV (of France and Navarre), 1589–1610. Edict of Nantes, 1598.		Execution of Mary, Queen of Scots, 1587. The Invincible Armada, 1588. East India Company, 1600.

LEADING EVENTS OF THE SEVENTEENTH CENTURY

France.	Germany.	Russia and Sweden.	England.
Henry IV murdered, 1610.	Thirty Years War, 1618-1648 :	Romanoffs in Russia, 1613.	James I, 1603-1625.
		Gustavus Adolphus, King of Sweden, 1611-1632.	Charles I, 1625-1649.
Louis XIII, 1610-1643.	1. Period of War in Bohemia, 1618-1623.		Petition of Right, 1628.
			Long Parliament, 1640-1660.
Ministry of Richelieu, 1624-1642.	2. Danish Period, 1625-1629.		Civil War, 1642-1649.
	3. Swedish Period, 1630-1635. Battle of Lützen; death of Gustavus Adolphus, 1632.		Execution of Charles I, 1649.
Louis XIV, 1643-1715.			The Parliamentary Republic, 1649-1653.
Ministry of Mazarin, 1643-1661.	4. Period of French Intervention, 1635-1648.		
			The Protectorate, 1653-1659.
	Peace of Westphalia, 1648.		Death of Oliver Cromwell, 1658.
			The Restoration, 1660.
Ministry of Colbert, 1661-1682.	The Great Elector of Brandenburg, 1640-1688.	Peter the Great, Tsar of Russia, 1692 (under regency until 1689)-1725.	Charles II, 1660-1685.
			James II, 1685-1688.
			The Revolution, 1688.
Revocation of Edict of Nantes, 1685.		Charles XII of Sweden. 1697-1718. Peter the Great visits England, 1698.	William III, 1689-1702.

24

LEADING EVENTS OF THE EIGHTEENTH CENTURY

France.	Prussia and Austria.	Russia and Sweden.	England.
Louis XV, 1715–1774.	Elector of Brandenburg crowned King of Prussia as Frederick I, 1701.	Charles XII defeats the Russians, Battle of Narva, 1700 ; conquers Poland, 1703.	Anne, 1702–1714.
Rousseau, 1670–1741.	Frederick William I, King of Prussia, 1713–1740.	Peter the Great founds St. Petersburg, 1703.	George I, 1714–1727.
Voltaire, 1694–1778.	Maria Theresa, Empress, 1740–1780.	Defeat of Charles XII, Pultowa, 1709.	George II, 1727–1760.
Social Contract of Rousseau, 1762. Suppression of Jesuits, 1764.	Frederick the Great, 1740–1786. Seven Years War, 1756–1763.	Catharine I, Tsarina, 1725–1727. Elizabeth, Tsarina, 1741–1762.	War between English and French in India, 1751–1754. Clive, Governor of Bengal, 1758 and 1767.
Louis XVI, 1774–1792. Ministry of Turgot, 1774–1776.	Joseph II, Emperor, 1765–1790.	Catharine II, Tsarina, 1762–1796.	George III, 1760–1820. "Old French and Indian War," 1755–1763.
Ministry of Necker, 1776–1781. Convocation of Estates General, 1789.	Frederick William II, King of Prussia, 1786–1797. Leopold II, Emperor, 1790–1792. Francis II, Emperor, 1792–1835. (Becomes Emperor of Austria, 1806.)	First Partition of Poland, 1772. Second " " 1793. Third " " 1795. Russia gets 6,000,000 inhabitants. Austria " 3,700,000 " Prussia " 2,500,000 "	Warren Hastings, Governor-General of India, 1774–1785. Cook's Voyages, 1768–1779. American Declaration of Independence, July 4, 1776. Treaty of Paris, 1783.
The French Republic, Sept. 22, 1792. Louis XVI executed Jan. 21, 1793. The Directory, 1795–1799. Establishment of Consulate, Dec. 24, 1799.	Frederick William III, King of Prussia, 1797–1840.		

LEADING EVENTS OF THE NINETEENTH CENTURY

France.	Central, Western, and Northern Europe.	Southern Europe.	England.
The Consulate, 1799-1804. The First Empire, 1804-1814. Treaties of Tilsit, July 7-9, 1807. Napoleon invades Russia, 1812. First Treaty of Paris, May 30, 1814. Return from Elba; beginning of the Hundred Days, March 1, 1815. Waterloo, June 18, 1815. Second Treaty of Paris, Nov. 20, 1815. Death of Napoleon, May 5, 1821. Revolution of July (27-29), 1830. Revolution of February (21-24), 1848. The Second Republic, 1848-1852. Coup d'Etat of Louis Bonaparte, Dec. 1-2, 1851. The Second Empire, 1852-1870. Crimean War, 1854-1856. Franco-Prussian War, 1870-1871. Sedan, Sept. 1, 1870. The Third Republic, Sept. 4, 1870-	Francis II abdicates crown of Holy Roman Empire; becomes Emperor of Austria, Aug. 6, 1806. Internal reorganization of Prussia; Stein; Hardenberg, 1807. University of Berlin, 1810. Bernadotte, Crown Prince of Sweden, 1809. (King as Charles XIV, 1818-1844.) Congress of Vienna, Nov., 1814-June, 1815. Denmark cedes Norway to Sweden; Peace of Kiel, 1814. Revolution at Berlin, March, 1848. Revolution in Austria, Mar.-Nov., 1848. Frankfort Parliament, May 18, 1848. Hungarian Revolution, 1848-1849. Schleswig-Holstein Wars, 1848-1851. Emancipation of serfs in Russia, 1861. Austro-Prussian War, 1866. Austro-Hungarian Arrangement, 1867. William I of Prussia proclaimed German Emperor, Versailles, Jan. 1, 1871. Assassination of Tsar Alexander II, 1881. Triple Alliance: Germany, Austria, Italy, 1881. Peace Conference at the Hague, May-July, 1897.	Napoleon, King of Italy, 1805. Revolution in Spain, Naples, Piedmont, 1820. War of Greek Independence, 1821-1829. Kingdom of Belgium, 1831. Reorganization of Switzerland, 1848. Battle of Novara, March 23, 1849. War of France and Sardinia against Austria, 1859. Italy acquires Venetia, 1866. Spanish Revolution and Military Dictatorship, 1868-1870. Opening of Suez Canal, 1869. Rome capital of Italy, 1871. Spanish Republic, 1873-1874. Turko-Russian War, 1877-1878. Congress of Berlin, June-July, 1878. Spanish-American War, April, 1898. Treaty of Paris, Dec. 10, 1898.	Union of Great Britain and Ireland (United Kingdom), 1801. Battle of Trafalgar, Oct. 21, 1805. George IV, 1820-1830. Catholic Relief Act. 1829. William IV, 1830-1837. First Reform Act, 1832. Abolition of Slavery throughout British Empire, 1833. Victoria, 1837-1901. Rebellion in Canada, 1837-1839. Repeal of Protective System, 1846-1852. First International Exposition, at London, 1851. Siege of Sebastopol, 1854-1855. Indian Mutiny, 1857-1858. Irish Land Acts, 1870, 1881-1885. Victoria proclaimed Empress of India, 1876. South African War, 1899-1902. Edward VII, 1901-

LIST OF EMPERORS, KINGS, AND PRESIDENTS—NINETEENTH CENTURY

FRANCE.

The Consulate: Nov., 1799–Dec., 1804.

The First Empire:

Napoleon, Emperor of the French, 1804-1814 (d. 1821).

The Restoration:

Louis XVIII, 1814-1824.
Charles X, 1824-1830 (d. 1836).
Louis Philippe, 1830-1848 (d. 1850).

The Second Republic:

Louis Bonaparte, President. 1848-1852.

The Second Empire:

Napoleon III, Emperor of the French, 1852-1870 (d. 1873).

The Third Republic:

Government of National Defense, 1870-1871
L. A. Thiers, President, 1871-1873
Marshal MacMahon, " 1873-1879
Jules Grévy, " 1879-1887
Sadi Carnot, " 1887-1894
Casimir-Périer, " 1894-1895
Félix Faure, " 1895-1899
Émile Loubet, " 1899–

ITALY.

(House of Savoy.)

Kings of Sardinia.

Victor Emmanuel I, 1802-1821.
(Napoleonic period, 1805-1813.)
Charles Felix, 1821-1831.
Charles Albert, 1831-1849.
Victor Emmanuel II, 1849-1878.
(King of Italy, 1861.)
Humbert, 1878-1900.
Victor Emmanuel III, 1900–

SPAIN.

Charles IV, 1788-1808.
Ferdinand VII, 1808.
Joseph Bonaparte, 1808-1813.
Ferdinand VII (rest.), 1813-1833.
Isabella II, 1833-1868.
Military Dictatorship, 1868-1870.
Amadeo I, 1870-1873.
Republic, 1873-1874.
Alfonso XII, 1874-1885.
Maria. 1885-1886.
Alfonso XIII, 1886–

RUSSIA.

Alexander I, 1801-1825.
Nicholas I, 1825-1855.
Alexander II, 1855-1881.
Alexander III, 1881-1894.
Nicholas II, 1894–

PRUSSIA.

Frederick William III, 1797-1840.
Frederick William IV, 1840-1861.
William I, 1861-1888.
(German Emperor 1871.)
Frederick III, Emperor-King, 1888.
William II, " 1888–

AUSTRIA-HUNGARY.

Francis II, 1792-1835.
(Became Francis I, Emperor of Austria, in 1806.)
Ferdinand I, 1835-1848.
Francis Joseph, 1848–
(King of Hungary, 1867.)

INDEX

HISTORY.

The Life of the Ancient Greeks.

With special reference to Athens. By CHARLES BURTON GULICK, Ph. D., Assistant Professor of Greek in Harvard University. 12mo. Cloth, $1.40.

"Very attractive for reference reading."—*Miss Rebecca Kinsman, Miss Winsor's School, Boston, Mass.*

"I shall be glad to recommend it to students for their reading."—*Dr. F. K. Ball, Phillips Exeter Academy, Exeter, N. H.*

A History of the Middle Ages.

By DANA C. MUNRO, A. M., Professor of European History, University of Wisconsin. 12mo. Cloth, 90 cents.

TEACHER'S MANUAL.

"I regard Munro's 'History of the Middle Ages' as an excellent work for the high school or academy. It is scholarly and interesting. In it the facts of history are woven together in such a manner as to show clearly the lines of cause and result."—*Miss Mary A. McClelland, New York Normal School.*

Medieval and Modern History.

By MUNRO and WHITCOMB.

In preparation, TEACHER'S MANUAL.

A History of the American Nation.

By ANDREW C. McLAUGHLIN, A. M., LL. B., Professor of American History in the University of Michigan. With Maps and numerous Illustrations. 12mo. Cloth, $1.40.

TEACHER'S MANUAL.

"In the front rank of single-volume histories."—*Alfred W. Rogers, May 31, 1902, Principal High School, Winthrop, Mass.*

"I have come deliberately to the conclusion that for high-school use it has no superior."—*George W. Knight, Professor of American History, Ohio State University, Columbus, Ohio.*

"It is by far the best text yet published. It is in every way accurate, scholarly, and practical. Having used it myself in high-school classes, I know that it meets the needs of the students."—*A. H. Tuttle, Instructor in American History, Ohio State University, Columbus, Ohio.*

D. APPLETON AND COMPANY, NEW YORK.

TWENTIETH CENTURY TEXT BOOKS.

A History of the American Nation.

By ANDREW C. McLAUGHLIN, Professor of American History in the University of Michigan. With many Maps and Illustrations. 12mo. Cloth, $1.40.

"One of the most attractive and complete one-volume histories of America that has yet appeared."—*Boston Beacon*.

"Complete enough to find a place in the library as well as in the school."—*Denver Republican*.

"This excellent work, although intended for school use, is equally good for general use at home."—*Boston Transcript*.

"It should find a place in all historic libraries."—*Toledo Blade*.

"Clearness is not sacrificed to brevity, and an adequate knowledge of political causes and effects may be gained from this concise history."—*New York Christian Advocate*.

"A remarkably good beginning for the new Twentieth Century Series of text-books. . . . The illustrative feature, and especially the maps, have received the most careful attention, and a minute examination shows them to be accurate, truthful, and illustrative."—*Philadelphia Press*.

"The work is up to date, and in accord with the best modern methods. It lays a foundation upon which a superstructure of historical study of any extent may be safely built."—*Pittsburg Times*.

"A book of rare excellence and practical usefulness."—*Salt Lake Tribune*.

"The volume is eminently worthy of a place in a series destined for the readers of the coming century. It is highly creditable to the author."—*Chicago Evening Post*.

D. APPLETON AND COMPANY, NEW YORK.

TWENTIETH CENTURY ENGLISH TEXTS.

Three points of excellence have given these Texts their remarkable success:

Their scholarly and judicious editing

Their singularly tasteful format and durable cloth binding

Their exceedingly reasonable prices

Wherever these features are appreciated these books are adopted, because they are truly

THE MODEL ENGLISH TEXTS

10 Volumes. 12mo. Cloth. Uniform Binding

ILLUSTRATED

Splendidly Edited   **Beautifully Made**   **Lowest Prices**

The Most Advanced Thought on the Teaching of English

Nothing more characteristic of **Twentieth Century** ideas on text-making than these classics.

SPECIAL OBJECTS

To facilitate power of expression; to cultivate taste for best reading; to interpret appreciatively great masters.

Exposition is not burdened, not one-sided. Develops the *motif* of play, poem, novel, inductively. Omits everything *that does not bear*. Sharp, animated, and suggestive; introductions and notes luminous and informing. Mechanical devices and typographical arrangements are material aids. A judicious division of commentaries, etc., avoids danger of over-editing, but gives all honest help for most careful study.

D. APPLETON AND COMPANY, NEW YORK.

TWENTIETH CENTURY TEXT-BOOKS.

A Text-Book of Geology.

By Professor ALBERT PERRY BRIGHAM, of Colgate University. 477 Pages. 295 Illustrations. 12mo. Cloth, $1.40.

This superb text-book is the best account for secondary schools of the earth's marvelous origin, of the processes that brought the ordered world out of chaos, and of the phenomena of geologic evolution—considered dynamically, structurally, and historically. The planet's life history is told with directness, brevity, and pedagogic fitness. The text is supplemented with 295 exquisite photographic illustrations, many taken by Professor Brigham for this work. An exceptional success in text-book writing and text-book making.

"Brigham's Geology is the cleanest cut and best pedagogical text-book for the high school that I have seen."—*C. H. Richardson, Hanover, N. H.*

"Most interesting. Decidedly the most practical book that I have seen for use in high schools."—*Miss S. A. Edwards, Philadelphia High School for Girls.*

I consider it the best written and best illustrated book I have ever seen for secondary schools."—*C. F. Warner, Mechanics Arts High School, Springfield, Mass.*

"The most attractive text-book of Geology for secondary schools that I have seen. The illustrations are a delight."—*Belle Sherman, Ithaca High School, Ithaca, N. Y.*

"It is magnificent. I consider it superior to any other book of the kind in illustrations, text, and adaptation to field work."—*Mrs. L. L. W. Wilson, Philadelphia Normal School.*

"In every way fully equal to any of the splendid series of Twentieth Century Text-Books. Many of the illustrations are new and their execution is perfect."—*R. I. Schiedt, Professor of Geology. Franklin and Marshall College, Lancaster, Pa.*

D. APPLETON AND COMPANY, NEW YORK.

TWENTIETH CENTURY TEXT-BOOKS.

MODERN LANGUAGE SERIES.

Editors: H. A. TODD, Ph. D., Columbia University; H. S. WHITE, LL. D., Cornell University; W. F. GIESE, A. M., University of Wisconsin. Illustrated. 12mo. Cloth.

First Book in French.

By C. A. DOWNER, Ph. D., College of the City of New York. $1.10.

Les Forceurs de Blocus.

By JULES VERNE. Edited by C. Fontaine, L. D., De Witt Clinton High School, New York. 30 cents.

Longer French Poems.

Edited by T. ATKINSON JENKINS, University of Chicago.

Le Barbier de Séville.

By BEAUMARCHAIS. Edited by Antoine Muzzarelli, New York. 35 cents.

Die Journalisten.

By FREYTAG. Edited by T. B. Bronson, A. M., Lawrenceville School. 45 cents.

Die Jungfrau von Orleans.

By SCHILLER. Edited by L. A. Rhoades, Ph. D., University of Illinois. 60 cents.

A German Reader.

By H. P. JONES, Ph. D., Hobart College. $1.00.

Minna von Barnhelm.

By LESSING. Edited by C. B. Wilson, A. M., University of Iowa. 50 cents.

A First Book in Spanish.

By W. F. GIESE, A. M., University of Wisconsin. $1.20.

SEND FOR CIRCULARS AND SAMPLE PAGES.

D. APPLETON AND COMPANY, NEW YORK.

Botanical Works

By Professor J. M. COULTER, Head of Department of Botany, University of Chicago, and Others.

Plant Studies.

An Elementary Botany. 12mo. Cloth, $1.25.

Plant Relations.

A First Book of Botany. 12mo. Cloth, $1.10.

Plant Structures.

A Second Book of Botany. 12mo. Cloth, $1.20.

Plants. A Text-Book of Botany. 12mo. Cloth, $1.80.

Teachers' Manuals, free, accompany all these texts.

Analytical Keys to Flowering Plants.

12mo. Limp cloth.

Northern States. By Professor COULTER. 25 cents.

Pacific Slope. By Prof. W. L. JEPSON, University of California. 45 cents.

Rocky Mountain Regions. By Prof. AVEN NELSON, University of Wyoming. 45 cents.

A Laboratory Manual of Botany.

By OTIS W. CALDWELL, Ph. D., Eastern Illinois State Normal School. 12mo. Cloth, 50 cents.

Seed Plants. Part I. Morphology of Spermatophytes. By JOHN M. COULTER, Ph. D., University of Chicago, and CHARLES J. CHAMBERLAIN, Ph. D., Instructor in Botany in the same. Illustrated. 8vo. Cloth, $1.75. 188 pages.

The Twentieth Century Botanical Course is now complete. It stands alone in its progressive pedagogical treatment of a great department of science. Its brilliant success in practical secondary school work has demonstrated the value of its principles and the attractiveness of their presentation.

D. APPLETON AND COMPANY, NEW YORK.

Printed in Great Britain by
Amazon.co.uk, Ltd.,
Marston Gate.